JUNE 1940–APRIL 2014

"He was a courageous and dedicated human rights defender, and his death marks the loss of an important voice in the struggle for justice and human rights in Malaysia. Amnesty International joins national and international activists in mourning his loss and expresses its deepest condolences to his family."
— *Amnesty International*

"He stood tall among the top leading lawyers in the world."
— *Datuk Param Cumaraswamy, former United Nations special rapporteur and former Bar Council president*

"Karpal Singh used his keen mind, legal training, and passion for justice to doggedly promote respect for human rights in Malaysia. For decades, he was an unyielding force for the rights of all."
— *James Ross, legal and policy director, Human Rights Watch*

"We've lost a colleague; an indefatigable fighter for justice; d legendary Karpal Singh! Our sincere condolences to d family. RIP. Anwar."
— *Datuk Seri Anwar Ibrahim, Opposition leader, PKR, in a tweet*

"In politics, he was an implacable leader; in law, a committed advocate."
— *Najib Razak, Malaysia Prime Minister*

"Until the end, Karpal fought for his principles. When he gave his views, he was very candid and it didn't worry if his comments could get him in trouble or offend people."
– *former Solicitor-General II Datuk Yusof Zainal Abiden*

"[Karpal] was a very outstanding criminal lawyer, he was one of the most prominent Malaysians that the country has produced. Despite his indisputable legal prominence, he shared his life with the party and was willing to commit himself to opposition politics, which is a very difficult vocation, because he passionately believed in the party, and also basically the people, that the voiceless should be heard, the dispossessed and defenceless should be protected, and the poor should be uplifted. I think that was his passion."
– *Lim Guan Eng, Penang Chief Minister*

"I feel the Malaysian Bar has lost a courageous member who stood to defend the Rule of Law at tremendous personal costs. Karpal has left this world but he will never leave our thoughts. His legacy will remain deeply entrenched in the legal and political arena."
– *Datuk V Sithambaram, lawyer*

"Despite his towering and larger than life reputation and achievement, he was always respectful, unexpectedly funny, and had time, often late evening, to chat and discuss cases or legal issues with his junior lawyers."
– *Eric Paulsen, executive director, Lawyers for Liberty*

"In his days at the Johore Bar, Karpal was most enduring, humble and approachable, as well as soft-spoken, polite and cheerful. It is not quite correct to say that he was aloof and ferocious as a tiger. Rather, he was mild-mannered, cool and calm. The ferocity in the man only erupted

like the Merapi if someone's rights were trampled upon or if some poor soul was bullied by the powerful. He gave hope to the defenceless, voice to the voiceless, and succour to the meek and the oppressed. He forsook his fees from the impecunious and for whose human rights he fought for. He did so without detriment to himself or to the laws."
— *S Balarajah, Johore Bar*

"The Malay proverb of "A tiger dies leaving its stripes, a man dies leaving his name" is apt for the late Karpal Singh. For one, metaphorically, the "Tiger of Jelutong" has left behind his stripes; secondly, in reality, he leaves behind a great name as a politician who is respected by both his allies and enemies alike. It is rare for one to be able to fill this proverb metaphorically and in reality, and it is as such this shows the greatness of the one who has departed us."
— *Datuk Dr Mujahid Yusof Rawa, PAS (Pan-Malaysian Islamic Party) member and MP for Parit Buntar*

"There are few who would dare to fight from a position of nothing and yet Karpal Singh did it knowing that he had all the odds stacked against him. He stood firmly for justice and the truth. He was prepared to speak out for what he believed in against a greater authority in many instances of legal confrontations in his career."
— *KK Wong, Malaysian Insider reader*

"He proved that realising aspirations is not about how far you can go, but how far you are willing to go. He makes a sheer mockery of what we call "struggles", as however much sympathy we give to him for the pain he has to go through, he channelled the sympathy right away to the defendants he had to represent at the dock of a criminal court."
— *James Chai*

"He was a humble and very down-to-earth leader despite his position."
– *Tan Bak Chooi, owner of Ju Huat coffee shop where Karpal used to hold his press conferences in Penang*

"I have deep scepticism to politics revolving around personality. But in times when our institutions can disappoint us, failing to check the powers that be and worsening the excesses of power, personalities like Karpal Singh can do a lot of good."
– *Hafiz Nor Shams*

"Equality, social justice and the rule of law are just some of the many things he stood for, unflinching in his principles. Some might not have known the gentleman, but he had set a benchmark of which many would intend to follow."
– *Jay Jay Dennis, law student*

"The battles he had fought and the sacrifices that he had made for the downtrodden Malaysians must be remembered. He spoke with reason and not emotions as some cheap politicians do."
– *Ravinder Singh*

"Karpal Singh, who died in a car accident in the early hours of April 17th at the age of 73, was a rarity in the venomous world of Malaysian politics: a man respected by many of his opponents as well as those on his own side."
– *Obituary by* The Economist

"Malaysia has lost a man of principle and a defender of justice."
– Harakah Daily

KARPAL SINGH
TIGER OF JELUTONG
THE FULL BIOGRAPHY

TIM DONOGHUE

with forewords by
Gobind Singh Deo and Mark Trowell QC

Marshall Cavendish
Editions

Copyright © 2014 Marshall Cavendish International (Asia) Private Limited
Text © Tim Donoghue

Reprinted 2022

First published 2013 as *Karpal Singh: Tiger of Jelutong*
This new edition published 2019 by Marshall Cavendish Editions
An imprint of Marshall Cavendish International

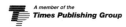
A member of the
Times Publishing Group

Other Marshall Cavendish Offices
Marshall Cavendish Corporation, 800 Westchester Ave, Suite N-641, Rye Brook, NY 10573, USA • Marshall
Cavendish International (Thailand) Co Ltd, 253 Asoke, 16th Floor, Sukhumvit 21 Road, Klongtoey Nua,
Wattana, Bangkok 10110, Thailand • Marshall Cavendish (Malaysia) Sdn Bhd, Times Subang, Lot 46,
Subang Hi-Tech Industrial Park, Batu Tiga, 40000 Shah Alam, Selangor Darul Ehsan, Malaysia

Marshall Cavendish is a registered trademark of Times Publishing Limited

National Library Board, Singapore Cataloguing-in-Publication Data

Name(s): Donoghue, Tim. | Singh, Gobind, author of introduction. | Trowell, Mark, author of introduction.
Title: Karpal Singh : tiger of Jelutong : the full biography / Tim Donoghue ; with forewords by Gobind Singh
and Mark Trowell QC.
Description: New edition. | Singapore : Marshall Cavendish Editions, 2019. | First published: 2013. | Includes
bibliographical references and index.
Identifier(s): OCN 1065533801 | ISBN 978-981-4841-45-0 (paperback)
Subject(s): LCSH: Singh, Karpal. | Politicians--Malaysia--Biography. | Lawyers--Malaysia--Biography.
Classification: DDC 324.2209595--dc23

Printed in Singapore

Photographs courtesy of Tim Donoghue and Karpal Singh unless otherwise stated.
Photograph of Karpal Singh and Tim Donoghue on inside back cover courtesy of Jeremy Teo.

Tributes on pages i–iv have been compiled from the open domain.

For
Michael

CONTENTS

FOREWORD TO THIS EDITION

Karpal Singh is a Malaysian icon. He was my father. He was born in 1940 in Penang, Malaysia. Despite difficult times, my father worked his way to the University of Singapore where he read law. He subsequently set up a legal practice in Kedah and then Penang and Kuala Lumpur building what most of us in the legal fraternity will remember as a controversial, yet most inspiring legal career.

He had a penchant for championing the plight of the downtrodden and oppressed. He took on weak and what some would describe as "hopeless" cases. It didn't matter so much if one could afford to pay him fees for legal representation. That was secondary. To my father, everyone had a right to be heard. Due process and proper application of law were essential aspects in a democratic system of administrative justice which he believed in.

Fundamental liberties guaranteed in the Federal Constitution which many saw as merely directory were most significant, almost sacred, to him. In fact, I recall his last day in Parliament on 10 April 2014. In an altercation he warned the Dewan Rakyat (House of Representatives) not to "play the fool" with the Federal Constitution, making it patently clear that in Malaysia, even Parliament was subservient to the Constitution. Indeed, the Federal Constitution is supreme and Karpal Singh worked tirelessly to remind everyone of the need to defend it as such at all times.

Politically, Karpal Singh played a pivotal role in building the Democratic Action Party (DAP). He was a State Assemblyman in Kedah and Penang and Member of Parliament, and the chairman of the DAP but resigned as chairman after he was convicted for an offence of sedition in 2014.

Known to be one who always spoke his mind, which drew severe consequences at times, even political detention and prosecution, he remained steadfast in what he believed to be right. His resilience and persistence resonated with the people and earned him the name "Tiger of Jelutong".

Despite the challenges it faced, including possible deregistration at one point not too long ago, the DAP during the chairmanship of Karpal Singh and working with two other parties, Parti Keadilan Rakyat (PKR) and Parti Islam Se-Malaysia, managed to form the state government of Kedah, Penang, Selangor, Perak and Kelantan in 2008, and Penang and Selangor in 2013.

In 2018, the DAP working together with PKR, Parti Amanah Negara, Parti Pribumi Bersatu Malaysia and Parti Warisan Sabah managed to defeat Barisan Nasional, the party which ruled Malaysia for 61 years since its independence to form a new Federal government of Malaysia. An incredible achievement indeed, and one which became possible with the combined leadership, guidance and inspiration of dedicated people like Karpal Singh. If my father were alive today, he would be gratified to see such a result come to pass in the country he chose to stay in and fought so hard for.

In 2005, my father was involved in a motor vehicle accident which caused him severe spinal injuries. Despite being wheelchair bound, he fought back. He was not one to be outdone by such a blow in life nor the disability it caused him. He returned to active legal practice. In 2008 and 2013, he again stood for elections for Parliament winning both times with comfortable majorities.

At 1am on 17th April 2014, I received news that he was involved in a fatal motor vehicle collision in Kampar, on his way home to Penang.

News of his passing shocked our family and the nation. Tens of thousands of people made their way to pay their last respects at our family home in Western Road, Penang, where his remains lay. He was accorded a State funeral by the Government of Penang. The massive scale of grief expressed by people from all walks of life underscored the huge impact he had on the people of Malaysia.

His story is one to remember and to learn from. This book provides an accurate account and tells it as it should be told. It traces extensively the different stages of his life, the difficult beginnings, the challenges he faced as a lawyer and politician, his perseverance and determination to overcome everything and anyone who stood in his way of success.

This is the story of Karpal Singh.

Indeed he is the Tiger of Jelutong. He is deeply missed, and he will never be forgotten.

GOBIND SINGH DEO
MINISTER OF COMMUNICATIONS AND MULTIMEDIA, MALAYSIA
AND DEPUTY CHAIRMAN, DEMOCRATIC ACTION PARTY
NOVEMBER 2018

Karpal, pictured near the old Federal Court building
in Kuala Lumpur, during his 2002 sedition case.
Photo courtesy of Mark Trowell QC.

FOREWORD

Karpal Singh was one of Malaysia's most prominent lawyers and a controversial figure both in the law and politics. He was an outspoken advocate of human rights in Malaysia for more than 40 years.

Often these distinct roles seemed to merge. That may be because politics and the law are inextricably linked in Malaysia. He is regarded as a true Malaysian 'patriot' who had a direct and progressive influence on his country's political and legal process.

Except for a short period out of office, Karpal Singh was a member of parliament for more than 30 years. Karpal was the National Chairman of the Democratic Action Party (DAP), one of the component parties of the opposition alliance known as Pakatan Rakyat.

He was deemed by Amnesty International to be a prisoner of conscience after having been jailed for two years in October 1987 under the draconian provisions of the now-repealed Internal Security Act.

Together with other opposition members he was swept up in what was known as 'Operation Lalang' for allegedly 'inciting racial tension'. Many observers regarded the operation as an excuse by the government of Dr Mahathir Mohamad to strengthen the hand of the executive and extend control over newspapers that had provided news coverage favourable to the opposition. At that time (as is still the case now in Malaysia) public assembly without a police permit was declared illegal.

Karpal was affectionately known as the 'Tiger of Jelutong' from his time as MP for the parliamentary seat of Jelutong. The nickname fitted his fiery temperament and the tenacious way in which he defended his clients. It also characterised his style as a member of parliament. Echoing Elvis Presley, his favourite saying was: "If you are looking for trouble, you have come to the right place".

He rarely, if ever, took a backward step and on several occasions was suspended from parliament on various issues of conscience. On one occasion he was even removed from the parliamentary chamber with a police escort.

Karpal was never known to do anything quietly and that not only reflected his approach to life, but also was the basis of his strength and resolute nature. He had a fiery temperament, but at times was gentle and humorous. I saw all of these qualities over the decade or so that I knew him.

Karpal was tragically injured in a traffic accident in 2005 as a result of which he suffered severe spinal injuries and was forced to use a wheelchair. Despite his disability, he still carried on a busy legal practice and remained a significant opposition member of parliament. It was a remarkable testament to his courage and determination.

Karpal Singh was twice charged with acts of sedition, first in 2002 and again in 2012. These charges span a turbulent decade in Malaysia's history. I was an observer at each of these trials and they provide some insight into the means by which the government has since 1948 used the legislation to stifle free speech and peaceful assembly. They also illustrate how Karpal Singh, both as a lawyer and politician, continued to challenge the government and assert his right to free speech.

The Sedition Act is a relic of British colonial rule. It was enacted in 1948 to deal with a perceived communist insurrection, but remained in force after Independence in 1957. Effectively, the Act has over the past 50 years been adapted and extended well beyond the intended scope of the original legislators.

It provides that a person can be convicted on the basis that what they said had a "seditious tendency" — which is an extremely vague phrase. It includes any words spoken which would "bring into hatred or contempt or to excite disaffection against" the government or engender "feelings of ill-will and hostility between different races". It doesn't matter if the words spoken are true or false. The defendant doesn't need to intend that the words spoken had one of the results identified in the Act.

Legislation of this type hardly seems appropriate in a modern democratic nation, which Malaysia claims to be.

The first charge of sedition brought against Karpal arose from his representation of former Deputy Prime Minister Datuk Seri Anwar Ibrahim at his first trial on allegations of sodomy in 1998.

During the course of the trial, Karpal raised the prospect that Anwar was being poisoned while in custody. That revelation had come about after his lawyers obtained a report confirming that traces of arsenic had been found in Anwar's body. During the hearing Karpal submitted that he suspected 'people in high places' to be responsible for the poisoning; the clear implication was that he meant Prime Minister Dr Mahathir. He was subsequently charged in 2000 with the offence of sedition.

The sedition charge stirred up the international legal community.

Many organisations expressed outrage. It was the first time that a lawyer in any Commonwealth country had been charged with sedition for remarks made in court defending a client.

The prosecution eventually fizzled out when the newly appointed Attorney-General Tan Sri Abdul Gani Patail withdrew the charge on the morning of the trial, but not before Karpal had launched a broadside at the presiding judge Datuk Seri Augustine Paul — who had also presided at Anwar's first trial.

Karpal told Justice Paul that he had acted more as a prosecutor than a judge in Anwar's trial and that he should be 'observed' by the international observers who were at court, which included me and other foreign lawyers. Understandably, Karpal's remark enraged the judge who claimed that it was an attack on his integrity and impartiality. Karpal refused to back down and continued to provoke the judge, but despite threatening Karpal with contempt of court he refrained from doing so.

Karpal told me later that he wasn't going to miss the opportunity of taking the judge to task for what he believed was inappropriate behaviour in the Anwar trial and to 'keep him in check'. Augustine Paul died in January 2010. Both had been students at the University of Singapore. Some people criticised Karpal for speaking graciously of him after his death, but Karpal was not one to carry grudges.

The second charge of sedition brought against Karpal arose from comments he made at a press conference on 6 February 2009 about the late Sultan of Perak, Sultan Azlan Shah, who had intervened to remove the Perak Chief Minister after making personal inquiries whether the state government still enjoyed a majority in the parliament following declarations by three government members that they had resigned from the ruling party.

Karpal said during the press conference that the Sultan's removal of the chief minister and appointing a replacement was beyond his constitutional powers and could be questioned in a court of law. The prosecution claimed these words had a 'seditious tendency' by bringing hatred or contempt or exciting disaffection against the Sultan.

Karpal claimed that he was doing no more than offering a legal opinion that the Sultan was subject to the Malaysian Constitution. Once again, he was in court asserting the rule of law and standing by the principle that every Malaysian was subject to it.

The case reflects the special status given to the rulers of Malaysia. Dr Mahathir in the 1980s had effectively removed the legal immunity of the rulers by legislative means and many harsh things had been said about the rulers at the time.

Karpal at his trial maintained that he was doing no more than the former PM had done 20 years before and that his prosecution was entirely selective. He was convicted and sentenced to a fine that effectively disqualified him from being a member of parliament. The appeal is still pending.

Since 1998 Karpal has continued to represent Anwar Ibrahim. He did so at the first series of trials when Anwar was convicted of sodomy and corruption. In 2004 the sodomy verdict was overturned on appeal resulting in Anwar's release from prison.

There was one moment at the appeal that was entirely characteristic of Karpal. He asked the three appeal court judges to give special status to the international observers saying we were there to 'see justice done'. Of course the implication was clear, but the judges did not take the bait saying it was unnecessary to give us special status because it was a court open to all members of the public. But the old fox had made his point.

In 2008 Anwar was again charged with an offence of sodomy. This time the alleged victim was one of his staff members who claimed to have been sexually assaulted by him.

Anwar claimed that the charge was politically motivated and an attempt to again damage him politically upon his successful return to politics. Anwar was found not guilty on 9 January 2012, almost two years after the trial started.

Karpal successfully led the defence team during an often-gruelling process despite being wheelchair-bound and relying on his son to handle the legal papers. He was more than once threatened by the judge with contempt, but he casually shrugged off those threats.

Again I was an observer at that trial. I recall him, at one stage during the hearing, claiming that one of the judge's threats of contempt had 'intimidated' him. I thought at the time that this must surely be no more than a bit of theatre because I could never imagine Karpal Singh being intimidated by anyone — let alone a judge.

Ultimately, the trial judge Justice Zabidin Diah found that the DNA evidence submitted by the prosecution was unreliable, and acquitted Anwar. The prosecution filed an appeal against the acquittal, which was upheld by the Court of Appeal in March 2014. Anwar was sentenced to five years' imprisonment.

Karpal was to argue the final appeal before the Federal Court, but his death has meant that others — including his son Ramkarpal — will now argue the case.

Karpal Singh appeared as counsel in most of Malaysia's significant cases over the last 44 years or so. But it was not just the big cases that mattered to him. His reputation for defending the 'little man' was well deserved. His offices at 67, Jalan Pudu Lama, Bukit Bintang are housed in a modest narrow four-storey building on the high side of the road. On the inside walls are photos of Karpal at different stages of his career and testimonials from grateful clients.

In the dark panelled reception area there is a large wooden plaque recording the appreciation of the National Union of Cinema and

Amusement Workers of West Malaysia. There are also framed newspaper articles recording past court victories or political events along the walls of the stairs leading to Karpal's book-filled office on the first floor.

Before he died, Karpal said that if he was gone then "100 Karpals would take my place". If that were only true, but he really is irreplaceable. He will be sadly missed.

Tim Donoghue's well-written biography of Karpal Singh, now in its second edition, records the life of a truly significant figure in Malaysian politics. It also records the personal side of the man. His account follows the incredible twists and turns of a larger than life character not only because of his involvement in politics, but also the law. Karpal's life reflected the modern history of Malaysia and the events that have shaped it as a nation since Independence more than 50 years ago. Karpal was very much an integral part of that history. It makes this biography relevant and important. It is not only the story of the man we knew as the 'Tiger of Jelutong' — but also of Malaysia itself.

MARK TROWELL QC

PERTH, AUSTRALIA

MAY 2014

Karpal and his legal team celebrate yet another hard won historic verdict at the Jalan Duta courthouse in Kuala Lumpur. It is 9 January 2012, and this time Anwar Ibrahim has been found not guilty of sodomy in the salacious Sodomy II High Court trial. Anwar is pictured here (obscured) behind lawyer-son Ramkarpal's right shoulder. Karpal, with a big grin on his face, is being pushed by lawyer-politician son Gobind. Wife Gurmit and Karpal's personal assistant Michael Cornelius are also enjoying the moment.

PREFACE

Lightning, in the form of motor vehicle accidents, struck three times in Karpal Singh's life. His own life came to a devastating halt in a motor vehicle crash on the North-South highway in the early morning hours of Thursday, 17 April 2014. Death for Karpal and his personal assistant Michael Cornelius was instant when the Toyota Alphard in which they were both passengers clipped the right rear of a northbound truck during a passing manoeuvre.

Karpal's death was reminiscent of his father Ram Singh's demise 40 years earlier. Ram, too, died instantly when the rickshaw in which he was the sole passenger was hit from behind by an out-of-control car in the 'Golden Temple' city of Amritsar in northern India in May 1974.

Three decades later, in the early hours of 29 January 2005, Karpal suffered the second major vehicle accident of his life. He became a tetraplegic when a car driven by Penang banker Lau Yee Fuat ploughed into the back of a taxi outside Karpal's Penang home. This accident consigned Karpal, who was the sole backseat passenger in the taxi and who was not wearing a seatbelt at the time, to nine years of pain and immobility.

During five decades practising law in Malaysia, Karpal became the country's most prominent lawyer-politician. He was an outspoken, fearless advocate for justice and human rights in Southeast Asia. He was best known internationally for his forthright defence of numerous international drug traffickers such as Australian Kevin Barlow, who went to the Pudu Prison gallows in July 1986. Until 1986, he regularly appeared before the Privy Council in London on a number of appeals, including the landmark Teh Cheng Poh case.

He juggled a prominent legal career with politics, particularly in Penang, where he became the outspoken MP for Jelutong in the Federal Parliament for 21 years and the MP for Bukit Gelugor for 10 years.

Known by the nickname the 'Tiger of Jelutong' for his uncompromising approach to politics and the law, the wounded tiger emerged from his 2005 accident in a wheelchair. The experience turned him into an even more powerful advocate for political and legal change. During the last nine years of his life the tetraplegic was a man who realised he had nothing to lose except life itself. He feared no one as he went about his work in Malaysia's courts and parliament.

His new condition required him to be patient and he came to slowly accept the fact he would be totally dependent on others for even the very basic fundamentals of life. Many people confronted by the situation Karpal found himself in in 2005 simply curl up and die. But this man had learned from his criminal law professional lifestyle that there was no need for anyone without a death wish to rush to the gallows. He relished the fact the ultimate judge had granted him a temporary reprieve on life.

After the accident he took on even more top-level anti-establishment cases, such as the defence of Anwar Ibrahim in the Sodomy II case. Karpal also saw bitter irony in the fact that prosecution lightning struck prominent opposition leader Anwar Ibrahim three times in terms of two separate sodomy cases as well as one of corruption over the past 15 years.

In latter years he also took on the Altantuya Shaariibuu case, involving a Mongolian woman who was blown to smithereens in a remote Selangor forest with military explosives on an October 2006 night. In taking on a watching brief for the dead woman's family in Mongolia, with the assistance of his three lawyer sons Jagdeep, Gobind and Ramkarpal and his lawyer daughter Sangeet Kaur, the family law firm stood very much alone in Malaysian legal circles. Karpal, with the total backing of his wife Gurmit Kaur throughout all his trials and tribulations, took on criminal and constitutional cases other lawyers feared and stayed well clear of.

Karpal conservatively admitted to having at least 50 clients die on Malaysian gallows. More importantly, he saved hundreds of others by repeatedly launching successful legal challenges.

He himself was charged twice with sedition. The first occasion, which saw the charge withdrawn, related to his spirited defence of Anwar, when he raised the possibility that the opposition leader had been poisoned while in custody.

The second sedition charge arose from comments made at a press conference in his Kuala Lumpur office on 6 February 2009, concerning the late Sultan of Perak. That charge was upheld when he was convicted by Malaysia's High Court on 21 February 2014 and sentenced two weeks later to a fine of RM4,000 on 11 March. At the time of his death, he had filed an appeal against the conviction.

Karpal's legacy as a catalyst for hard-won legal and political change in Malaysia is well positioned to live on via his adult children. At the Bukit

Gelugor by-election held on 25 May 2014, third lawyer son Ramkarpal Singh polled 41,242 votes. He won the seat that his father had held since 2004 by a majority of 37,659 votes.

Over the years I had a habit of turning up unannounced on the red carpet of his first floor office in Kuala Lumpur late at night.

On the last occasion I did this, in early September 2013, he looked up from behind his desk and said, "Ah, my friend, you are back."

Karpal's life story, primarily because of the incorrigibility of the man, was one I could never put behind me as a journalist. I realised early on back in 1987 that the tiger was always available for a chat late at night. He was a man of extraordinary patience and I tested that patience while coming to grips personally with the challenges involved in the writing of this book.

Following his conviction on 21 February I texted Karpal the same day and said, "Have just heard the news. I have no doubt you will prevail in the appeal stages. I can hear the tiger roaring from here."

As always, when he found himself with his back to the political and legal wall, he was politeness personified and that sense of humour of his came through in his response.

"They have wounded the tiger," he replied, "but will have to pay very dearly for it. Regards. Karpal Singh."

And on 11 March, just before he was sentenced for sedition, I texted this message: "Karpal, bestest for today. Keeping a close eye as always on the situation. Tim."

The last time I spoke with Karpal was on St Patrick's Day, 17 March at 7:20 p.m. Michael picked up my call, as he always did, and said, "Ah Mr Tim! You hold on, eh." He then put the phone to Karpal's ear. In this conversation we spoke about the support he had received from the

New Zealand Law Society which issued a statement on 27 February, parts of which are reproduced here.

> The New Zealand Law Society has joined LAWASIA and other legal organisations in expressing its concern at the recent conviction of Malaysian lawyer and politician Karpal Singh, on sedition charges....
>
> LAWASIA says that while appreciating that the conviction is a matter for the courts, its concern arises where the Malaysian government had, in 2011, indicated its intention to repeal the Sedition Act, "which is widely regarded as draconian and a relic of colonial era laws".
>
> The New Zealand Law Society and LAWASIA support the view of the Malaysian Bar that "the decision to proceed with the prosecution of YB Karpal Singh under a law that the government has slated for repeal is inexplicable and raises the spectre of selective prosecution."
>
> LAWASIA says it notes that the United Nations Basic Principles on the Role of Lawyers indicate at Article 23 that lawyers "have the right to take part in public discussion of matters concerning the law, the administration of justice and the promotion and protection of human rights...".

In that same phone call Karpal also left me in no doubt that he planned to appeal his sedition case all the way through to the highest appeal court available to him.

I'm proud to say the last substantial hard news interview Karpal

xxviii   KARPAL SINGH: TIGER OF JELUTONG

ever gave was with Aimee Gulliver, a colleague of mine from the Fairfax newsroom in Wellington, New Zealand. She was on a secondment job for the *Malaysiakini* wire service and arrived in Kuala Lumpur on 8 March 2014, the same day a Malaysian Airlines Boeing 777-200 went missing on a flight from Kuala Lumpur to Beijing.

On 20 March, I emailed Karpal: "Suffice to say, Karpal…any assistance you are able to accord Aimee during her time in Malaysia would be greatly appreciated by myself…with thanks and best wishes to Gurmit Kaur and the wider family. Tim."

Karpal promptly replied: "I will communicate with Aimee Gulliver immediately."

Gulliver subsequently interviewed Karpal.

On 11 April, six days before he died, Karpal thoughtfully emailed Gulliver thanking her for the "superbly written, hard hitting" interview, which appears in its entirety in the epilogue to this book.

This book is the brutally true life-and-death story surrounding a proud, modern-day Sikh warrior.

When Karpal died his legal sword was still out of its scabbard. This was hardly surprising for his Sikh parents had taught him well about Guru Gobind Singh, the man after whom Karpal's second lawyer son is named. The Guru once famously said, "When all modes of redressing a wrong having failed, the raising of sword is pious and just."

As the long-serving National Chairman of the opposition Democratic Action Party (DAP) political party, Karpal's political activities over the years saw him imprisoned twice in the late 1980s under Malaysia's now abolished draconian Internal Security Act legislation. Throughout his life Karpal successfully fought to overturn such legislation and to make Malaysia's royal families accountable under law. He did it all while operating in a might-is-right political and legal environment where the predominant rule of the game is smash or be smashed.

Politically, on 5 May 2013, Anwar Ibrahim's opposition coalition mounted a credible challenge for political change in Malaysia's 13th general election by winning the popular vote, but missing out on political power. Karpal retained his Bukit Gelugor seat by a 41,778 vote majority. After this result he made it clear he had no intention of retiring from politics or the law. "A good lawyer dies in the saddle. The same applies equally to a politician. They should work to the last. If you slow down, you die. In this life, you have to fight," he told me on election night 2013.

At the time of his death on 17 April 2014, Karpal had Anwar's Sodomy II appeal files in his vehicle.

Indeed Karpal was not a man to utter words in order to retract them later.

For sure, the smiling 'Tiger of Jelutong' fought to the very last.

Haere ra Karpal.

1 POVERTY TO OBLIVION

The Calcutta-based long-range B-29 bombers flew over the narrow channel between Butterworth and Penang Island in northern peninsular Malaya in January 1945.

For many in Penang, looking at the planes from a distance, the sight of the American Superfortresses with their glistening nose cones represented proof freedom from the rigours of Japanese wartime occupation was nigh. For others, who perceived themselves to be within the target zone of bombs about to be dropped, the planes represented yet more terror for a tired, cowed Asian community.

It was hardly surprising that the desperately poor family of the young Karpal Singh fitted into this latter category. From the gates of the workshop where he worked as a watchman during the Japanese occupation, Karpal's father Ram Singh Deo was among those who looked up and saw the bombers approaching. The sight of the planes had him running as fast as he could along Light Street past the Esplanade towards the three-storey house on Green Hall where he and his young family rented two small ground-floor rooms.

By the time Ram arrived at the ramshackle apartment the Superfortresses were bombing the nearby St Xavier's Institution, which came in for special treatment as it had been commandeered and used as the headquarters for the Japanese detachment in Penang.

"Come quickly!" Ram instructed his wife Kartar Kaur and three young sons Baksis Singh, Santokh Singh and Karpal. Ram grabbed toddler Jernal Singh while Kartar jogged along with baby daughter Ajit Kaur on her hip.

Looking up into the blue sky, in one of his earliest childhood memories, four-year-old Karpal saw bombs raining down on the school his parents one day wanted to send him to.

As the rat-infested drains outside their home were already full of prostrate Sikh friends and neighbours seeking refuge from the flying debris, Ram and his family had little option but to move along. Between the earth-shaking explosions, Ram shouted at his wife and turbaned sons to follow him.

They were terrified. They ran past the entrance columns of the Supreme Court building, the stone monument to 19th-century colonial lawyer James Richardson Logan, across Farquhar Street and into the looted remains of the roofless St George's Church. Built in 1818 by the East India Company, the oldest Anglican church in Southeast Asia had itself been targeted by a Japanese bomber in December 1941.

Four years later, with the tide of war going out on the Japanese, Ram gambled that the Americans were unlikely to subject the remains of the Parthenon-like church shell to a second bombing. The fact the superstructure of the church remained essentially intact did not say much for the impact of Japanese bombs in 1941, but Ram had no doubts about the destructive force of American bombers seeking out 'targets of opportunity' in early 1945.

He pushed his boys into the throng on the stones near the area where the refurbished Francis Light Memorial stood in front of the old church. Kartar, a proud, strong and forthright Sikh, huddled her five children around her.

On the wall of the small Francis Light Memorial building is a plaque, often covered in bird dropping. This plaque, honouring the empire-building Englishman, goes some way to explaining the colonial wartime problems Ram and his family found themselves caught up in.

In memory of Francis Light, the plaque reads. *In his capacity as Governor the settlers and natives were greatly attached to him and by his death had to deplore the loss of one who watched over their interests and cares as a father.*

In the 18th century Francis Light had been Penang's first governor under the British, and in early 1945 he was still apparently looking after the descendants of his subjects. Those who huddled into the church and churchyard near his memorial stone were unharmed when a misdirected American bomb exploded directly across the street from Karpal's childhood home.

Before the war the heavily bearded Ram and his wife considered sending their sons to St Xavier's Institution, run by the Christian de La Salle brothers in a Moorish conglomeration of architecturally incompatible-looking buildings. But by the time the Superfortresses headed back out over the Straits of Malacca, the school had been reduced to a pile of rubble. Destroyed were the three-storey building facing Farquhar Street, the ornate chapel above the school hall and three classroom blocks.

Thoughts of his children's schooling were far from Ram's mind as he gingerly guided his young family back through the dust and devastation to the remains of their home at 23 Green Hall. Eight poor Sikh families had shared the home but no one would ever live there again. The house, while it had not incurred a direct hit, was rendered uninhabitable by damage to foundations from the vibrations as the Superfortresses rained their bombs down on the nearby makeshift Japanese barracks and a row of shop-houses across the street. Remarkably, all the Sikh residents of the apartment had escaped with their lives.

Covered in dust and surveying the tottering ruins of their small soon-to-be-demolished apartment, the young Karpal and his siblings were to find out what it meant to be Sikhs in post-Japanese-occupied Malaya. With nowhere else to go and possessing only the clothes on their backs, his parents could take some consolation from the knowledge they would at least be welcome at the Sikh temple in Brick Kiln Road.

The Sikh priest, in his white robes, blue turban and curling moustache, welcomed Ram and his family with open arms. Like most *gurdwaras* throughout Asia, there are to this day rooms set aside for accommodation. Hospitality for the homeless and travellers is an important part of the Sikh religion.

For the remainder of 1945, home for the family was a small room in the Penang *gurdwara*, its sole furniture an elevated wooden sleeping bench. In this poor but happy environment beneath the Sikh flag, Karpal and his siblings would sit on the red-tiled floor, their backs supported by large square white columns, studying introductory courses in Gurmukhi script.

The American bombing shattered the material aspects of Karpal's boyhood world and saw him embark on life's journey with no worldly goods whatsoever. His parents never did have a home to live in together

Kartar Kaur and Ram Singh Deo, in a photo taken shortly before Ram's ill-fated trip home to the Punjab in May 1974.

(*above left*) St George's Church, Penang, where Ram and his family took shelter during the American bombing; (*right*) the Francis Light Memorial which stands in front of the church.

they could call their own. But what they did give their third son and his brothers and sisters was an incorrigible and adventurous spirit.

It was a spirit honed out of total abject poverty in the Punjab, a spirit with an ability to transcend even the destructive capacity of B-29 bombers. While others in equally difficult situations crumbled around them, Ram and Kartar relied on a set of Sikh principles to guide them.

On the day they became homeless, Karpal's family and friends walked to the sanctuary of the *gurdwara*, past a derelict mansion once owned by business tycoon Cheong Fatt Tze.

From there they made their way along Penang Road where they had earlier seen decapitated heads of Chinese citizens, displayed by the Japanese occupation forces on the metal fence spikes surrounding the Penang Police Station.

They also passed through the grounds of the Supreme Court where somehow Justice Lim Cheng Ean, a respected member of the Straits Settlement Legislative Council before the war, continued to dispense justice in a humane manner during the Japanese occupation.

The grounds of Light Street Convent immediately behind their destroyed home had a more sinister significance for Karpal and his brothers. During the occupation, they had heard stories of Japanese soldiers administering water torture there to suspected sympathisers of the Malayan People's Anti-Japanese Army.

These stories involved Japanese soldiers forcing water down the noses and throats of their mainly Chinese victims until their bodies were bloated. With their victims tied to a board, their heads placed below their feet, the gang of rostered torturers would club the stomachs of their vomiting choking victims and repeat the process over and over until, sometimes, the gurgles ceased.

The Japanese routinely used such methods against American prisoners of war. Water-board torture was also a favoured means of ridding themselves of local Chinese they viewed as expendable. The Malay and Indian communities in Malaya generally fared better during the occupation than the Chinese, whose homeland had been at war with the Japanese since the mid-1930s.

The Japanese in Malaya dealt with suspected pro-mainland Chinese sympathisers ruthlessly. Thousands of Malayan Chinese simply disappeared during the occupation years. The Japanese supported the Indian independence movement by assisting the head of the provisional government of Free India, Subhas Chandra Bose, to establish units of an Indian National Army (INA) in Malaya.

Chandra Bose, as well as furthering his own independence cause by advocating military force in association with the Japanese, also managed to save the lives of a great many Indian migrants in Malaya who were quick to associate themselves with the INA. Philosophically Ram, a religious man primarily intent on survival for his family, was very much a quiet supporter of the INA.

Against this background there were limited wartime prospects for this proud Sikh family man. Among them he could work as a watchman on the Esplanade at a Japanese mechanical workshop; join Chandra Bose's INA division based in Penang; or accept the realities associated with a forced posting to the death railway in Burma, where starvation and exhaustion were the norm. Thousands of Tamil rubber tappers from Malaya far less fortunate than Ram died while working on the death rail projects.

In the early days of the occupation Ram and his Sikh friends harboured a certain respect for the Japanese, particularly the manner, speed and efficiency many of them exhibited in cycling their way down the Malayan peninsula to Singapore. There they achieved a notable victory over Lieutenant-General Percival's allied forces.

The European civilian population in Malaya, with the exception of a number of Christian brothers, a French priest who ran an orphanage for Tamil boys on Penang Road and a number of medical personnel, had won few friends among the Indian, Malay and Chinese communities of Penang when they boarded a whites-only train at Butterworth. En masse they fled down the peninsula on this train to the sanctuary of the so-called 'fortress Singapore'.

In the eyes of Ram and his Sikh, Indian, Chinese and Malay friends, when the British civilians boarded that train they also took with them any real hope of re-establishing a credible long-term, post-war colonial administration in Malaya.

The Japanese were quick to capitalise on this anti-British attitude and used the INA for propaganda purposes, while the Indian soldiers who enlisted in it saw it as a means, among other factors, of helping their extended families survive the hardships of occupation.

The Malayan Indian community was further motivated in its support for the INA when news filtered through of the British decision to imprison the entire Congress Party leadership in India.

In this environment Ram and his family were very much supporters of the INA, particularly members of the unit from Penang who fought alongside the Japanese in the quest for Indian liberation against fellow Indians, in the campaign in Burma in 1944.

As a way of showing this support Ram took his eldest son Baksis to a meeting addressed by Chandra Bose at the Indian Association field in Penang in 1943. There was standing room only during the speech on the club's grass field. Father and son came away impressed by what they saw, even though they found difficulty understanding, for language reasons, a lot of what the imposing character on the dais had to say.

A cousin of Ram, Tara Singh, died while fighting for the INA in the disastrous Burma campaign. Before Tara left for Rangoon and the Imphal front, under the leadership of Shah Nawaz Khan, a formal photograph was taken at a studio in Penang of Tara and Ram with the latter's sons Baksis, Santokh and Karpal. To this day the memory of the tall member of the Number One Guerilla Regiment in Burma, Tara, is much respected by Ram's descendants. Tara is remembered as a man who did what he had to do to achieve self-government for India.

Throughout the Japanese occupation, personal survival was the major preoccupation for the Malayan population. Thanks to Ram's and Kartar's efforts, all members of their family survived the hardships of life under Japan's Greater East Asia Co-prosperity Sphere in Malaya.

The early respect the local Asians had for their liberators from British colonialism soon gave way to distrust when they saw the daily atrocities and the food queues, which did little to prevent starvation. By the end of the war the population of Penang had endured enough of the Japanese.

his sons Baksis and Santokh stood in endless food queues
Road, Ram supplemented the family diet by obtaining rice
n his Japanese employers and growing vegetables himself.
e farmer born in Samana, just a few miles from the Golden
Amritsar, used the subsistence economy survival skills he had
i boy on the land in India.
family belonged to the Deo clan in northern India. He had
education, but realised as a young man he would have to leave
of a home in India if he was to break out of generations of

wn father Hakam Singh died a young man, which threw extra hardship and responsibility on Ram's shoulders to help his older brother Maghar with the endless work of growing wheat and rice on the family farm. As he lived his austere life, highlighted by regular daily readings of the holy book the *Adi Granth*, Ram heard the stories of Malaya being a land of milk and honey, with good prospects for enterprising young

Sikhs in the police force as bullock cart drivers or as security personnel in prosperous tin and iron mines.

Kehar Singh, a friend from the nearby village of Varpal, was one who spoke so enthusiastically of life in Malaya that Ram finally approached his older brother to obtain permission to emigrate. This bold request was granted on the clear understanding that money would be sent home to the family on a regular basis. Accompanied by his mentor Kehar, Ram set off for Malaya.

The first stage of the journey involved a train trip to Calcutta, where the enterprising young bachelors purchased bunk-class tickets on a steamer bound for Penang. After disembarking, Ram tried his luck at a mine outside Ipoh, working briefly as a guard for a Chinese concern, before returning to Penang where he was employed as a guard in the Penang Municipal Workshops.

He held this position for four years, returning to the Punjab in 1932 to complete formalities for his arranged marriage to Kartar. The simple ceremony took place at Kartar's home in the village of Khosay Randhirke, some 40 miles from Amritsar.

Soon after the marriage Ram resumed his job in Penang, leaving his wife behind in India. Their first son Baksis was born in 1933. He was almost two by the time Kartar decided to join her husband.

Life in Penang was a challenge for her at first; she found difficulty adapting from the single-race easygoing Sikh village lifestyle to the vibrant, communal, multi-racial Green Hall community.

She had understandably been reluctant to leave her village in the Punjab. She had grown up there, cooking food on cow dung-fuelled fires and blooming among the poorest of India's poor in a situation where two brothers — Ram and Maghar Singh — respectively married her and her sister Angrez Kaur. The brothers were given control of the land when they married the sisters, and for this reason, too, Kartar found it doubly difficult to give up her birthright by immediately following her husband to Malaya.

A dedicated Sikh throughout her life, Kartar remained absorbed in her religion in Malaya, dividing her time and energies between her young family and the Brick Kiln Road *gurdwara*.

Karpal was born on the eve of extraordinary times in Asia when he arrived in this world at the Penang Maternity Hospital, Macalister Road on 28 June 1940.

As a boy during the Japanese occupation Karpal was very much protected by his parents from the fear and deprivation which constituted everyday life, but he and his elder brothers had to take many horrifying sights for granted. An early memory involves battered bodies being transported to a hospital morgue and mass graves following an American bombing in the Sungai Pinang area. The victims in this case had been squashed to death after they took shelter in deep drains from the bombs of the Superfortresses. A bomb landed in the middle of a street, forcing the concrete drains where these people were sheltering to implode violently.

When the war ended Karpal was five years old. Unlike his brother Baksis, who was 12 in 1945, Karpal had not attended a Japanese school where the pupils studied the Japanese language and began their school day by singing the national anthem of the occupation forces. On a number of occasions, when in the company of his older brothers Baksis and Santokh, Karpal was instructed to bow to the Japanese flag whenever he passed sentries on duty on the streets of Georgetown. When passing the sentry stationed permanently outside Light Street Convent he and his brothers learned to bow the deepest of bows; they knew from bitter experience that failure to do so would earn them repeat bowings, slaps, kicks and the occasional whack with a rifle butt.

The brothers also saw members of Chinese families being asked to sit in the middle of Georgetown's streets by the Japanese occupiers. People would be picked out at random and forced onto lorries at bayonet point. Many were never seen or heard from again. The men selected by such means were sometimes beheaded. The fate of womenfolk left behind was often little more appealing as some of them were consigned to be 'comfort women' for the Japanese.

Karpal was just three when he found himself at the centre of a 'comfort woman' drama at his Green Hall home 18 months into the Japanese occupation. One afternoon a drunken Japanese soldier burst in on the household when the youngster was asleep in one of the ground-floor rooms. The soldier's intentions were obvious and all the womenfolk inside the house fled to avoid the none too subtle drunken overtures of this member of the Imperial Japanese Army. It was only when she was on the street outside her home that Kartar remembered her sleeping toddler still in the communal home.

Karpal's older brother Santokh remembers this crisis being quietly resolved by their father's cousin Tara, who went inside the house and discreetly shadowed the drunken young Japanese away from his prey. The tall and powerful Tara finally cajoled the man out of the house, where he eventually found his way back to his barracks. The intervention allowed the toddler to sleep soundly throughout the 30-minute drama. It was a much-relieved Kartar who rushed back into the house to find her son unharmed.

The incident highlighted the constant threat of violation experienced by Karpal's mother and her female friends. Like the Chinese, they lived with the prospect of being selected as 'comfort women' for the Japanese at a moment's notice.

The occupation was tough on Karpal's mother. Unlike her husband, she had no real opportunity to participate in the everyday activities of the short-lived regime. For her the occupation meant a denial of such basic rights as sustenance, security and safety for herself and her family.

Karpal's parents took every opportunity to prevent their young sons from witnessing the gruesome sights but his parents soon discovered it was impossible to shield their boisterous and carefree youngsters all the time from the daily atrocities of life under the Japanese.

In September 1945 the official surrender saw the Japanese occupiers of Penang marching down Brick Kiln Road in front of the Sikh temple with their hands on their heads. Karpal and his brothers were among the crowds who threw stones, jeers and taunts at the former masters and perpetrators of misery.

The months after the Japanese surrender were difficult ones for Ram. Bandits of many political shades came out of their hideouts in the surrounding jungles and began targeting those they perceived to have been too closely allied with the Japanese during the occupation.

The reality of Ram's situation, and thousands like him, had been that he had had little choice other than to work for the Japanese. So when the British returned, expecting to continue their colonial administration where they left off in 1941, Ram was in no hurry to publicise the fact he had been forced to work as a watchman by the Japanese at a workshop next to the historic Fort Cornwallis on the north-eastern tip of Penang Island.

Karpal's tumultuous early childhood years proved a useful apprenticeship for the rigours associated with his subsequent criminal law and political career. When confronted by major health problems in his adult life, Karpal often thought of the lesson learned from his parents during the family's wartime trials. It was a lesson in how to survive against all odds.

2 SINGAPORE FLING

The reality of life in 1946 Penang was of education-deprived Malayan youngsters, six- to ten-year-olds, queuing up to belatedly begin their formal education.

Like his peers from impoverished backgrounds, Karpal was just another overaged undernourished youngster by the time his parents found a Standard 1 position for him. He finally began school in 1948 when he was enrolled at St Xavier's Institution across the road from the court building in Penang.

Conditions at the bombed-out St Xavier's were challenging to say the least. The makeshift assembly hall for 1,500 pupils was simply the protective shelter and shade provided by a large rain tree (*albizia*). Karpal and his fellow Standard 1 pupils were taught in a thatched hut with a dirt floor; whenever the tropical rains came, the roof leaked and the classroom became a quagmire. It was years before the ashes and rubble left behind by the B-29 bombers were finally replaced by new classroom blocks.

In school, Karpal did well academically, particularly in English and History, but his performance on the sports field was mediocre. Looking back, his former teachers observed there was nothing to suggest that the quiet, conscientious, outwardly diffident student would develop into anything out of the ordinary.

The post-war years saw Ram move his family out of the Brick Kiln Road temple and into a former stable that had been converted into the Macalister Road Universal Cars garage. The steadily expanding family of nine children moved into a set of rooms adjoining the garage (along with the family cow housed in the back yard), and Ram worked as the watchman for its British owners. Amar Kaur, Simindar Kaur, Manjit Singh and Balwinder Singh completed Ram and Kartar's line-up of six sons and three daughters. The family lived in the converted garage for eight years.

As their financial situation improved slightly there was a further move in 1953 to a two-storey rental in Herriot Street owned by the widow Gurbachan Kaur. This woman was concerned for her safety, having to live alone during the first communist emergency years with terrorists known to be active in the predominantly Chinese Jelutong area. She suggested that Ram's family move in with her, and for the next 20 years Gurbachan became a second mother to Karpal and his many siblings.

When his own father died in 1974, Karpal was to repay the debt of gratitude his family owed to their surrogate mother. He and his wife Gurmit purchased a new house for his own mother — the only house she owned in her lifetime — and handed the Herriot Street property back in its entirety to Gurbachan and her heirs.

Ram's children were often called upon to help their father with his expanding herd of cows. The demands of helping to feed, water and milk the family cows inculcated a strong work ethic in Karpal. Apart from his dilatory university days in Singapore, he retained this attribute throughout his working life. A practical work ethic and hard-headedness inherited from his mother were also to stand him in good stead when placed alongside the education he received with its strong emphasis upon Sikhism at home and the arts at school.

At 5:00 a.m. every morning of his life Ram would rise from his stringed *charpoy* bed, douse himself with cold water from a bucket and recite aloud from memory the prescribed *Japji* morning prayer pieces from the Sikh *Adi Granth* holy book. The monotones invariably worked better than any alarm clock and while his father chanted his prayers, Karpal developed the early morning habit of memorising his homework while walking back and forth under a streetlight in front of the Herriot Street family home.

The quiet diligence he brought to his lessons early in his school career ensured he escaped the dreaded Monday morning *rotan* roll call. St Xavier's pupils breaking school rules came in for special attention from 'Lau Hor' (the old tiger), otherwise known as discipline master Brother Michael Paulin Blais. Lau Hor's use of the *rotan*, however, did not have the same impact as the corporal punishment methods employed by the family's Sikh priest and Gurmukhi script teacher. This heavily bearded gentleman regularly horrified his pupils by holding the wayward among them by the ankles — like chickens — and dangling them precariously over the first-storey temple balcony. Unlike the judicial *rotan* floggings still regularly administered in Malaysia, Brother Michael's *rotan* delivered just enough pain to make its recipients think at least briefly about mending their ways.

Karpal's parents were quietly encouraging their son to consider a career in medicine, but at home he was developing a reputation for speaking his mind, a characteristic that later pointed him in the

Karpal's family. (*Standing from left*) Jernal Singh, Santokh Singh, Baksis Singh and Karpal Singh; (*sitting from left*) Balwinder Singh, Amar Kaur, Kartar Kaur (mother), Manjit Singh, Ram Singh Deo (father), Ajit Kaur and Simindar Kaur.

direction of law. School days coincided with Chin Peng's 1948–60 communist emergency in Malaya. Many recent former students of St Xavier's Institution involved themselves in the armed forces in the quest to remove Chin Peng's communists from the Malayan and southern Thai jungles.

Measures adopted by the colonial British government during the emergency — at its height there were 300,000 allied servicemen up against a few thousand jungle-based communist guerrillas — meant all Malayan citizens over the age of 12 had to carry an official identity card.

In July 1952, just a year after Britain's liberal High Commissioner to Malaya Sir Henry Gurney was ambushed and gunned down while being driven in his car north of Kuala Lumpur, Karpal Singh became Malayan citizen number 1,836,265.

When St Xavier's officially celebrated the end of the communist guerrilla war, Karpal and his fellow school leavers of 1960 recalled the deeds of a former schoolmate TS Sambanthanmurthi. An undercover policeman, he penetrated the communist ranks as a double agent during the emergency, living as a terrorist unsuspected by his red comrades in the jungle. He was subsequently awarded the George Cross for his efforts at a secret ceremony in Kuala Lumpur.

Malaya won its independence from the British in 1957, towards the end of Chin Peng's guerrilla war. It was a time when the now tranquil war cemeteries in places like Batu Gajah outside Ipoh had almost seen the last of white planter, police and military funerals.

While *merdeka* (political independence) was a time of great rejoicing for the Malay community, it was also a time of uncertainty for Ram and Kartar. They had to choose whether to follow their white sahibs to Britain, or return to rural India with their family and run the risk of alienating fellow ancestral property owners, or throw in their lot permanently in Malaya by becoming permanent citizens.

Malaya's Chinese had earlier had their future options limited when they were forced to cut ties with mainland China in 1949 when the communists came to power there.

In the wake of Independence Ram and Kartar decided to place their family's future citizenship in Tunku Abdul Rahman's administration. The new government pledged constitutional protection for members of the Indian and Chinese communities. The new political structure allowed for Malaysian Indian Congress (MIC) and Malaysian Chinese Association (MCA) participation alongside the dominant political power base of the United Malays National Organisation (UMNO).

Karpal, as a bright 20-year-old, was presented with the award of runner-up to dux Fong Wang Pak at St Xavier's prize-giving in 1960 when his schooldays ended.

In the eyes of his parents second best was not good enough for Karpal. They still wanted him to study to be a doctor, specifically at the Punjab University Medical College in India, where he would also be exposed to the culture of his ancestors. His parents knew if they could persuade him to study medicine in India he could live with friends and family and graduate as a qualified doctor relatively cheaply.

Kartar had another reason for wanting her son to study medicine: she and a friend in the Punjab had earmarked Karpal for an arranged marriage to a Sikh medical student.

Despite the pressure to become a doctor, Karpal's wish to study law held sway at a family conference involving his parents, oldest brother Baksis and himself. At secondary school he had decided upon a career in law, in part as a result of his history studies, which showed him how many political leaders had used their expertise in law to further their political ambitions. The family resolved he would attend the University of Singapore and study law. It was a big commitment for a poor family, and in making it his parents were singling Karpal out for a special role in the family.

In an ideal world he might have been sent to the United Kingdom to study law at the Inner Temple, Gray's Inn, Lincoln's Inn or the Middle Temple but Ram's family simply did not have the money to fund such an education. With the assurance of financial support from Baksis, who studied radiography in Kuala Lumpur from 1960 to 1961, Karpal became a resident of Dunearn Road Hostel and a law student at the University of Singapore in 1961.

Away from the secure home environment for the first time in his life, Karpal initially exhibited the same dedication to study displayed at secondary school. However, his hitherto sheltered existence had not prepared him for the tough rites of passage associated with the start of university life.

The 'ragging' indoctrination to student life left this product of a good St Xavier's Catholic education shocked when senior Chinese and Indian residents of his hostel abused him with a flurry of four-letter words in the presence of a lady handling hostel enrolment procedures. On this occasion Karpal asked his abusers to leave him alone as he could recall having done nothing to upset them. Nor could he understand why the dutiful Chinese clerk did not answer his questions and appeared to tolerate the verbal volley of filth from his accusers. He discovered later the lady was deaf and had agreed to oblige the 'raggers' by removing her hearing aid whenever a new hostel entrant arrived.

Throughout his life Karpal was a quick learner and it was no coincidence that by the time he left university, he was known among freshmen as 'King Ragger'. There are a few judges on the Malaysian bench today who have special cause to remember their introduction to university life from King Ragger such that not all the marginal decisions go his way.

King Ragger met his match in an unusual showdown with a man who went on to become a prominent Singapore criminal lawyer Subhas Anandan. Freshman Anandan did not take kindly to what he perceived to be Karpal's bullying tactics, so he organised for friends from the Sembawang naval base to visit the university and teach the upstart Sikh a lesson. The showdown between the two men was to take place at Union House at about 7:00 p.m. and Anandan was surprised when Karpal did not front for the big pre-arranged scrap. What the Singaporean student did not know, however, was that Karpal's friends had overpowered him and tied him up in his room 15 minutes before the fight.

For years Anandan thought Karpal was a coward who had chickened out of a big ragging scrap at the eleventh hour. Later, having been briefed on the reason for the no-show, Anandan asked Karpal to fly to Singapore to represent Singapore Workers' Party Chairman Wong Hong Toy in a

(*above left*) King Ragger (right) in action during his university days in Singapore, putting a Sikh necktie hold on a 'newbie', 1963; (*right*) Karpal in his hostel room.

contempt of court case. The two men reminisced over their crazy student antics. Anandan told Karpal he was glad his friends had tied him up and prevented him from keeping the appointment for what would have been one hell of a scrap.

In 1962 a significant change occurred in Karpal's approach to his studies. His hostel friends were the first to recognise the young Sikh's leadership, advocacy and political skills by electing him President of the Dunearn Road Hostel and as a member of the university's student union. The young student leader clearly enjoyed the political opportunities provided by his newfound freedom and the confidence his peers had placed in him.

Nevertheless, while the student politician regularly skipped lectures and was clearly enjoying himself on a voyage of self-discovery in Singapore, he continued to enjoy the financial backing of his family. However, his success in student elections did oldest brother and financial benefactor Baksis no favours whatsoever. The judgement on Karpal's fitness to be called to the Malaysian Bar took eight years to deliver. Surprisingly, Baksis never once threatened to cut off the money supply during his brother's student days.

Karpal at the Taj Mahal, Agra, on his first trip to India in 1963.

In the mid-1960s, there was always an annual day of reckoning for Karpal after yet another set of unsuccessful exam results was posted on the university notice board. He would have to apologetically face his oldest brother (who in turn reported to their father) and explain to him the vicissitudes of university life and why he had failed yet again. With an understanding smile upon his face and a characteristic knowing roll of the head, Baksis would explain to his younger brother that he had been hearing about certain things. He repeatedly told him the future hopes of the family lay upon his law-student shoulders and would then urge him to do better the following year. Ram's reaction to his son's failure at exam time was one of confidence in the young man's ability and of patience. As a watchman, Ram had learned much about patience.

The excursion into university politics did provide Karpal with an unexpected and valuable real-world lesson in how to deal with tough political opponents. It came in 1963 when the People's Action Party leader in Singapore Lee Kuan Yew, seeking to expand his party, led Singapore into the Federation of Malaya.

Lee Kuan Yew's hard-line political style resulted in problems of academic freedom and university autonomy for students and staff at the University of Singapore. The university authorities introduced a vetting system whereby students had to prove their suitability to embark upon study courses. Karpal reacted to the requirement by organising a series of demonstrations opposing the vetting processes. The move, which failed to change the policy in any way, saw him suspended from his hostel for two weeks, along with 14 other student residents.

The student politician and president of Dunearn Road Hostel addressing his peers.

The perennial student was nicknamed Gandhi by his father, after the non-violent lawyer leader of Indian nationalism, who Ram observed also went through a period of adolescent rebellion.

When Karpal discovered the university authorities had sent a letter of complaint to Ram regarding his son's political activities the rascal student leader realised he could expect no Gandhi-like pacifism, reason or tolerance from his father. A looming family crisis was narrowly averted when someone close to Karpal's family, then a post office worker in Penang, intercepted the official letter of complaint from the Singapore authorities addressed to Ram. Thanks to this loyalty Ram never did get to read the official Singapore version of his wayward son.

To the university authorities in Singapore went the distinction of imposing the first of what would be Karpal's numerous suspensions of a political nature. This first clash with officialdom, in comparison to the major suspensions from the Malaysian parliament and Penang State Assembly to follow, was a relatively minor affair. Karpal, never one to shy away from righting a perceived wrong, would make sure he squared the ledger with Lee Kuan Yew in his own way later in life.

The suspension from the Dunearn Road Hostel was lifted following talks between Student Union President Gilbert Chai, his executive and the Chancellor of the University of Singapore Dato' Dr Lee Kong Chian. Karpal, who lived in a garage during the suspension and was fed well via the back door of his university hostel by sympathetic kitchen staff, remained unrepentant for his part in organising the 'autonomy day' demonstrations.

The official University of Singapore Dunearn Road Hostel 1963–64 *Psyche* magazine quoted the student leader, who summarised the suspension in a diplomatic yet typically uncompromising fashion:

> There was actually no question of disobedience at all. It was just the observance of a fundamental principle of one's rights, namely the right to question legitimate authority which one upholds with respect and dignity. The deprivation of this right is tantamount to dictatorship. The imposition of the suspension order was arbitrary because none of the students were given a fair hearing before the order was imposed.

At this stage of his life the questioner of all forms of authority had clearly embarked down a lifetime road. The confident anti-establishment manner he exhibited during and after the 'autonomy day' demonstrations impressed his peers, and the student leader had little difficulty consolidating the hostel presidency position.

Over jugs of Tiger Beer at the nearby Wahab's Highway Inn,

Karpal on his Matchless motorbike;
(*above*) Karpal finally graduates from
the University of Singapore in 1968.

Karpal focused on the need for a nightclub at the all-male hostel and the discussions materialised in 1965 into the establishment of the Kosmo Club, where students could entertain their guests in comfortable surroundings.

Also at university he purchased an old and noisy World War II army surplus Matchless motorbike. Knowing little about how to ride or maintain a motorbike, he got his machine for SGD150, the deal being struck beneath the palm trees overlooking the university's soccer and hockey pitches. When he saw the new owner disappear over a bank in the university grounds while on his first test ride, the vendor took the money and ran.

So loud in fact was the motorbike that at the end of every university term Kartar swore she could hear her son riding on the causeway over the Straits of Johor to begin the long ride home up the peninsula.

Whenever he headed home from Singapore on the bike, he always had a passenger on the back, whose main role was to help push-start the machine and pick up parts from the road as various pieces of mechanical equipment became detached.

On one memorable journey the law student detoured via Kuantan, the capital of the east coast state of Pahang, with student friend A Mariadas as pillion. Such was the noise of the machine it attracted the unwelcome attention of a dozing water buffalo. Woken from its monotonous cud-chewing, the savage ox-like creature charged in the direction of the noisy motorbike. Its rounded horns and fat muddy black coat brushed the handle bars and terrified the swerving rider and his passenger. Shaking, Karpal took some time to bring his severely jolted machine to a halt.

With the motorbike stationary it was discovered that Mariadas (who later became an Ipoh lawyer) had lost his glasses in the encounter. Great was their concern when they realised the glasses lay on the road between them and the buffalo, which was gazing menacingly at the riders over its steaming elongated nostrils. Given the situation, Karpal believed there was clearly no need to recover the glasses on this occasion. He was, therefore, surprised to see Mariadas venture out into no man's land to retrieve them. The beast fortunately remained motionless during the recovery operation and in no time at all rider and fully-sighted pillion were once again speeding towards Kuantan, harbouring new respect for the boldness and charging ability of water buffaloes.

Not all trips home contained such drama and in the latter years of his university life, there was an added incentive to nurse his motorbike home as safely as possible. He could not help but notice, every time he returned to Penang, how much the girl whose father kept a herd of cows next to Ram's herd in the Ayer Itam area had changed since he first set eyes on her in 1958.

Gurmit Kaur was the ninth of Sohan Singh Gill and Puran Kaur's 13 children. She was a secondary school pupil at a convent school in Penang when she first unofficially met Karpal. Her father was just

13 and her mother 14 when they married in the Punjab in 1923 before establishing their home in southern Thailand where, through hard work, Sohan established himself as a planter. Then her parents set up a home in Penang, Malaya when Gurmit was aged eight, primarily to enable the younger children to complete their education in good schools.

As is common in many families, there were initial differences between the prospective in-laws. Karpal and Gurmit were, therefore, required to date each other discreetly in their early days of courtship.

The law student was under pressure from his family to finish his degree. He was not aided in this quest when, in 1966, he was elected Assistant Secretary-General of the Student Union Council in Singapore. That year he also suffered the humiliation of failing his exams and finishing bottom of his class.

It seemed to some of his lecturers, among them Professor Tommy Koh, that the 'Sikh fellow' from Penang had no real desire to graduate, as this would have meant having to say farewell to the security of the university. Koh (later to become Singapore's ambassador to the United States) sat Karpal down one day and said to him, "Look here, Karpal, don't you want to go home?"

Karpal responded, "Well if you fellows will not let me go home, what can I do about it?"

The result of this conversation saw Koh obtain an agreement from Karpal to attend lectures and complete assignments in between carrying out student political activities such as publishing student journals, organising debating tournaments, presiding over university beauty queen competitions and packing as many people as possible into hostel rooms and Austin 7 cars.

Karpal's lifelong friend Daniel Raphael (an electrical engineer nicknamed 'Dynamo' by Karpal's mother) was among the first to recognise his schoolmate's legal potential. "I told him during his university days he would be a good lawyer. He had always been a very logical straightforward person," Raphael said of his friend.

With Koh's continued cajoling support, Karpal graduated from the University of Singapore with an LLB Hons in 1968. All that remained for him now to be called to the bar was to complete nine months 'reading in chambers' in a law firm.

The prospect of being called to the bar and organising his marriage to Gurmit in the Brick Kiln Road *gurdwara* became the two major priorities in the 28-year-old's life. He foresaw little difficulty in being able to achieve both objectives harmoniously in the short term as he rode his old motorbike out over the causeway into Johor Bahru for the last time. He also considered himself fortunate to obtain a junior position with a respected Chinese lawyer Lim Huck Aik, who specialised in civil work in Penang.

All was well in Karpal's world until one day in November 1968 when he was stopped in the street by leading Penang criminal lawyer Jagjit Singh, who asked the keen young university graduate why he had decided to work for a Chinese law firm.

Jagjit told Karpal he was a good friend of his father, and as a newcomer to the profession he should have first sought to broaden his criminal law experience by seeking work with Jagjit Singh & Co. Karpal was invited to call by his office at any time after hours so he might gain some understanding of the real workings of a criminal law practice in Malaysia. The reason behind the invitation left Karpal feeling strangely uneasy about the elderly Sikh lawyer's motives. He made a point of diplomatically dropping by to visit the senior lawyer in his Penang office from time to time.

It did not take too long for the aspiring lawyer's suspicions to be confirmed. Shortly before he was due to be called to the bar in the Kuala Lumpur High Court in 1969, Karpal was advised by the Malaysian Bar

Council that Jagjit was formally opposing his call.

Experienced Malaysian lawyers say Jagjit's move against the young man's call was unprecedented. It was motivated, they said, by a fear of possible future competition.

In his letter of complaint to the Malaysian Bar Council, Jagjit alleged Karpal had passed himself off as a fully-fledged lawyer while negotiating for Penang office space. This was in anticipation of establishing a sole practice after being called to the bar.

The matter was heard before Justice Ong Hock Sim. Karpal explained to the High Court judge how he had negotiated in good faith for the office space with the landlord, who was an old Indian moneylender. Following this explanation Justice Ong dismissed the senior Penang lawyer's objection.

"Call this man to the bar," Justice Ong said in no uncertain terms before going on to warmly welcome him to his new profession. It was perhaps fitting that the man who was destined to become Malaysia's most noted criminal and constitutional lawyer should himself have received his call to the bar in such controversial circumstances.

Nothing in Karpal's life, it seemed, was destined to proceed smoothly. Since then, the name Karpal Singh was never far from controversy in Malaysian political and legal life.

There was a sequel to the Jagjit Singh incident, but on this occasion the inexperienced practitioner had nothing to do with the righting of the wrong. The solution was implemented by his uneducated father and administered during a trustees meeting at the Brick Kiln Road *gurdwara* in Penang, soon after Karpal's call to the bar.

Jagjit, a respected member of the Sikh community, was chairing the meeting of trustees, many of whom were illiterate, when the behaviour of a particular trustee came under scrutiny regarding the unauthorised transfer of temple funds from one bank account to another. Despite no suggestion of theft or misappropriation, Ram expressed concern that temple funds should not be used in such cavalier fashion. Lawyer Jagjit supported the movement of the funds and in doing so said to Ram, "Do you know who I am? I am a lawyer."

Ram quietly responded, "Do you know who I am? I am the father of a lawyer." The funds were quietly returned to the appropriate bank account a few days later.

Jagjit apparently regretted his opposition to Karpal's call to the bar because he told friends and acquaintances after the incident how he went to the trouble of having the young man's horoscope read one day in Alor Setar. "My God! That man's going to go very far. Don't tangle with him," he rather belatedly advised friends and associates.

Following the 'unprecedented' challenge to his call to the bar Karpal thought better of opening his own practice in Penang immediately. He accepted a junior position with the criminal law firm of Raja Ridzuan in Alor Setar, south of the Thai border.

His first case in Alor Setar involved the theft of a buffalo and the result was a morale-boosting victory. He worked for Raja Ridzuan in Alor Setar until he opened his own office in Penang in 1971.

With his legal career soundly launched Karpal was now in a position to think about taking on other responsibilities, such as marriage to Gurmit. Here again there were problems for the young lawyer in the build-up to the marriage as Karpal's mother was not in favour of the union.

For their part, Gurmit's parents viewed Karpal as being the top prospect in Penang for their daughter. They had seen him develop and were impressed by his personal attributes and academic qualifications.

Gurmit was then working as a reservations clerk for Malaysian Airlines in Penang. On 30 July 1970 her third oldest brother Jagir Singh gave his second-to-youngest sister away to Karpal, with the bride wearing the traditional red sari.

On 30 July 1970 Karpal married into another large Sikh family. The members of Gurmit Kaur's family are pictured above. (*Standing from left*) Gurmit Kaur, Anokh Singh, Bhagwan Singh, Jagir Singh, Harcharan Singh, Balvinder Singh; (*seated from left*) Amarjit Kaur, Gurdiap Kaur, Sohan Singh Gill (father), Puran Kaur (mother), Jagjit Kaur, Sarvinder Kaur; (*seated on floor from left*) Manjinder Singh, Manjit Kaur, Prakash Singh.

There were 100 guests at the Mandarin Hotel wedding reception. The couple enjoyed an extended honeymoon in a beach hotel at Batu Ferringhi before moving into a Burma Road flat. From there Karpal commuted to his law office in Alor Setar.

On 3 May 1971 their first son Jagdeep Singh was born.

He did not know it at the time of his marriage, but Karpal's family — and Gurmit in particular — would be tested in ways few people are these days. There had been many times over the years when Karpal was grateful he stood up to his family and chose the woman he wanted to marry. This was a choice he refused to allow his mother, until that time the dominating influence in his life, to make for him by way of a traditional arranged marriage.

(*left and below*) Karpal and Gurmit at their marriage registration, 30 July 1970.

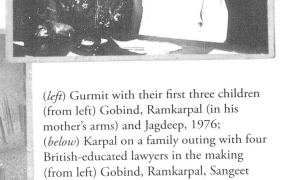

(*left*) Gurmit with their first three children (from left) Gobind, Ramkarpal (in his mother's arms) and Jagdeep, 1976; (*below*) Karpal on a family outing with four British-educated lawyers in the making (from left) Gobind, Ramkarpal, Sangeet and Jagdeep, 1983.

Once upon a time: The family law firm in business, (from left) second son Gobind, brother Manjit, Karpal, and oldest son Jagdeep. Gobind is also MP for Puchong while Jagdeep is DAP assemblyman for Dato Keramat.

Third lawyer son Ramkarpal has been groomed for a career in politics. This was obvious for all to see when he addressed approximately 100,000 people at a political meeting in Penang on 3 May 2013. One year later, he won the Bukit Gelugor seat that his father had left vacant.

Mankarpal, the youngest of Karpal's and Gurmit's five children, is the only one of the four sons who has not become a lawyer. He studied mathematics, operational research, statistics and economics at Warwick University in the UK.

Sangeet Kaur works out of the Karpal Singh & Co. Kuala Lumpur office. Since 2005 she had worked closely with her father on a number of important cases, including Anwar Ibrahim's Sodomy II case.

3 JUSTICE FOR FATHER

In the early 1970s the lawyer's retired parents were living the good life of proud doting grandparents in Penang when Ram decided it was time to once again visit family members in the Punjab. In particular he wanted to pay homage at Sikhdom's holy Golden Temple shrine in Amritsar.

Soon after his arrival in May 1974, in his traditional, long, white sarong-like *lungi* and short-sleeved *kameez* over-garment, peaked turban and battered sandals, Ram was killed instantly in a tail-end collision. The high seat of his rickshaw was hit by an out-of-control car and he was thrown head-first onto the pavement of a railway overbridge.

The telegram bringing the news from the Punjab left Ram's extended family in Malaysia devastated. The husband, father and grandfather had been in high spirits and perfect health as he left Penang days earlier. Amidst the family's grief was the consoling thought that he had met his death in the place where he would have most wanted to die — at home in Amritsar.

Upon hearing this news, Karpal and his elder brother Santokh made hurried arrangements to fly to the Punjab themselves. They considered it their duty to officiate at the funeral pyre service of their father.

At the back of his sons' minds was a niggling thought that their father might have been a victim of the terrorist foul play prevalent throughout the Punjab at that time, or that he might have found himself caught up in a land dispute. Murders of a territorial nature are not unusual in India, particularly in cases where absentee landlords return from overseas seeking to reclaim their rights.

Nothing could have been further from the truth in Ram's case, as he had successfully established a new life for his extended family in Malaya and — from 1963 — Malaysia. Nevertheless the dutiful lawyer son resolved that there would be justice for father in the latter's homeland if there was any hint of foul play surrounding his sudden death.

The normal feelings of grief aside, the emergency trip to the Punjab could not have come at a worse time for Karpal. In May 1974 he was involved in one of his first murder trials in Alor Setar. The presiding judge proved sensitive to the defence counsel's personal predicament and, after the dismissal of the jury, Karpal was granted leave to fly to India to attend his father's funeral.

The unease surrounding the death of their father was exacerbated soon after the brothers arrived as they had difficulty establishing the whereabouts of the body. They went first to their mother's remote village of Khosay Randhirke, where they were informed the cremation ceremony had taken place earlier in the day at their father's village of Samna Pind. The task of lighting Ram's funeral pyre had gone to his older brother Maghar. Thoughts of foul play surrounding a father's death were quickly dissipated when the two Malaysians met their uncle and aunt Maghar and Angrez, and their cousins Bhola Singh, Sucha Singh and Ajit Singh at their father's village.

The two brothers were much moved by their grieving relatives during the final stages of Ram's *path da bhog* (funeral rites). Karpal was particularly struck during this, his second visit to India, by the obvious piety and poverty of the supportive relatives as he recalled the discipline and simplicity of his father's life.

It was a reflective Karpal who looked down on the remains of his father's smashed skull and breastbones, the remnants of the cremation. Looking at his own right wrist he recalled the symbolism of the *kada* (steel bracelet) given to him by his father in Penang's Brick Kiln Road *gurdwara* years earlier. Never forget your roots, his father had said as he placed the *kada* on his son's wrist. These words took on new meaning as the son stood in the Punjabi fields tilled by his father and his ancestors for centuries. Had it not been for a father's enterprising decision to leave for a new life in Malaya 48 years earlier, Karpal's life would inevitably have been played out in a mud hut, an annual crop cycle dictated by monsoons and the blazing sun.

On the day of his death on 18 May 1974 Ram had risen early, as he always did, and walked from his birthplace through the wheat and rice fields to the Golden Temple without telling anyone of his plans. On this final journey he walked past the shrine of one of Sikhdom's most revered martyrs Baba Dip Singh Shahid, a warrior who made his reputation as a disciple of Guru Gobind Singh in the wars against 18th-century Afghan invaders.

The Golden Temple legend surrounding Baba Dip Singh Shahid has it that the Sikh had his head cut off in battle near Tarn Taran, outside Amritsar. Clutching his head in one hand, the decapitated Sikh continued to fight his way back into the temple complex before finally succumbing to his injuries. For millions of Sikhs worldwide the story was an inspiring one. It was one of the reasons Ram returned from Malaysia to revisit the temple whenever he could.

Normally when he went out of his way to walk in Baba Dip Singh Shahid's bloody footsteps Ram was accompanied by a family member, but on the day of his death the man in his 70s, who never knew his true age, walked alone to the temple. He bathed in Sikhdom's sacred waters before hailing a rickshaw to get to his bank in Amritsar. After withdrawing money from the bank, earmarked for use to upgrade his brother's mud hut in the village of Samna Pind, Ram's rickshaw wallah rode across a railway bridge before making a left turn and heading down a small incline. A car following behind lost its brakes on the incline and smashed into the back of the rickshaw. The rickshaw wallah survived with minor injuries.

The car driver delivered Ram's lifeless body to a nearby hospital before travelling to Samna Pind and breaking the news to the old man's relatives.

Maghar never recovered from his younger brother's death. He died later in 1974, reportedly of a broken heart, after blaming himself for the accident. Maghar erected a humble monument in Ram's honour among the family fields where his ashes blended in with the soil. There, for the remaining months of his life, he would go and share his meals and talk to the spirit of his brother who had returned to his own Sikh roots to die.

Some of Karpal's relatives in Punjab. His cousins Bhola Singh
(far left) and Ajit Singh (far right) at the village of Khosay
Randhirke, 2011.

(*above left*) The author at Ram Singh's memorial erected by Ram's brother
Maghar in Samna Pind, Punjab, July 1999; (*right*) Ram's nephew Sucha Singh
(with turban) at the exact spot in Amritsar where Ram died; the rickshaw
in which he was travelling was struck from behind by a runaway car. *Photos
courtesy of Gabrielle Donoghue.*

4 SCHOOLBOY KILLERS

The beginnings of Karpal's career as a practising lawyer in Alor Setar coincided with a troubled period of Malaysian history dominated by the Kuala Lumpur race riots of 1969. As a result of these bitter and bloody riots between members of the Malay, Indian and Chinese communities, the disparate Communist Party of Malaya found itself with a flood of untrained applicants looking for jungle guerrilla work.

This increased militancy at the time of the second emergency years in Malaysia provided the springboard for Karpal to launch a legal career of national prominence.

As well as being a young father and husband in the early 1970s, Karpal found himself as the unofficial lawyer of choice for communists on the wrong side of the law.

In the eyes of many of his fellow lawyers, representing such people in Malaysia at this time was not a financially sound career move. In recent history Karpal would have been about as popular, in American military circles, as the lawyers who represented Iraqi president Saddam Hussein before his internationally televised trip to the gallows in Baghdad.

While most other lawyers shied away from taking on the briefs of communist insurgents, Karpal relished the prospect of such high-profile work in the death penalty environment.

It was no coincidence therefore that when three men went to their deaths on Pudu Jail's gallows on 15 March 1980, two of them were clients of Karpal. March 15 is a significant date in Malaysia's capital punishment history — there had been no judicial hangings in Malaysia for 11 years until that day. The three men were hanged under the 1960 Internal Security Act (ISA) and Essential (Security Cases) Regulations 1975 (ESCAR).

During his five decades of practising law Karpal had more than 50 clients go to their deaths on prison gallows. Looking back, he said the country's busiest gallows at Pudu, Kajang and Taiping prisons had hosted two distinct groups of condemned since 1980.

The first group can broadly be termed the 'communists' or 'security prisoners' of the 1980s, while the second group continues to routinely number among its ranks common criminals such as drug traffickers and murderers. Karpal recalled how the Vietcong victory over the Americans in Vietnam brought renewed confidence to followers of Malaysian communism, and the government justified its enactment of the ESCAR following numerous terrorist attacks throughout the country.

Under the ISA, the death penalty became mandatory for anyone found in possession of firearms in any area declared a security area, and in any part of the country when circumstances raised 'a reasonable presumption that the individual intends, or is about to act, or has recently acted, in a manner prejudicial to public security'.

One of the attacks resulting in the hard-line legislation occurred one morning in June 1974 when Malaysia's Inspector-General of Police (IGP) Tan Sri Abdul Rahman Hashim was being driven to work in his Mercedes along Kuala Lumpur's Jalan Raja Chulan.

After the car came to a stop near the busy Jalan Tun Perak intersection, two well-dressed young men walked out of the crowd and pumped seven bullets into the nation's top policeman. Their mission completed, they calmly disappeared into the anonymity of the throng heading towards the highly organised chaos of the Puduraya bus terminal.

Soon after the IGP had been taken to hospital, his son Najib Rahman, a newspaper reporter, arrived on the scene and saw his father's blood in the back seat of the car. His presence personalised what was clearly a national tragedy.

Communist rebels from the Betong West communist group subsequently claimed responsibility for this bold attack, but no one was ever convicted for this crime. There was little doubt, though, in the mind of the chief investigating officer Assistant Commissioner of Police Mokhtar Marahakim that the murder had been the work of communist terrorists.

The police had no firm leads on the brazen gunmen until 17 months later when the Ipoh-based Chief Police Officer (CPO) for the state of Perak Tan Sri Khoo Chong Kong and his driver Sergeant Yong Peng Cheong were also gunned down in similar broad daylight circumstances in the town of Ipoh.

On 13 November 1975 at 12:55 p.m. the CPO, sitting in the back seat, and his driver were heading along Ashby Road in the CPO's official vehicle. At the junction of Ashby Road and Fair Park Road they stopped at the traffic lights, whereupon two youths on a motorcycle pulled up beside them, dismounted and opened fire at the occupants inside the car. After leaving both the driver and the CPO dead, the young killers threw pamphlets on the road, turned their motorcycle back in the direction they had come from and made good their escape.

Among those who gave evidence before the Ipoh High Court against the 'schoolboy killers' — dubbed such as they were wearing school uniforms — were sugar cane seller Lee Kok Wah and workshop assistant Ramli bin Hussain.

On the day of the shootings, Lee had been selling sugar cane near the road junction. He told the court he had heard gunshots and seen a person squat by the side of the CPO's Volvo, while another person holding a gun backed away to cover the scene. Lee said he then saw two people leave on a motorcycle. One of them had earlier fired a few shots at the back seat of the car through the rear side window while the other had gone to the front of the car and fired shots.

Ramli bin Hussain had been a pillion rider on a motorcycle that stopped at the traffic lights alongside the CPO's car. When the lights turned green the rider Gopinathan proceeded through the intersection. Ramli then heard gunshots behind him. He turned around and saw two men wearing school uniforms of the nearby Anderson School holding pistols and calmly going about the methodical execution of their targets.

The police got a break when a hopelessly lost Ipoh man Ng Foo Nam was apprehended in the jungle in the Thai-Malaysian border area. At the time he was trying to find his way back to his communist camp headquarters. The rigorous interrogation of Ng at the Ipoh police station led police to Ng's accomplice in the Perak police murders. Lim Woon Chong was arrested at his Kuala Lumpur residence in November 1976. Both men were charged with the Ipoh murders under the ESCAR. They were also charged with possession of Llama 7.65 pistols and seven rounds of 7.65 mm ammunition. The charges against them carried a mandatory death penalty.

In the three months leading up to the CPO's shooting in Ipoh, there had been a bomb explosion in an attempt to destroy the National Monument and a grenade attack on the Police Field Force Platoon Headquarters in Kuala Lumpur. Such attacks understandably evoked a strong anti-communist mood throughout the country, and in March 1976 Prime Minister Tun Hussein Onn said his major preoccupation was the security of the nation.

Lim's father Lim Tian approached Karpal to represent his son in the forthcoming Ipoh High Court trial. From this point onwards Karpal became the unofficial lawyer for an increasing number of communist party members, all of whom faced the death penalty.

Early on in his dealings with the communists, Karpal realised they were very different clients from the common criminals he dealt with. During the five years he knew them, the 'schoolboy killers' Lim and Ng made numerous attempts to convert Karpal away from his Democratic Action Party (DAP) political affiliations.

Buoyed by the communist victory in Indochina against the United States, Lim and Ng told Karpal of their desire to eliminate the leaders of the Malaysian police force. By doing that, they told their lawyer, they would keep the communist cause in the headlines. They argued that the victory of the revolution would occur only when country folk surrounded the cities and seized political power through armed struggle.

Karpal disagreed with his clients on their methods of achieving social change in Malaysia. Indeed it was chilling for Karpal to realise that Lim and his fellow communists practised what they preached. The bodies of police officers, particularly over-zealous Chinese ones, would often be found in drains alongside city streets in Kuala Lumpur, and the lawyer sympathised with the problems the authorities had in maintaining law and order in this 'wild west' environment. Based on information from his communist clients it appeared that there was an understandable reluctance, particularly among Chinese members of the police force, to exhibit too much diligence in attempting to solve a number of police murders at this time.

Lim and Ng inevitably went to the gallows on 15 March 1980 under the 1960 Internal Security Act regulations, a rehash of the 1948 emergency regulations enacted at the height of the communist insurgency under British colonial rule. (The communist rebellion featured thousands of ruthless killings, and after Independence in 1957 the new authorities saw a need to perpetuate emergency legislation to combat terrorism. This led to the passing of the Internal Security Act in 1960 to combat communist Chinese subversion in a young nation struggling to find its financial, social and economic feet.)

Following the Kuala Lumpur race riots of May 1969 there was widespread support for the Agong (king) Sultan Ismail Nasiruddin when he promulgated, under the umbrella of the ISA, emergency regulations empowering him 'to make essential regulations for securing public safety, the defence of Malaysia, the maintenance of public order and of supplies and services essential to the life of the community'.

Although parliament resumed control from the National Operations Council in February 1971, emergency powers remained in force, and an ESCAR amendment to the ISA was promulgated on 4 October 1975 in response to ongoing underground activities of communist and other subversive elements.

Against this background, the ESCAR trial of Lim and Ng began before Justice Fred Arulanandom in the Ipoh High Court on 19 July 1977 amidst extremely tight security.

Karpal's client Lim was flown by military helicopter from Pudu Jail in Kuala Lumpur to Ipoh before the trial began. Justice Arulanandom and the prosecutor Abu Talib Othman (who later became Malaysia's

Attorney-General) were under constant armed guard throughout the trial. Prosecution witnesses had their identities protected by the erection of screens, meaning they could only be seen by counsel and the judge while giving evidence in court. Karpal and fellow lawyer ST Lee, who defended Ng, along with everyone else attending the trial, were thoroughly searched upon entering the court compound on a daily basis.

From the outset Lim and Ng made it clear they had no intention of co-operating with the court and did little to help their cause by ignoring Justice Arulanandom's orders to stand at the beginning and end of court sessions. Contempt of court meant nothing to the defendants for the only orders they took any notice of were from their masters who had instructed them to eliminate Perak's CPO; by carrying out this order they believed they had achieved the purpose of eroding the morale of the security forces inside Malaysia.

The relationship between Justice Arulanandom and Karpal during this trial was also somewhat strained. The trial followed an altercation in the Penang High Court a year before when the judge had chastised Karpal during a *habeas corpus* case, saying courts were 'not circuses for legal acrobatics and counsel are not entitled to consider themselves ringmasters'.

Karpal reacted by discharging himself from the case the following day, saying 'there is a possibility Your Lordship may be biased in view of Your Lordship's comments yesterday'. The comment evoked a warning from the judge at the time that Karpal might find himself in jail for contempt if he was suggesting the court was biased.

During the police investigation in the tense build-up to the trial of Lim and Ng,

Justice Fred Arulanandom.

the defendants proudly told police in cautioned statements that they were instructed by an agent to assassinate the CPO. Lim, in particular, appeared to the police to have been almost boastful of his deeds.

Karpal knew there was not much he or any other lawyer could do for the two proud members of this top communist assault unit. All associated with the case knew it and halfway through the trial, Karpal and ST Lee discharged themselves when the Malaysian Bar Council passed a resolution, moved by Karpal himself, advising its members not to represent clients charged under the ESCAR.

The Bar Council held that people charged with security offences had great difficulty proving their innocence, as many of the normal checks and safeguards regarded as important to ensuring a fair trial were not part of trials under the ESCAR. The Bar Council viewed these 'one-sided' trials as being 'show trials, no trials'. It described the regulations as oppressive and against the rule of law.

Before leaving the Ipoh High Court the lawyers explained to their clients at length the reasoning behind their decision to leave them on trial for their lives without lawyers. Also, that Justice Arulanandom was sitting alone in the trial without a jury, and upon the inevitable conviction being entered he would be required to impose the maximum penalty of death. Karpal explained to Lim and Ng the significance of prosecution witnesses giving evidence *in camera* and hearsay evidence being admissible in their trial.

Lim and Ng knew they would be convicted and, notwithstanding this, were prepared to give up whatever slim hopes they held of retaining life when they accepted fully the decision of Karpal and his fellow counsel to discharge themselves from their trial. They told Karpal to do what he had to do without fuss or bother.

"You only die once, Mr Karpal," Lim said. "You do what you have to do and we'll do what we have to do."

In Karpal's eyes the 'schoolboy killers' were far from being schoolboys. He could not agree with their terrorist methods but nevertheless respected the fact that his clients were prepared to sacrifice themselves for their cause. Even when facing the inevitable prospect of a death sentence Lim and Ng were prepared to endorse the sentiments of the Bar Council resolution.

Nor did it come as any surprise to Karpal when he was once again threatened with contempt of court proceedings being brought against him by Justice Arulanandom as he formally discharged himself from the case. The lawyer was told he should not use the court as a political forum and was roundly admonished for pulling out midway through the trial.

In his decision on the case the judge made a stinging attack on defence counsel Karpal, ST Lee and SP Annamalai (who would much later in life be stabbed to death near Karpal's office in Green Hall, Penang):

> Mr Karpal Singh and Mr Annamalai discharged themselves and even after being released by the court came to court and Mr Karpal Singh wanted to address the court. This resulted in the two accused interfering with the court on the ground that the court was preventing Mr Karpal Singh appearing for the accused. This resulted in further interference with the court by the accused. This case which should have concluded in August 1977 was only concluded in January 1978 as a result of these machinations. Counsel discharging themselves from a case have a duty to impress upon and explain to their clients that they are doing it of their own volition and the courts have nothing to do with their decision. Conduct such as this by members of the Bar

who are officers of the court to deliberately interfere and obstruct the administration of justice and the functioning of the court is not only no credit to the Bar but brings the matter of integrity of the Bar into question. Unless those responsible for the discipline and conduct of members of the Bar play a more active part in enforcing ethics, etiquette and discipline on the 'black sheep', society may look to other sources for such control and this may mean a further diminishing of the credibility of the Bar.

As a former president of the Bar Association of Perak and a Malaysian delegate to the United Nations general assembly in 1981, Justice Arulanandom did not think as highly of Karpal as did the communists on the latter's client list.

By discharging himself from the case Karpal had endeavoured to highlight in a very public way the fact that he considered his clients were not receiving a fair trial under the ESCAR in Justice Arulanandom's court.

The decision of the lawyers to discharge themselves resulted in numerous incidents during the trial, particularly when the court decided to appoint WE Balasingam to represent both defendants. Defendant Lim stood up and threw a slipper at the judge at this point, shouting as he did so for Balasingam to get lost.

"He's not our lawyer. We want our lawyers back," Lim screamed.

Not to be outdone, Ng shouted out in Mandarin that there was no justice in Justice Arulanandom's court. He was immediately ordered below into a holding cell by the judge.

When the fracas had died down the judge then ordered Lim to stand and say what he wanted to say. Predictably, Lim refused to stand and said the judge could hear him sitting down or not at all and he did not want Balasingam as his lawyer. Given one last chance by the judge to act according to the rules of court etiquette, Lim reacted by telling the judge to stand up himself and 'get lost'.

Lim was ordered into the holding cell alongside Ng, and for the first time in Malaysian judicial history a criminal trial continued without the presence of the two accused in the dock. Balasingam officially represented Lim and Ng for the remainder of the trial and it came as no surprise to the defendants when the death penalty was finally delivered upon them on 23 March 1978.

With the two committed communists firmly ensconced inside the thick stone walls of death row in Pudu Jail, the authorities then set about solving the 1974 killing of Malaysia's IGP Tan Sri Abdul Rahman Hashim.

In 1977 Lim was charged with the IGP's murder. On 13 March 1980, the day before he was scheduled to be executed at dawn for the murder of the Perak CPO and his driver, Lim applied to the High Court in Kuala Lumpur for stay of his execution to give him time to clear his name on the IGP's murder charge. In his affidavit accompanying his application for stay of execution Lim matter-of-factly said:

> I respectfully state I have had nothing to do with the murder of the IGP ... In the name of God I say I am innocent. I wish to establish my innocence in respect of the unfounded charge against me. The Public Prosecutor should either proceed with the pending trial relating to the alleged murder of the IGP or withdraw the charge against me. It is a matter of honour not only to me but my family that I be given an opportunity by the honourable court to establish my innocence in respect of this charge before I am executed.

Ng, too, informed Karpal the day before he went to the gallows alongside Lim that he had nothing to do with the IGP's 1974 murder. Senior federal counsel TS Sambanthanmurthi (the George Cross winner from Karpal's old school in Penang) withdrew the charge of murder against Lim and in a hastily arranged hearing, Justice Harun Hashim acquitted and discharged Lim on the IGP murder charge. This was to allow Lim's execution to proceed as scheduled the following morning.

Karpal believed Lim's and Ng's story emphatically for one reason — men who know they are going to die within 18 hours have no cause to lie. To this day, the 1974 killers of Malaysia's IGP in Kuala Lumpur have never been brought to justice. The Malaysian authorities, however, will always continue to disagree with Karpal and his communist clients. In parliament on 6 June 1982 the Minister of Home Affairs Datuk Musa Hitam said the file on the IGP's murder had been closed as the police held Lim and Ng responsible for the crime.

Of all the clients he has lost to the gallows, Karpal said none have faced the hangman more bravely than the communist 'schoolboy killers' who accepted full responsibility for the killing of the Perak CPO and his driver.

The lawyer embraced Lim and Ng as they said their farewells the night before they walked through the double doors of the *bilik akhir* (last room) to the gallows at the end of Pudu Jail's Block D. Karpal apologised to his clients for not being able to save their lives. He would never forget how Lim looked him in the eye and laughed. "Look here, Mr Karpal, this is something we have expected and we'll get along with it. Why all this ceremony? Tonight we'll sing. Tomorrow morning we'll put on the rope and go."

After the execution of a client Karpal routinely inquired with the death row jailors at the Kajang, Pudu and Taiping prisons about how the hangman went about his work and how his clients handled their

Pudu Jail's hanging chamber at the end of
Block D, the death row; (*right*) This was the
last view of the world many of Karpal's clients
ever saw, taken from the doorway of cell 1 in
the *bilik akhir* (last room) in Pudu Jail. The
doorway to the gallows was two metres to the
left of the bottom of the staircase.

ultimate ordeal. When he spoke to the Pudu jailors on the morning of
Saturday 15 May 1980 he was not surprised to learn that Ng and Lim
had passed their final night singing communist songs. And when the
hangman and his assistant arrived in the death cells about 6:00 a.m. and
pinioned their arms behind their backs — thus starting the execution
process — Ng and Lim told prison staff to get on with their work quickly
and efficiently as they too had work to do on the other side. They sang
a communist song as the trapdoors opened beneath them.

Also executed with Ng and Lim on that day in 1980 under the
ISA was Lee Hong Tay, who had been found guilty in January 1977 of
illegally possessing two revolvers, a pistol and 27 rounds of ammunition.

Following the triple execution, the communist radio station Suara
Revolusi Malaya (Voice of the Malayan Revolution), broadcasting from
its base in southern China, paid a special tribute to the work of martyrs
Lim, Ng and Lee. Given the 'root out the reds' mentality permeating
Malaysia in the 1970s and 80s, nothing was going to save Lim and Ng

from the gallows, even though there were legal grounds to their June 1979 Federal Court appeal which focused on parliamentary procedural issues.

Karpal, in his argument before Lord President Tun Mohamed Suffian Mohd Hashim, submitted the Agong's 1969 proclamation of emergency had not been laid before the senate and therefore was not effective. For a bill to become law it must receive the assent of the House of Representatives, the senate and the Agong, he submitted.

For his part in his submissions the Solicitor-General Tan Sri Ong Hock Sim argued the proclamation had, in fact, been laid before the senate on 22 March 1971.

In his decision the Lord President acknowledged problems with the Hansard record when he said:

> Unfortunately the votes and proceedings of the senate for 22 March 1971 made no mention of the proclamation as having been laid before it. Nevertheless … it must have been so laid, because: (a) it had been laid before the Lower House earlier and it was difficult to suppose that it could then not have been laid before the senate as claimed; (b) it appeared in the Senate Order Paper for 22 March 1971; (c) the date of the laying before the senate was duly entered in the Register and the votes; and (d) proceedings of the senate for 22 March 1971; recorded a speech from the Throne in which His Majesty explicitly referred in the second paragraph to the proclamation.

The appeal court also heard evidence from Ghazali bin Haji Abdul Hamid, the senior Malay translator in the office of the secretary to the senate. He provided documentary evidence of the proclamation being presented to the senate on 23 February 1971 and being laid before it on 22 March 1971. However, the fact remains that in the official Hansard record of Upper House parliamentary proceedings there was never any record of the proclamation having been laid before the senate.

Karpal remained adamant the proclamation was never laid there. In his view the court chose to turn a deaf ear to his submission because of the possible far-reaching repercussions, such as the release of all condemned ISA prisoners, if the appeal of the 'schoolboy killers' against the death sentence was allowed. This decision was little consolation for Lim and Ng and the other 50 or so death row security prisoners awaiting execution.

Another unusual ISA case involving Karpal was heard by the Alor Setar High Court in 1977. It involved the defence of army storekeeper George Abraham who faced the death penalty for being in possession of a sporting event starter pistol. Fear reverberated throughout the Malaysian sporting community while the two-week case was heard.

The former territorial army corporal based in Alor Setar, a town south of the Thai-Malaysian border, was accused by police of participating in subversive activities and supporting communist terrorists by supplying them with bullets and arms. The prosecution submitted the starter pistol could be adapted to shoot a live bullet and therefore fell within the definition of a firearm under the ISA. Karpal pointed out a starter pistol was designed for athletic and swimming events and was incapable of causing injury to anyone.

In acquitting Abraham of the charge the judge said he did not think 'parliament intended to stretch the definition of a firearm so wide as to embrace any component part of an object resembling a firearm unless they are component parts of an ordinary firearm or part of an object that can be usually adapted by an ordinary intelligent person into a barreled weapon'.

The fact this 'silly case', in Karpal's view, reached court at all highlighted the intensity of the government and police campaigns of those difficult days against alleged communists and their sympathisers.

In their training camps on the Thai-Malaysian border, communist recruits were advised by their superiors to contact Karpal if ever they were arrested and in need of legal advice. This message was further reinforced in prisons up and down the Malaysian peninsula, particularly among inmates on death row where Karpal was developing a reputation among the nation's desperadoes as the best criminal lawyer in Malaysia.

Condemned Chinese communists, like Lim and Ng, trusted Karpal to do his absolute best for them, even though they disagreed with his 'moderate' politics. They viewed him as politically anti-establishment and someone who would not sell them out. To them he was a man advocating in a court of last resort. Many, knowing they were going to die, felt better about going to their deaths in the knowledge that at least they had a fighter for a lawyer.

Karpal also knew he and his clients were involved in a high stakes political game beyond a defence lawyer's control. Coincidentally, of course, Lim, Ng and Lee went to the gallows just hours after Malaysia officially welcomed Chinese Foreign Minister Huang Hwa to Kuala Lumpur in March 1980.

Another case in this 'mission impossible' category was the landmark case of Penang carpenter Teh Cheng Poh who, in November 1976, was charged under the ISA and ESCAR with possession of a .38 revolver and five rounds of ammunition.

The case came Karpal's way in unusual circumstances when lawyer friend Albert Lee Him approached him on the verandah at the top of the old wooden stairs in the Penang High Court in January 1976. Lee informed his friend he had been assigned the Teh Cheng Poh case and

Karpal's first Federal Election victory was in 1978 against
Albert Lee Him (*right*), who was gracious in defeat.

told him how he was disturbed by the prospect of taking it on. He had
no experience in ESCAR cases where the client's life was on the line.
Karpal was in the process of explaining to a determined Lee how he
had enough problems of his own without taking on those of his friend
when at that point deputy public prosecutor Ghazi bin Ishak entered
the conversation.

With the revolver at the centre of the case found in Teh's belt after
the armed robbery of a Penang alcohol and sundries shop and a shot
fired during the hold-up, Ghazi was in an understandably confident
frame of mind. He suggested 'the big hero and the champion lawyer of
Penang' should handle the case himself.

Ghazi, a competent prosecutor, was told to 'shut up and mind
your own business' while Lee went on with his pleadings. In the finish,
however, it was Ghazi's goading which led to Karpal agreeing to put Lee
out of his misery.

"Right-o, Ghazi. I'll take you on," Karpal said.

In squaring off on this occasion both prosecutor and defence lawyer had no idea what they were letting themselves in for over the next five years.

A more immediate problem for Karpal, however, involved placating the Penang shop owner who threatened to cut off the lawyer's alcohol supplies. Karpal was a regular customer at the shop and its owner was not happy when he learned Karpal was representing the man who had held him up at gunpoint.

The lesser armed hold-up charge was set down for hearing in the Magistrate's Court, while the ISA charge for possession of a weapon and ammunition would be heard in the Penang High Court.

During his first meeting with Teh, the carpenter told Karpal something he already knew — on the facts of the case the carpenter described himself as a dead man. Teh told Karpal his hopes for life lay in his lawyer being able to fight the charges purely on the law.

Karpal took the first legal initiative in the November 1976 trial when he argued before Justice Arulanandom that the High Court had no jurisdiction to try an alleged armed robber such as Teh under the ISA. There was no element of subversion or organised violence in the robbery and the case more appropriately belonged at the Magistrate's Court level under the Firearms (Increased Penalties) Act.

Ghazi bin Ishak did little to assist Teh's cause when he observed knowingly that there was a background to the case he did not wish to disclose because it would prove unfavourable to the accused. Justice Arulanandom commented it was the prerogative of the Attorney-General alone to decide whether cases should be tried as serious security cases, and the trial proceeded to its inevitable conclusion with the ever-polite Teh going out of his way to thank the judge for passing the death sentence upon him.

In 1977 the Federal Court upheld the conviction on appeal and

Teh prepared to make his final journey from Penang Jail to the gallows at Pudu Jail in Kuala Lumpur. Apart from the final obligatory appeal to the Penang Pardons Board there was one other legal avenue left to Teh — an appeal to the Privy Council in London.

The Malaysian authorities were clearly serious in their intention to hang all prisoners charged under the security regulations and men destined for the gallows were beginning to stack up on the death row at Penang, Taiping and Pudu.

Alongside proven and committed communist killers, such as Lim and Ng, on death row in the late 1970s were men who had been sentenced to death for the mere possession of bullets, weapon parts and pistols. Their lawyers knew something had to be done and done quickly if their clients were to have any chance of escaping the gallows.

In conversation with his fellow Penang lawyers, Karpal suggested an appeal should be made to the Privy Council on the grounds the ESCAR 1975 were invalid and unconstitutional. He discussed with his colleagues how the original draconian regulations had been promulgated by the Agong during a state of emergency, when parliamentary institutions were suspended following the May 1969 race riots in Kuala Lumpur.

Parliament was dissolved on 20 March 1969 and the general election was held on Saturday 10 May 1969. On Tuesday 13 May 1969, following publication of most of the election results, the Kuala Lumpur riots broke out. The Agong proclaimed a state of emergency under article 150 (1) of the constitution. Simultaneously he promulgated the Emergency (Essential Powers) Ordinance 1969, giving himself wide powers for securing public safety including power to make provisions departing from the Criminal Procedure Code and the Evidence Act.

By section seven of the ordinance he suspended all uncompleted elections to the Lower House of parliament. All of this was done at a time when the Malaysian parliament was not sitting. Parliament did not sit again until 20 February 1971, when the government felt security had improved and it took back control of the country from the National Operations Council.

But why, Karpal asked of his legal colleagues, should the Agong be allowed to continue ruling by decree via regulation after parliament had resumed sitting? Surely once parliament sat the Agong had no more power and the regulations were void.

To Karpal the argument was simple and compelling, yet his colleagues kept referring him back to regulation 21 of the ESCAR 1975, a regulation specifically excluding the right of appeal to the Privy Council in security cases. In their minds the doors had been firmly slammed on Privy Council appeals involving security cases, for had not the Federal Court already ruled the regulations valid?

Yet Karpal continued to argue that the Federal Court had been wrong and he resolved to take the matter further. Before he could do so, however, an appellant was needed and he passed the word round among security prisoners on death rows in Penang and Kuala Lumpur. It was not an attractive proposition to the death row inmates. But just when Karpal was giving up all hope of being able to take the appeal to London, the 'common criminal' Teh Cheng Poh expressed an interest from his death cell in Penang Jail to at least discuss the job description.

Teh was an understandably worried man when he spoke to Karpal. He had heard from death row authorities that if he decided to appeal to the Privy Council, he would very likely be the first to go to the gallows if the case failed.

He asked for his lawyer's advice and was told the case was good but the consequences could also be dire no matter how the Law Lords found. Even if Teh won the appeal it would be a simple matter for parliament to resort to constitutional amendments to overcome the Privy Council decision.

"Put it this way, if I were you I would leave things as they are at the moment. I don't want to have your death on my hands," Karpal told Teh.

The criminal looked his lawyer in the eye and said, "Mr Karpal Singh, you take it up! You take it up! I am with you. I will sign."

Teh's agreement represented a clearing of the first hurdle.

The second far more difficult task involved obtaining leave from the Federal Court in Kuala Lumpur to lodge the appeal.

Early in 1978 the Chief Registrar of the Federal Court was Justice Anuar Zainal Abidin and it was his approval Karpal required before any appeal could be forwarded to London. The formal application for leave to appeal, in writing, was initially dismissed by Justice Anuar on the basis that the regulations spelled out clearly there was no right of appeal to the Privy Council in security cases under regulation 21.

Undaunted by this setback and realising the precarious situation Teh now found himself in, Karpal flew from Penang to Kuala Lumpur to urge Justice Anuar to reconsider his position. Karpal elaborated on his submission, namely that all the emergency regulations promulgated by the Agong during and after the period of National Operations Council rule — including regulation 21 — were void once parliament had resumed sitting in 1971. Upon reconsideration the judge agreed there was merit in the submissions and leave was granted for Karpal to take Teh's appeal to the Privy Council.

This case was the last of importance on a constitutional matter to be heard by the Privy Council from Malaysia; the right of litigants to appeal to the highest court in the Commonwealth on constitutional matters was removed by a 1976 amendment to the Courts of Judicature Act 1964.

Teh's status on death row was very much enhanced when permission was granted for the former Penang carpenter to, in effect, legally take on the Malaysian monarch. Execution plans for all security prisoners were placed on hold pending the outcome of the case and, at the very least,

Teh's peers knew their lives would be extended for the period of the appeal process.

Great indeed then was the rejoicing among the 44 security prisoners on death row in December 1978 when word of the Privy Council's decision in the Teh Cheng Poh case filtered through the prison grapevine from London. Amidst singing and cheering the condemned men learned Teh's death sentence had been set aside and his earlier High Court trial was referred to as a nullity. On death row in Penang Jail, Teh and his lawyer were hailed as heroes. Karpal was viewed as a legal guerrilla prepared to take on the full force of the state on behalf of his clients. The case was sent back to the Federal Court in Kuala Lumpur to consider whether or not a retrial should be ordered.

The Law Lords had agreed with Karpal's submission that the ESCAR was unconstitutional. In the Privy Council public gallery, when the appeal was being heard by the Law Lords was Malaysia's Attorney-General Tan Sri Abu Talib Othman. His personal presence in London indicated just how seriously the Malaysian government viewed the case. The choice now facing the Attorney-General was whether to uphold the rule of law or resort to retrospective legislation to overturn the Privy Council decision.

Surrounded by British QCs as he removed his borrowed wig and drank a celebratory whisky, Karpal knew, even as he quietly enjoyed the moral high ground, how the Malaysian government would react. His thoughts turned to the bravery of a common criminal in Penang who had entrusted him with his life by allowing him to proceed with the Privy Council appeal.

On his return to Malaysia Karpal urged the government to release Teh from Penang Jail and remove the other 43 condemned security prisoners from their death row cells. When he visited Penang Jail he was met by profuse thanks and an extremely happy man.

Karpal, pictured outside the Privy Council in London, following the December 1978 hearing of the Teh Cheng Poh case which declared the Malaysian security regulations unconstitutional.

Following the visit between lawyer and client in Penang Jail there was an ominous silence for a month. During this time Malaysia's law draughtsmen were working overtime to enable Prime Minister Tun Hussein Onn's government to unveil its Emergency (Essential Powers) Bill to parliament on 17 January 1979. This legislation validated all the regulations earlier declared void by the Privy Council and dashed the hopes of the condemned security prisoners.

When he saw for himself exactly how Malaysia's parliament re-established its supremacy over the courts, Karpal was forced to acknowledge that his legal challenge had failed. Speaking as the MP for Jelutong elected to parliament in 1978, he attacked Prime Minister Tun Hussein Onn asking him how, as a lawyer himself, he could mastermind the retrospective legislation. In future Karpal knew he would have to broaden his strategy from a purely legal to a political campaign if he were to have any hope at all of saving his condemned security clients.

He reacted to the introduction of the retrospective legislation by suing the entire Malaysian cabinet on Teh's behalf in a civil suit. In authorising the suit Teh knew he was simply fast tracking his date with the hangman. This suit asked the Agong to revoke the Emergency (Essential Powers) Ordinance 1969 declaring the whole country a security area — but it never reached court.

Within the space of a month Karpal and Teh had experienced a mood swing from euphoria, following the win in the Privy Council, to almost total depression. In lengthy discussions with his older brother Santokh, Karpal reflected on winning a battle in London while losing a war in Malaysia.

Karpal temporarily wondered about his country of residence and his choice of profession. He viewed the government's decision to legitimise the execution of people for acts which were not offences until the passing of the retrospective legislation in January 1979 as an insult to the Law Lords in London and an ultimate abuse of power.

He also remembered the goading from his friend, deputy public prosecutor Ghazi bin Ishak, son-in-law of Prime Minister Tun Hussein Onn. This goading had led him to take on the Teh Cheng Poh case in the first place. Ghazi, being an intelligent man, had the good sense never to goad Karpal again. It was a reaction shared by the members of an obviously embarrassed Malaysian government.

Teh, though, earned the respect of even the hard-core communists on death row, for in picking up the Privy Council appeal cudgels despite knowing the consequences, he gave his condemned colleagues hope.

For Teh the next step saw him back in the dock in the Federal Court in Kuala Lumpur on 27 April 1979, where a retrial for his case was ordered. An early date for his second trial was arranged for August 1979 and at the end of this Justice Gunn Chit Tuan sentenced Teh to death for a second time. Just as he had done at the end of his first Penang High Court trial, the carpenter, with a quiet smile upon his face, thanked the judge for sentencing him to death. In mitigation Karpal urged Justice

Gunn to recommend mercy to the judges who would hear the Federal Court appeal.

Teh's second appeal to the Federal Court against his death penalty failed on 24 January 1980. The appeal was heard before Chief Justice Raja Azlan Shah (a man who would become the ninth Agong of Malaysia), Justice Michael Chang Min Tat and Justice Tan Sri Eusoffe Abdoolcader.

In February 1981 his second appeal to the Penang Pardons Board was turned down and Teh went to the gallows on 4 March 1981, alongside two other security prisoners Low Kok Eng and Tan Tiang Peng. All three had been found guilty of possession of pistols and ammunition under the ISA.

When finally forced to deliver Teh up to the gallows Karpal congratulated his client for the tenacity he had shown during the five years the two men had known each other. In response the Penang carpenter thanked his lawyer for doing everything possible to save his life.

Teh could still manage a wry smile when Karpal reminded him how his bravery had brought the Malaysian government to its knees in the Privy Council and how he, a simple carpenter whose crime had been to hold up a liquor store with a pistol, still had a suit pending suing the whole Malaysian cabinet.

As he left Pudu Jail and Teh on that Wednesday afternoon in March 1981, Karpal knew deep down that what he had done had not been good enough. There was more work to be done. The hanging of Teh meant little hope of survival for any of the remaining security prisoners by traditional legal or constitutional means.

Teh's widowed mother would have no one to look after her in her old age. The sight of this woman at the mortuary the following morning, dressed in her black sackcloth, reminded Karpal rather too vividly of this fact.

5 STOP THE HANGING

Within a decade of embarking upon his career in Malaysia, Karpal had carved out a reputation for himself as a young criminal lawyer very much on the way up.

The Privy Council ruling in the Teh Cheng Poh case declaring the Essential (Security Cases) Regulations 1975 (ESCAR) unconstitutional gave the lawyer ammunition in the fight against the security regulations, but it did nothing to stop the hangings once the might-is-right government response had kicked in. At least his capital punishment clients knew they had a no-beg-your-pardon lawyer when it came to taking on the government.

But for Karpal it was still disconcerting to know by the end of 1981 that 31 of the 64 people sentenced to death had been hanged under the Internal Security Act 1960 in accordance with the ESCAR. It was equally clear to the advocate, by now based in Penang having returned from law practice in Alor Setar, that an international political campaign was required to bring further pressure on the Malaysian government. Without such a campaign, Karpal observed, everybody convicted under the ESCAR would go submissively to the gallows.

While Teh Cheng Poh found himself at the forefront of Karpal's Privy Council legal campaign, the choice of Tan Chay Wa as standard-bearer for the broader international political campaign operation was an easier one.

Tan Chay Wa, a Singaporean, was the first foreigner to be sentenced to death under the ESCAR on 19 January 1981 in Johor Bahru for possession of a pistol and ammunition. Karpal first heard of the case when he was approached by Tan's brother Tan Chu Boon, mother Tan Gim and other family members in 1979.

The mother and son agreed with Karpal's analysis at the time that it was largely a waste of time fighting ISA cases in the Malaysian courts when the government had the ultimate eleventh-hour weapon at its disposal of simply being able to change the law. The lawyer suggested the best way to save their son and brother was via an international awareness campaign, and Tan Chay Wa's family agreed.

Tan, a bus driver, had fled across the causeway from Singapore to Johor Bahru in 1976 when Singapore police came looking for him and his wife, wanting information on their alleged communist activities. Tan's wife Tan Gek Cheng remained behind in Singapore and was detained for five years without trial under the Singapore ISA.

On 2 June 1979 Malaysian police arrested Tan Chay Wa during a raid on a Johor Bahru cucumber farm. He was initially detained under the Malaysian ISA at Kamunting Detention Camp, just outside Taiping. He was later charged with possession of a .32 Llama special semi-automatic pistol and seven rounds of ammunition. Police said they found the evidence on him during the raid on the cucumber farm.

Apprehended by seven Special Branch officers while running from a hut on the farm towards a rubber plantation, Tan Chay Wa was searched by Inspector SS Tan, who said, in evidence, he found the pistol tucked in Tan Chay Wa's waistband.

The death penalty against Tan was upheld on appeal by the Federal Court in Kuala Lumpur on 7 September 1981, with the defence having little to go on apart from a discrepancy with the serial number of the pistol being listed as 425910 during the committal proceedings in the Magistrate's Court and later listed as 425940 at the High Court trial stage. Justice Mohamed Yusof Abdul Rashid put the serial number discrepancy down to a simple typing error. He was unmoved by Karpal's submission that this inconsistency in the prosecution's case was too serious to be ignored and there could be no absolute certainty of guilt. Tan's explanation, from the dock, of running from the hut because he was afraid of being arrested by police as he was involved with the underground movement did little to impress the judge either.

Coinciding with the conviction of Tan Chay Wa and others like him, Malaysian and Singaporean students in the United Kingdom and elsewhere began to take an interest in what they publicly described as 'human rights abuses' in Southeast Asia.

Under the campaign auspices of the Federation of United Kingdom and Eire Malaysian and Singaporean Student Organisations (FUEMSSO), support for the condemned in Malaysian jails came from the United Nations Secretary-General, the EEC, United States political leaders, British parliamentarians and trade unions, including the Transport & General Workers Union, the National Union of Public Employees and the National Union of Miners.

FUEMSSO engaged Karpal to look after its interests in Malaysia. The campaign to stop the hangings received a propaganda boost when Deputy Prime Minister Datuk Musa Hitam reportedly said in March

1982 that the Malaysian government would be prepared to adopt out to other countries ISA detainees and that Malaysia would be prepared to allow 'these champions of human rights' to have its detainees if they really wanted them.

This statement evoked concern among other members of Prime Minister Dr Mahathir Mohamad's government that the People's Republic of China might interpret the comments as an open invitation to fly all the condemned security prisoners to China's would-be Hawaii equivalent, Hainan Island, or a Chinese mainland bolt-hole.

It was no surprise, therefore, when DPM Musa qualified his earlier reported statement three months later on 1 June by saying Malaysia would not give up for adoption ISA detainees who had been found guilty by the courts. He also made his position on capital punishment perfectly clear: "We believe in capital punishment. We do not tolerate violence, that's why the ISA carries a mandatory death sentence."

In the months between the issuing of the deputy prime minister's two statements, the enterprising British-based students and Karpal busied themselves looking for foreign countries prepared to adopt Tan Chay Wa and his other condemned colleagues.

A French church-based organisation, the Ecumenical Service for Mutual Co-operation (CIMADE), agreed to adopt the condemned men with backing from the French socialist party. Belgium also agreed to issue them with visas if the Malaysian authorities agreed and the EEC Foreign Ministers' Council made a collective appeal for clemency to the Malaysian government. In Britain FUEMSSO kept up the relentless campaign by organising a deputation of prominent British lawyers to a meeting with the Malaysian High Commissioner in London led by two QCs Lord Tony Gifford and (New Zealand-born) John Platts-Mills.

The Belgian and CIMADE offers clearly embarrassed the Malaysian authorities as they did not anticipate Tan Chay Wa and his colleagues receiving any real support at an international level.

The activities of the UK-based students was a huge morale booster for Karpal, who faced a daily barrage of personal criticism from friends and associates wanting to know why he chose to represent 'communist terrorists'. Philosophically very much opposed to their modus operandi he was indeed a man alone with his communist clients as the great majority of the Malaysian population wholeheartedly supported the tough anti-communist measures of the government.

The government certainly did not thank Karpal for his commitment to represent the communists, particularly his handling of those cases where the defendants were found not guilty. Security trial defendants acquitted in ISA cases were routinely re-arrested, detained and recharged under the same act, and at least twice during this period the ESCAR was used to impose the death penalty on people originally sentenced to lesser terms of imprisonment.

Tan Seng Song, for instance, was convicted of armed robbery and sentenced to life imprisonment and 18 strokes of the *rotan*. He was then charged under section 57 of the ISA for unlawful possession of firearms. This meant he was charged under ESCAR procedures and was found guilty and sentenced to death.

Lee Yong Seng was perhaps the unluckiest security prisoner of them all. In October 1974 he was charged under the Firearms (Increased Penalties) Act 1971 and sentenced to seven years jail and six strokes of the *rotan*. He appealed against the sentence and approval was granted for a retrial. The public prosecutor then amended the charge to one under section 57 of the ISA. The High Court found him guilty and imposed the mandatory death penalty.

In Penang, Karpal's role in the international political campaign — apart from representing the everyday needs of his numerous security clients on death row — was essentially to keep the pressure on the

Malaysian government via publication of FUEMSSO's lobbying activities.

Predictably there was a cool response from the government to the pleas from foreign organisations and individuals. At a government level, FUEMSSO's activities were viewed as an insult to Malaysian legal autonomy.

For his part Karpal made much of the fact Malaysia had exhibited clemency during the Indonesian confrontation of 1964 when communist guerrillas had fought alongside the Indonesians. He argued that the commuting to life imprisonment of a number of ISA death sentences imposed during this period had earned international respect for Malaysia and its first Prime Minister Tunku Abdul Rahman.

In his June 1982 submissions to the Pardons Board on Tan Chay Wa's behalf, Karpal accentuated CIMADE's involvement and described Malaysia's intention to proceed with execution plans by spurning the French adoption offer as morally indefensible.

He kept up the intensity of the international campaign by speaking at the University of London on 3 July 1982. He told his audience of the betrayal felt by many of his clients who had divulged information to Special Branch police officers in return for verbal undertakings of detention of no more than two to four years under the ISA. As events unfolded they were subsequently charged in court under the ESCAR and, in some cases, induced confessions were used against them.

One man treated in this fashion was Sum Kum Seng, who co-operated with the police following his arrest for possession of firearms at Kampung Gabok in Seremban. He was sentenced to death on 25 September 1980, lost his appeal to the Federal Court in January 1981 and was executed on 28 November 1981. The oldest in a family of seven boys and two girls, Sum Kum Seng was told by police there was a good possibility he would be released following a short term of imprisonment if he co-operated.

In another case Lau Kee Hoo was also allegedly told by police he would be treated leniently and not tried in court when he signed a cautioned statement. He led police to the site of a buried biscuit tin on his oil palm holding. The tin contained six grenades, five detonators, two communist flags and a booklet — more than enough to send him to the Pudu Jail gallows in 1984.

It was hard for a lawyer working in a routine death-sentence environment — where the accused apparently were deemed to be guilty until they proved their own innocence — not to feel disillusioned when pleas for mercy from the condemned and their families were constantly ignored.

Karpal considered penalties under the ISA too harsh, especially on those who were sentenced to the gallows because their crime mostly was to be caught in possession of firearms and ammunition, even though the weapons had not been used for any criminal purpose. It was clearly a different issue if the weapons had been used for the cold-blooded killing of police officers.

The High Court execution warrants authorising and requiring the officer in charge of Pudu Jail to hang security prisoners by the neck 'until they be dead' flooded into Pudu Jail in early 1981. How could the hangings be stopped?

There were successes in the courts because by the end of 1981 some 37 defendants had had their death sentences commuted to life imprisonment. But little mercy was shown to the remaining 64 who lost their Federal Court appeals. Their numbers were being reduced on a weekly basis by a government which responded to the pleas of such international organisations as Amnesty International and the International Commission of Jurists by politely suggesting they mind their own business.

On the scheduled eve of a client hanging, Karpal had long made a practice of sending an appeal for clemency to His Majesty the Yang di-Pertuan Agong as a last-ditch attempt to prevent the hangman from doing his work between 5:30 and 6:00 a.m. the following morning.

'Only God has the ultimate right to take life which he in the first place created. No other person or body has the right to usurp that prerogative,' he informed the Agong in his telegrams.

Sometimes, after the execution had been carried out, there would be a polite response to the appeals for royal clemency advising they had with regret been declined.

The frustration Karpal experienced in being for the most part a lone voice on behalf of the condemned and having a number of clients go to the gallows in such a short time was evident in the telegram Karpal sent to the United Nations Secretary-General Kurt Waldheim on 5 March 1981:

> In the name of God please intervene immediately to put a stop to continued hangings in Malaysia in ISA cases. 18 hanged so far. More to follow. Kindly prevail on Malaysian government to adhere to Article Three of UN Declaration of Human Rights which reads: 'everyone has the right to life, liberty and security of person' and Article Five of the Declaration which reads 'no one shall be subjected to torture or cruel, inhuman or degrading treatment or punishment.'

The most difficult part for the lawyer was having to deal with the families of the condemned prisoners. They formed their own committee in 1980 to lobby the government and sought to have the sentences of their loved ones commuted to life imprisonment on humanitarian grounds. In 1981, allowing for one-third remission for good behaviour, 20-year life imprisonment sentences in Malaysia meant a minimum of 13 and a half years in jail.

As a group, the communists stoically accepted death on the gallows as an occupational hazard. But their young children and widows, dressed in the traditional Chinese black sackcloth of mourning, most certainly did not share the same unswerving philosophical commitment to the violent overthrow of the Malaysian government as their dead husbands and fathers.

The 25th anniversary of independence from Britain on 31 August 1982 gave the authorities an opportunity to release a number of ISA detainees held without trial, and three prisoners had death sentences commuted to life imprisonment by the Agong. Desperate to find a chink in the law enabling his remaining condemned security prisoners to live when all other means of appeal had been exhausted, Karpal mounted another constitutional challenge to the death penalty under the ISA in August 1982.

The thrust of his argument — on behalf of farmer Lau Kee Hoo, who was charged with being in control of six home-made grenades in July 1977 — was that the death penalty in itself was not unconstitutional, but a mandatory death penalty was, as it contravened the Malaysian constitution.

Under the ISA, which has now been repealed, the death penalty was mandatory with no question of any mitigating factors. As an aside to his main argument Karpal submitted the judicial taking of human life should be in the rarest of rare cases and not a weekly occurrence. He also argued that putting to death those found in mere possession of firearms under the ISA placed law enforcement officers in danger as the death penalty actually encouraged gunmen to engage in shootouts when confronted by police.

The issue was referred to the Federal Court by the High Court in August 1982. In response, the full bench of the Federal Court headed by Lord President Tun Mohamed Suffian agreed with Attorney-General Tan Sri Abu Talib Othman's submission that the 'mandatory' death sentence was constitutional.

The Federal Court agreed with the Attorney-General when he submitted that it should decide only on whether the 'mandatory' death sentence was constitutional and not concern itself with the morality, harshness or desirability of any legislation.

This case stalled all hangings for two months in Malaysia, including the execution of one man who had had his last meal and thought he had just six hours to live. At the unsuccessful conclusion of this challenge the way was once again clear to steadily trim the death-row queue.

Those on Pudu Jail's death row were housed in four separate compartments on the ground floor of the notorious Block D. Men and women scheduled for imminent execution were housed in the section closest to the gallows known as the *bilik akhir* (last room).

The door of cell number one in this seven-cell section was situated just two paces from the double door entrance to the gallows. Prisoners who had lost their appeals were often accommodated in sections two (six cells approximately ten metres away from the gallows) and three (ten cells approximately 30 metres away from the gallows). Those sentenced to death at a High Court level were routinely housed in the 12 cells of section four. At its furthest point this section was approximately 50 metres away from the gallows. All prisoners on death row had a clear view of the gallows doors when the doors between the four sections were left open.

The hangings of the men housed in the *bilik akhir* resumed in

January 1983 and among those to go at this time was the man who spearheaded FUEMSSO's international political campaign against the death penalty — Tan Chay Wa.

When he embraced Tan for the final time and thanked him for his international political campaign efforts, Karpal knew he was saying goodbye to a committed political idealist. But what he did not envisage at this farewell meeting was the prospect of Singaporean authorities preventing the committee member of the Malayan National Liberation Front, the assault unit of the Malayan Communist Party, from resting in peace. Soon after his brother's execution, Tan Chu Boon was initially sentenced to one year's jail (which was reduced on appeal) in Singapore for having a subversive document in his possession, namely his executed brother's tombstone. The inscription on the tombstone incorporated a poem written by Tan Chay Wa. The poem, according to his brother, highlighted the dead man's noble qualities.

FUEMSSO's international political campaign died on the gallows alongside Tan Chay Wa and all the remaining security prisoners knew that nothing any lawyer could do would save them.

The hangings in Kuala Lumpur continued throughout the Chinese New Year festive period in February 1983 with desperate last-minute appeals from Karpal on behalf of Liew Weng Seng and others to the Agong, the prime minister and the 'father of the nation' Tunku Abdul Rahman — all falling on deaf ears.

The first woman to be executed under the ISA since the communist emergency of 1948 to 1960 was seamstress Thye Siew Hong. Thye, who was represented by lawyer Sidney Augustine, and her husband Lim Re Song, represented by Karpal, were found guilty of possessing nine grenades in a Kuala Lumpur house in September 1977. As well as grenades, a large number of jungle-green uniforms were recovered from the couple's room, which the prosecution alleged belonged to communist terrorists. The husband and wife stood side by side on the gallows before falling to their deaths on 20 February 1983.

One of the worst facets of the ESCAR from Karpal's perspective involved the prosecution attitudes behind the 'anti-Chinese enforcement' of the regulations. Why was it, he asked himself, that Thye Siew Hong and her husband should hang, thereby leaving their young daughter an orphan, when 11 top leaders of the Rohaniah Islamic group could escape the gallows for a similar crime after being arrested under the ISA in 1978? Eleven automatic pistols, 74 rounds of ammunition, a hand grenade, 60 flags and military uniforms were seized from these people, yet they were not charged in court.

Similarly, in January 1980, 14 people including five leaders of Koperasi Angkatan Revolusi Islam Malaysia (KARIM) were detained under the ISA. Assorted ammunition (282 rounds), one hand grenade and an army bayonet were alleged to have been seized. Once again no charges were laid in court against any of these detainees.

How was it a Malaysian cabinet minister Datuk Mokhtar Hashim could use a gun for murder on 14 April 1982, yet escape the gallows via a Pardons Board reprieve when numerous others were keeping their gruesome early morning date with the busy Pudu Jail hangman for mere possession of firearms or ammunition? Karpal wondered. The former Youth and Sports Minister was convicted of murdering the Speaker of the Negeri Sembilan State Assembly Dato' Taha Talib. Datuk Mokhtar had his death sentence commuted to life imprisonment by the Pardons Board in 1984.

The case of Datuk Mokhtar and the subsequent royal pardon he received — resulting in his release from Pudu Jail in 1991 — was a reminder to Karpal of what happened to 22-year-old Lim Kwang Yeow. Lim went to the gallows for possession of a .32 bullet and a component part of a firearm, namely a .32 pistol magazine, after being sentenced to death in 1980 by the Muar High Court. Lim's appeal for clemency to the Pardons Board was rejected and he made the *bilik akhir* walk to the gallows in 1983.

What criteria did the Pardons Board adopt when considering appeals for clemency? a confused Karpal asked himself. As the then former DAP MP for Jelutong (he would lose this seat in 1999) Karpal was often labelled a supporter of anarchy by his establishment critics. Nevertheless, he had considerable sympathy for the acute problems the government faced from criminals like Botak Chin, who created chaos through murder, violence and intimidation.

The main thrust of Karpal's anti-ESCAR argument throughout was that deprivation of fair trials could not be justified no matter how heinous (or in Lim Kwang Yeow's case, how minimal) the alleged offences may have seemed.

Botak Chin, who was represented by Kuala Lumpur-based lawyer Jagjit Singh, was executed at the unusually early time of 2:00 a.m. on 11 June 1981 following his 1976 arrest in a blazing gun battle. The leader of the 360 Gang saw himself as a modern-day Robin Hood and masterminded a number of armed robberies in Kuala Lumpur during the mid-1970s, including a RM210,000 cash haul from the Selangor Turf Club on 26 October 1975. When he appeared before the High Court on 11 January 1977, Botak Chin became the first Malaysian to plead guilty under the ISA for possession of a .25 pistol and 33 rounds of ammunition. He sent a message to Karpal seeking his advice soon after taking up residence on death row in 1977, but Malaysia's most notorious criminal decided to retain the services of his court-appointed lawyer Jagjit throughout his imprisonment. One of his final instructions to his family was: 'Throw my ashes in the drains.'

On 16 March 1983 the Deputy Minister in the Prime Minister's Department Datuk Haji Suhaimi bin Datuk Haji Kamaruddin confirmed

39 people had been executed since January 1980 for offences carrying the mandatory death penalty under the ISA. By then all those whose appeals had been rejected by the Pardons Board had been executed and Karpal needed some glimmer of hope to give to the remaining 30 ISA convicts on death row.

It came from New Delhi on 7 April 1983 when a five-judge constitutional bench of the Indian Supreme Court headed by Chief Justice YV Chandrachud struck down as unconstitutional and void section 303 of the Indian penal code stipulating the death sentence "for life convicts committing murder". The court stated: 'A standardised mandatory sentence and that too in the form of a death sentence, failed to take into account the facts and circumstances of each particular case.'

Justice Chinnappa Reddi of the Indian Supreme Court described provision of the mandatory death sentence under section 303 as an anachronism out of tune with the march of time and the rising tide of human consciousness. "So final, so irrevocable and irresistible is the sentence of death that no law which provided for it without involvement of the judicial mind can be said to be fair, just and reasonable… section 303 is such a law and it must go the way of all bad laws," he said.

In Malaysia, apart from the ISA, the mandatory death penalty was also provided for murder, and in April 1983 it was also expanded to include drug traffickers.

It remained Karpal's view that Malaysia, in its zeal to stamp out serious crime, should not lose sight of the basic premise that its laws should be constitutional. He urged the Malaysian Federal Court to review its decision of September 1982 when it ruled the mandatory death sentence was constitutional. It was necessary in the public interest in the wake of the Indian Supreme Court ruling for the issue to be given fresh thought in Malaysia.

It was in fact raised again before a five-man bench in the Federal

Court during Lau Kee Hoo's appeal hearing against his death sentence in August 1983. In dismissing the appeal the court rejected Karpal's request to review its earlier ruling that mandatory death sentences under the ISA were constitutional.

Once the Federal Court had reaffirmed its decision there was no higher court as appeals in criminal and constitutional cases to the Privy Council in London had been abolished from January 1978.

The ISA death shuffle to the gallows continued until 1986 and by this time approximately 60 prisoners convicted of firearms offences had been executed. Behind the grim statistics were people like noodle seller Yap Seng Keat, who was found in possession of a revolver; fisherman Hussein bin Masa, found in possession of a home-made pistol; Chan Lup Wei, found in possession of a pistol and 102 rounds of ammunition; Ang Cheng Guan, found in possession of a firearm and ammunition; painter Lee Hong Tay, found in possession of two revolvers, a pistol and 27 rounds of ammunition; electrical goods salesman Lock Loi, found in possession of a pistol; Lau Kee Hoo, found in possession of six home-made grenades and five detonators; labourer Ishak bin Khalid, found in possession of a pistol and 14 rounds of ammunition; underground organisation member Tan Tiang Peng, found in possession of two .38 pistols and 36 rounds of ammunition; painter Soon Seng Sia Heng, found in possession of a revolver and 12 bullets; and tapper Chong Soon Koy, found in possession of a pistol and 37 rounds of ammunition.

Karpal found it an absurd situation where a parliament could dictate to the courts that certain categories of people, like those possessing weapons and ammunition, must be executed once convicted. The requirement for judges to impose a mandatory sentence infringes the separation-of-powers doctrine which is meant to ensure that judicial power remains in the hands of the judiciary and not with the legislature. For Karpal, any fettering of judicial power was not in the public interest. Judges, having the benefit of experience, should be left to decide on the range of punishments without having a mandatory sentence sword dangling over their heads.

The government view remains that the Pardons Board is in place to mitigate the severity of any mandatory sentence a court is required to impose. However, it should not be forgotten that the Attorney-General, who is also the public prosecutor, remains a member of the Pardons Board, while defence counsel enjoy no such representation. This fact remains a major source of irritation for Karpal.

Speaking generally, the Malaysian judiciary, according to Karpal, through its silence has a lot to answer for. Judges should have the courage to speak up when law does not measure up to expected standards of justice. Laws must reflect natural justice, as this in turn invests the law with fairness, a concept inherent in the thinking of any reasonable person.

Throughout the period of the ISA hangings, Malaysian judges, according to Karpal, were aware of the injustices evident in the ESCAR, yet few of them had the courage to condemn the legislation as not measuring up to accepted standards of international justice. In remaining quiet, Karpal argued, the Malaysian judiciary had chosen to function with blinkers on and take an easy road by pointing to divisions between judicial and executive power as the justification for their actions.

According to Karpal, such a doctrine should not render a judge completely impotent in the face of manifestly unjust laws. Judges could, under such circumstances, grudgingly apply the law but at the same time register their displeasure by calling for its repeal. By carrying the title 'Justice' before their names Karpal said it was incongruous for a judge to meekly apply legislation not containing the basic elements of justice and fair play as universally understood. In his mind a strong judiciary should be a bulwark against the excesses of an overly punitive executive.

The Malaysian public should be able to turn to its judiciary in anticipation of draconian legislation being frowned upon to such an extent the repeal of that legislation would become inevitable, Karpal said.

One Malaysian judge who stood up in the initial stages of ESCAR was Justice Tan Sri Harun Hashim, who said it would be better to shoot an accused triable under ESCAR rather than to actually try him.

The umbrella ISA legislation incorporating the emergency regulations remains very much a part of Malaysian legal life. In fact the first man in Malaysia to be convicted for waging war against the Agong was hanged on 4 August 2006.

Mohamed Amin Mohamed Razali was the leader of the Khalifah Mujahuddin Al-Ma'unah movement, which had a stated aim of overthrowing the government of Prime Minister Dr Mahathir Mohamad and setting up its own Islamic state. During the early morning of 2 July 2002, dressed as an army major, Mohamed Amin led a group of 29 men to raid armouries at two military camps in Perak state. The raid meant the by now well-armed group was able to hole up in Bukit Janalek in Sauk.

Mohamed Amin distributed the stolen weapons to his Muslim foot soldiers. Soon after the arms cache raids on the two Perak army camps, group members launched abortive attacks on two brewery properties, the national power grid and a Hindu Temple at Batu Caves just outside Kuala Lumpur. These attacks resulted in little or no damage to the carefully chosen targets. It was the subsequent sound of rifle fire during military training sessions at Bukit Janalek which alerted the authorities to the whereabouts of the group. From this camp the group waged war against a government force of 1,000 troops sent in to overpower them. In the shootout two government men were killed before the group was eventually surrounded and overpowered on 6 July 2002.

All the men involved in the Al-Ma'unah movement were tried under the ESCAR. Four of them were sentenced to death following their

Federal Court appeals, 15 others were given life sentences and the remaining ten were jailed for ten years. The leader of the group Mohamed Amin, who was tried under the ESCAR for waging war against the King, was represented throughout by Karpal.

Mohamed Amin lost his appeal against the High Court death sentence in June 2003. In its decision the Federal Court noted the action of waging war against the Agong had to be 'nipped in the bud'. Mohamed Amin went to the gallows at the Sungai Buloh Prison in Selangor. He was supposed to go to the gallows alongside three of his lieutenants a week earlier but the execution was delayed a week to give Mohamed Amin the opportunity of a final meeting with his mother, who was in Mecca to perform the *umrah* (pilgrimage) at the time.

The case of the Khalifah Mujahuddin Al-Ma'unah movement highlighted the fact that battling deviant Islamic sects remained an ongoing major problem for the Malaysian government.

Following Mohamed Amin's hanging, Karpal again called for ESCAR legislation to be repealed. The Communist Party of Malaya had officially laid down its arms after a ceremony in Thailand in 1989 and Karpal argued that there was now no justification for perpetuating the ISA in Malaysia as it had outlived its original purpose.

However this was not the way the Malaysian government continued to view the ESCAR legislation. Mohamed Amin was executed under it and during the 1998 political turmoil surrounding Deputy Prime Minister Anwar Ibrahim's sacking, approximately 20 people were detained briefly under the ISA during the police clampdown. Most prominent among the mainly Malay ISA detainees incarcerated in September 1998 was the man at the centre of it all — Anwar Ibrahim himself.

Inevitably, it was not long before Anwar's name made its way to Karpal's long-term client list.

6 REMOVE THE SCUM

The 330-kilometre drive from Kuala Lumpur to Penang on the four-lane North-South highway provides the modern traveller with a history lesson on a Malaysian economy once based on mining towns, rubber and oil palm plantations.

Times have changed since British-controlled days and under the leadership of Prime Minister Dr Mahathir in particular, Malaysia has developed dramatically into a strong independent economy in the past 30 years. Nowhere in the country is this more obvious than on the approach from the south looking towards Penang Island.

Well before the motorist arrives in Butterworth the rotund 65-storey Komtar skyscraper springs up like a pikestaff; the surrounding Chinese shops look like acolytes around a deity. It stands out even more as you cross Penang Bridge — itself a massive and impressive structure built by South Koreans in the early 1980s — and many wonder who could have been the driving force behind two such imposing projects.

The man, still often described as a 'buddha', who had the political and economic drive to see the projects materialise was Lim Chong Eu, Chinese political maestro and former state Gerakan political party chief on Penang Island. Lim, a Scottish-educated medical doctor who died in 2010 aged 91, is fondly remembered as the father of modern Penang. He was also the driving force responsible for implementing the island state's free trade zone. Possessing a keen sense of humour, one of his greatest satisfactions upon the completion of the bridge was to invite a political opponent (not Karpal) who had boldly stated he would be the first person to commit suicide by jumping from it if it was ever built, to do just that. There must have been many occasions in the early 1980s when Lim, as Chief Minister in the Penang State Assembly, would have hoped Opposition leader Karpal would consider taking up such a final option.

Karpal's uncompromising political career had its launch base in Penang after he served a single quiet term as an apprentice Kedah state assemblyman for the Alor Setar Bandar electorate in the north of the country. He won the Bandar seat on a Chinese-dominated multi-racial Democratic Action Party (DAP) ticket following the national race riots of 1969. The DAP, in fact, evolved out of Lee Kuan Yew's People's Action Party (PAP) in Singapore, and its first MP in Malaya was Devan Nair, who won the Bangsar seat in the April 1964 elections standing on a PAP ticket.

Two major political nemeses in Karpal's political life were the Penang State Assembly boss Lim Chong Eu in the 1980s and Malaysian Prime Minister Dr Mahathir. Karpal was MP for Jelutong from 1978 to 1999 and Dr Mahathir was PM from 1981 to 2003.

When Malaysia's fourth prime minister bowed out of politics in 2003, Karpal made a comeback to federal politics as the Penang electorate

MP for Bukit Gelugor in 2004. The political careers of the two men were inextricably linked with the authoritarian Dr Mahathir exercising power and Karpal challenging his use of that power every step of the way.

By way of background, after Singapore's withdrawal from Malaysia in 1965 and the PAP's deregistration in Malaysia, Devan Nair became the DAP's first Secretary-General while completing his parliamentary term. Karpal's impetus for throwing his weight behind the DAP in the 1970s came to him during the race riots of 1969 in Kuala Lumpur. He saw a future role for himself in the DAP as he believed it was essential for Malaysia's three major racial groups to work together as equals.

He had always been a strong opponent of those who advocate Malaysia becoming an Islamic state. For that reason Karpal initially had a personal problem with Anwar Ibrahim's formation of an opposition coalition comprising the DAP and the Islamic-dominated Parti Islam Se-Malaysia (PAS), among other groupings.

As recently as the 5 May 2013 general election, PAS members were still advocating federal parliament implementation of *hudud* Islamic law punishment issues. The possible implementation of sharia law remains a huge turnoff for members of Malaysia's Chinese and Indian communities. Karpal had still called upon Anwar to clearly state his position on *hudud* in a front page article in the *New Straits Times* a week out from polling day.

But back to why Karpal decided to throw his hat in with the DAP. By aligning himself with a significant political faction of the entrepreneurial Chinese community Karpal knew it would do his criminal law career no harm.

As a man who saw himself as a Sikh first and an Indian second, he was criticised by many in the Hindu community for turning his back on the Malaysian Indian Congress (MIC) party, a key Barisan Nasional component.

Karpal on the back of his jeep while campaigning in the
Bukit Gelugor electorate in the 2004 Federal election.

Membership of the MIC, Karpal argued, would have made political
life on the inside too comfortable. He knew his personal political agenda
would require him to rock the boat, seeking often unpopular legislative
change. Such change could not be achieved by allying himself with long-
standing Works Minister Samy Vellu's MIC political establishment.
Karpal was determined to paddle his own canoe in politics, with the
support of a few trusted friends, just as he would do in law.

A major drawback for Karpal in his first political campaign in 1974
in the Alor Setar Bandar constituency was that he could not speak Malay
well. In his youth he spoke English and Punjabi at home and English
at school. Given this linguistic disadvantage nobody expected Karpal to
win that Bandar seat but he overcame the problem via party-deprecating
humour while electioneering in the Malay kampongs. He simply told his
constituents to 'vote Mr Apollo'. 'Mr Apollo' was a play on the DAP's
rocket symbol, with its four boosters signifying the Malay, Chinese,
Indian and other ethnic communities working together in unison.

(*left*) DAP rocket symbol outside Karpal's home in Penang; (*above*) Karpal celebrates his first election victory in the 1974 Bandar electorate, Alor Setar state elections.

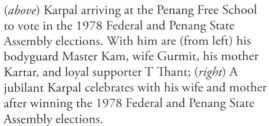

(*above*) Karpal arriving at the Penang Free School to vote in the 1978 Federal and Penang State Assembly elections. With him are (from left) his bodyguard Master Kam, wife Gurmit, his mother Kartar, and loyal supporter T Thant; (*right*) A jubilant Karpal celebrates with his wife and mother after winning the 1978 Federal and Penang State Assembly elections.

Lim Chong Eu headed the state government in Penang from 1969 to 1990 on a platform of major projects and industrial development. He inspired confidence in investors and prided himself in not becoming overly entangled in scoring political points. Life went along relatively smoothly and peacefully in Lim's Penang State Assembly world until the 1978 elections when Karpal was elected as assemblyman for Bukit Gelugor with a majority of 574 votes over Barisan Nasional's Datuk Tan Gim Hwa.

The comparatively young and politically inexperienced Karpal was appointed leader of the DAP and of the Opposition in the Penang State Assembly. In that year, he was also elected to the federal parliament as MP for Jelutong. He would hold the Bukit Gelugor seat in the Assembly for 13 years until being voted out while contesting a sacrificial marginal seat in an all-out DAP bid for state control in the 1990 elections, and the Jelutong seat for 21 years.

In this position he was to clash bitterly with Lim Chong Eu over a seven-year period before DAP veteran Lim Kit Siang moved north from Malacca to assume the Opposition leadership role in Penang in 1986.

The celebrated clashes between 'The Buddha' and 'The Singh' in the Penang State Assembly during those years have become part of Malaysian political folklore. On one occasion three truckloads of riot police were dispatched to the assembly building to remove 'The Singh'. Newspapers did well out of the ongoing spats between the two men by regularly featuring front-page photographs of officious-looking police officers throwing Karpal out of the Assembly on a regular basis.

As Opposition leader, Karpal revelled in the role of frustrating Lim Chong Eu whenever he could. In 1980 he had been shown the suspension door for a two-year period after describing Lim as a fraud. Later, amidst the heated rhetoric and polemics was a June 1981 allegation of impropriety against a Penang state official — an allegation that would not go away. Karpal, from his Jelutong seat in the federal parliament, alleged this state official had not revealed a conflict of interest when he sat on a board responsible for awarding a contract to a family member.

The affable Lim defended his employee by stating publicly on a number of occasions the allegations were rubbish. The wily old state politician then went on a character assassination rampage of his own, labelling Karpal's revelations in parliament — incidentally repeated the following day outside the house away from parliamentary privilege — as cowardly, irresponsible, malicious and dirty politics.

Lim's very public utterances of support for his employee did not, however, quite stack up against his subsequent decision to quietly transfer the official outside the state in early 1982. This was the same year when Karpal was returned to the State Assembly in the June 1982 elections.

The spats between the two men continued and reached their zenith in October 1984 when, in total frustration, Lim moved a motion proposing 'the House remove a scum in its midst' after Karpal had referred to him as 'an UMNO stooge and a robot'. In response Lim described Karpal as 'a bloody crook, a rascal and a DAP crook'.

There were expressions of outrage when Karpal suggested Lim and others like him in the Assembly were happy to abide by UMNO decisions because it accorded them non-hereditary titles like Tun, Tan Sri or Datuk, just as the award of Tan Sri was given to the Speaker Tan Sri Teh Ewe Lim. Several members described this comment as an insult to the Agong who awarded such titles.

In the tense atmosphere Lim had 'the scum', who characteristically refused to apologise in all major political showdowns, removed from the State Assembly building. With the none-too complimentary reference to the lawyer as 'the scum' publicised for the entire world to read, Karpal's second major suspension from the Penang State Assembly within six years was underway.

The major 1984 altercation occurred during debate on the rezoning of Catholic seminary land for commercial uses in Penang. During the debate on the issue Karpal alleged Lim was 'lying' about the timing of a decision.

On both occasions the suspensions dragged on until after the respective 1982 and 1986 elections because of Karpal's refusal to apologise for his remarks.

During the 1984–86 suspension period Karpal's political isolation was complete as he was also under suspension from the federal parliament over allegations made against the Agong.

However, even while in isolation, Karpal had his publicity-seeking ways and means to remind his critics from the columns of local newspapers he was still alive. When he suggested Penangites should celebrate the 200th anniversary of the first British Governor Francis Light's arrival in Penang in 1986 the perennial political bad-boy was shouted down from all sides.

In the 1986 State Assembly elections the Chinese voters of Bukit Gelugor overwhelmingly sent their man back in for a final round with Lim. Lim was quick to remind Karpal of the fact that his establishment exclusion predicament was 'unique'. He was, while still a young politician, the record holder for being suspended from both the federal parliament and the Penang State Assembly.

There is no doubting the fact that throughout the 1980s Karpal gained a deserved reputation as Malaysia's most hard-line opposition politician ever. He proved this when he decided to go for the Agong — the Sultan of Johor at the time — in the federal parliament in 1984.

Against this hard-line approach there were also a number of officially endorsed attempts to finish off the lawyer permanently in the courts. It was a tribute to the lawyer's legal ability — somehow in tandem with Lim Kit Siang, Malaysia's other great DAP political survivor — that he remained a considerable force in Malaysian political and legal life till the time of his death.

Looking back on their over-indulgence in ultimate hardball politics, the late Lim Chong Eu and Karpal came to see the funny side of their exchanges now with almost 40 years behind them.

In the heat of battle on one occasion Karpal, referring to his own Sikh heritage, dramatically informed the political maestro 'only brave men have beards'. Quick as a flash Lim responded 'and so do goats and bisons'. Pencils and pens were flung from both sides of the Assembly in this exchange when Karpal described Lim as a 'political animal'. Amidst shouts of 'sit, boy, sit' Chief Minister Lim responded by describing Karpal as the political animal from Bukit Gelugor.

"He is like a bull and I am a matador. I show a red cloth here he charges here and if I show a red cloth there, he charges there... there are some animals who will not learn even if you beat them," Lim said, laughing.

On another occasion Karpal disparagingly referred to his nemesis as 'an old fox'. Professing absolute outrage at this remark and in the process of demanding it be expunged from the official record, Lim informed the opposition leader he wanted him to know, "I'm not an old fox. I'm a very, very, very old fox."

On yet another occasion when Karpal pointed out to the Speaker that the 'old fox' was sleeping during the assembly debate, Lim opened his eyes, grinned and went back to sleep again.

Following Lim's death in November 2010, Karpal paid him a warm tribute describing him as a humorous man. Looking back on it there was not a lot of humour for Karpal at the time though. How could there be when truckloads of riot police would turn up outside the Assembly to remove just one man, namely himself, from the precincts?

While Karpal enjoyed mixing it up with Lim, he was not so happy

Karpal enjoying an unusually quiet moment with Penang's
Chief Minister, Lim Chong Eu in 1986.

about a racial slur contained in the verbal banter of the Federal MP for
Pasir Puteh, Wan Mohamed Najib Wan Mohamed. In Parliament on
24 July 1984 Wan Mohamed Najib uttered a colloquial Malay expression.
This expression, roughly translated, meant: 'If you see an Indian and a
snake, you hit the Indian first.' Karpal considered this statement to be
an insult to the Indian community and Malays themselves as no right-
thinking Malay would want to use such derogatory statements against
another community.

Perhaps the biggest scenes involving Karpal in the Penang State
Assembly occurred on two occasions in 1981 when the suspended
man dropped in unannounced on his former colleagues. The first was
on 13 May when the Speaker called the police for assistance and three
truckloads of riot police arrived.

There was another massive scene on 22 December when the 'gate-
crasher' paid a surprise visit again and sat down in the seat for the
member for Bukit Gelugor. The Speaker immediately called the police.
A corporal and a constable soon arrived and conferred with the clerk of

council Wong Hin Fatt. When the three men politely requested Karpal to leave, he responded in turn by ushering the policemen out of the chamber.

The gentle persuasion diplomatic approach continued when the next policeman Inspector Bhupinder Singh came into the debating chamber. The two men spoke to each other in Punjabi with the inspector pleading with his fellow Sikh to leave. In response Karpal asked the eminently reasonable inspector to remember how his junior colleagues had been unceremoniously evicted a few minutes earlier. "Now, you would not want that to happen to you, would you, Bhupinder?" Fortunately for Karpal, the inspector possessed a sense of humour and responded, "You're right. I would not," before discreetly withdrawing.

All hell broke loose, however, when Penang's Chief Police Officer Zaman Khan arrived soon afterwards. The man who went on to become the Director-General of Malaysian Prisons ordered five of his men to 'throw him out'.

How was Karpal going to handle this situation?

"Get out! Get out!" Zaman ordered as Karpal embarked on his humiliating walk towards the door.

While staring an inevitable defeat in the face Karpal could not believe his luck when he saw Zaman pick up his legal briefcase.

"You've got my bag in your hands without my prior knowledge, Zaman... Come on, Zaman, give me the bag," the Sikh bellowed back at the CPO.

There was a table in between the two men and CPO Zaman Khan pushed the bag onto the table. As luck would have it, from Karpal's perspective at least, the bag tottered off the edge and fell onto the floor.

At this point the lawyer knew there could yet be an honourable way out from the humiliating situation he had found himself in. He decided once more to go for broke.

"Zaman, you threw my bag… pick up my bag," he ordered.

Much to Karpal's amazement Zaman did pick up the bag and courteously handed it back to him.

Honour had been restored and Karpal quickly headed for the door, followed by five police officers. The scene greeting him from the steps leading out of the Assembly building did not look promising. The riot squad was once again in full attendance. There was a large number of other uniformed police officers outside the building, all with walkie-talkies blaring, describing the suspended politician's every move.

Karpal did not know whether he ought to feel flattered when many of these police officers proceeded to salute their quarry. He returned the compliment and walked directly to his car where an understandably very nervous driver was waiting with the engine running.

"Get the hell out of here," Karpal ordered. Once again he could not believe his good fortune in being able to extricate himself from yet another tight corner of his own creation.

Behind the orchestrated pandemonium Karpal's strategy in all of this mayhem was to focus attention on the issues he was not allowed to raise in the Assembly during his suspension periods. Whenever there was a need to focus national attention on a political issue he would simply pay his old friends who had suspended him from the Assembly a visit. The police too kept a close eye on him when the Assembly was sitting in Penang.

On one occasion Penang Police Headquarters were alerted when Karpal walked past the Assembly building with his wife and daughter. They were merely en route to the Immigration Office to include daughter Sangeet Kaur's name on their passports.

In late 1984 Karpal was back in hot water over an impending prosecution in the Alor Setar Magistrate's Court for his role in taking part in an 'unlawful' procession during the DAP's 'Save Bukit China' campaign.

(*left*) Karpal reverses the roles by escorting a policeman, who had been sent to evict him from the Penang State Assembly, out of the chamber on 22 December 1981; (*above*) "Pick up my bag, Zaman," the suspended Penang State Assemblyman orders Penang police chief Zaman Khan. *Photos courtesy of* The Star, *Malaysia.*

(*left and below*) It's always nice to have friends in the right places. Karpal is pictured here having a quiet word with Inspector Bhupinder Singh after being evicted from the Penang State Assembly.

In July 1984 the Malacca state government had unveiled plans for the commercial development of the historic Chinese cemetery site, one of the largest Chinese cemeteries outside mainland China itself. Three months later, on 20 October, the DAP launched its national campaign against the development beginning with a national marathon relay which would start from four locations — Penang, Alor Setar, Kuantan and Johor Bahru — with the runners all converging in Malacca. As DAP deputy national chairman, Karpal was assigned to officially flag off the marathon from Alor Setar.

DAP MP Fung Ket Wing was the first runner out of the blocks and just as he was getting under way, the support party walking along behind him were confronted by police and told to disperse. Karpal argued with the police, whose commanding officer at one stage told the group they would be 'smashed' if they did not disperse. During this exchange a police corporal approached the lawyer and pushed him on the shoulder. Karpal retaliated and pushed the policeman back. A shoving match ensued and this was the incident at the heart of Karpal's assault charge.

Karpal faced three charges: taking part in an unlawful procession, not dispersing after an order to disperse was given by a police officer, and assaulting a police officer in the execution of his duty.

Jointly charged with him on the unlawful assembly charges were 20 others: Kedah/Perlis DAP chairman George John, DAP MP for Sandakan Fung Ket Wing, Thean Kuek Leong, Beh Hock Lim, Oon Teik Chow, Lee Chuan Sam, Lim Lye Huat, Ngooi Ah Fart, Teoh Yong Chow, Teh Lai Yu, Han Young Heng, Ang Teik Hee, Yan Sing Lai, Lim Peng Guan, Loh Seng Keang, Lee Kwei Heng, Lee Hock Seng, Ang Keak Ooi, Lee Tek Heng and Lim Kean Puel.

There was just the one assault charge — and this was against Karpal.

Karpal was assisted with the Magistrate's Court defence of the 21 DAP people (including himself) by his younger brother Manjit Singh and S Assamaley, two men — both now deceased — who were always on call when Karpal found himself in real trouble.

During the hearing of the case the two junior counsel were to have serious doubts about Karpal's sanity when, in possibly another Malaysian first, he assaulted a police witness in court in front of Magistrate Radwan Ibrahim (who is now a High Court judge).

The prosecutor had put a constable in the witness box instead of the corporal who was involved in the shoving match with Karpal. In his testimony the constable claimed Karpal had assaulted him. Despite his best efforts Karpal was unable to get the constable to budge on his evidence. Karpal knew the shoving match had involved the corporal and himself, so he was both mystified and grateful when the prosecution decided to put the corporal in the witness box to say he had seen Karpal shoving the constable.

While cross-examining the corporal, Karpal recalled approaching the witness box saying, "Look here, you are the guy I hit. I hit you there and I am going to hit you again now."

At this point in his evidence Karpal said he hit the corporal in the chest in full view of the magistrate. The corporal threw his hands up in the air and fell backwards, protesting.

Radwan Ibrahim's reaction was one of immediate incredulity. "What? You hit him!"

Karpal walked back from the witness box to his seat while the magistrate repeatedly called upon him to apologise.

There would be no apology.

"I've said it time and again," Karpal said. "The question of an apology does not arise. You do not seem to understand, I will not apologise… I hit him to show what happened during the walk… I did not hit the other man, I hit him [the corporal]."

Radwan Ibrahim informed the lawyer he had not obtained the

court's permission to strike a witness and therefore he must apologise. The lawyer responded he had no intention of apologising. "I was only trying to show what actually happened," Karpal said.

The magistrate, who wrote down every word of Karpal's response to his request for an apology, clearly wanted time to ponder how he should handle this highly irregular and physical evidential development. He called for a 30-minute adjournment, with a bang of the door as he departed.

Manjit as a young lawyer at home in Alor Setar with his law books.

A worried Manjit and Assamaley asked their fellow lawyer what madness had possessed him to be so foolish as to assault a police witness in court. Karpal tried to explain that if he was going to go down he would prefer to go down on the basis of truth.

When the hearing resumed Radwan Ibrahim once again insisted on an apology, but it was still refused.

"The question of an apology does not arise. Demonstrating an incident before the court is allowed," Karpal argued.

The magistrate then turned his attention to the corporal in the witness box. "All right. He hit you. Do you want an apology?"

The policeman remained silent.

"He hit you," the magistrate repeated.

"Yes, he hit me," the policeman responded.

"I ask you again. Do you want an apology?"

After a long silence the corporal finally answered, "No, sir."

The magistrate had difficulty believing what was going on. "What? He hit you and you do not want an apology?"

"No, sir," the corporal responded again.

The magistrate, shaking his head, turned to the lawyer. "Mr Karpal Singh, what do we do now?"

Karpal was not about to have a second assault charge filed against him and he quickly responded. "Your Honour, we carry on from where we left off."

Radwan Ibrahim reminded Karpal that he had struck the corporal in open court whereupon Karpal responded, "Of course I hit him. I am not denying it. If you have to put me in [jail] then let me go in on the truth."

The magistrate then instructed Karpal to continue his cross-examination. By not seeking the apology the corporal was saying much about the quality of the evidence he and the constable had placed before the court.

Later, during an adjournment in the case, the corporal approached Karpal and begged for forgiveness. Holding up his hands in a gesture of prayer the policeman said in Malay, "Please forgive me. I ask for your forgiveness."

The prosecution, Karpal discovered later, apparently made the decision to put the constable into the witness box as their main witness because they did not trust the man who was actually involved in the game of push and shove with Karpal to stand up to cross-examination. This decision could not have been more helpful to Karpal because he knew no magistrate could convict him on an assault charge on the basis of the physical evidence presented.

Indeed at the close of the case for the prosecution on 10 October 1985 Radwan Ibrahim acquitted and discharged Karpal on the charge of using criminal force against the constable, without any reference to him having hit the corporal in court either.

Somehow Karpal had got away with the biggest physical risk he had ever taken inside a courtroom — hitting a policeman in the witness box right in front of a magistrate.

He could now turn his attention to defending his 20 colleagues and himself on the lesser charges of disobeying an order to disperse and participating in an unlawful assembly (without an appropriate police licence). Giving evidence from the witness box himself, Karpal said there was no organisation of any procession on the day in question. Some DAP members were present at the front of the DAP office from where the marathon began. To provide moral support for the first runner Fung Ket Wing, Karpal and the other 19 charged walked behind the runner on the sidewalk in twos and threes until they were stopped by the police.

In a joint statement from the dock, the supporters, with the exception of Karpal and Fung said:

> We were informed by the DAP leaders that a relay-marathon will be flagged off by the deputy chairman of the party Mr Karpal Singh at the DAP office at Jalan Kota, Alor Setar on 20 October 1984. At about 9 a.m. we all gathered outside the DAP office at Jalan Kota to witness the commencement of the relay-marathon. After Mr Karpal Singh flagged off the relay-marathon Mr Fung Ket Wing who was also present proceeded with the relay-marathon by jogging. As a show of moral support for the participants in the relay-marathon we followed Mr Fung Ket Wing at a distance together with Mr Karpal Singh. Outside the police station the police ordered us to stop. We saw Mr Karpal Singh talking to some police officers. We were all walking close behind Mr Karpal Singh in twos and threes on the sidewalk. There was no obstruction to the traffic. After about five minutes we proceeded towards the BP station led by Mr Karpal Singh and Mr George John. At the BP station the police again told us to stop. Once again we saw

Mr Karpal Singh talking to some police officers. While at the BP station Mr Fung Ket Wing, who was all alone ahead of us, joined us. Mr Karpal Singh then said, 'Let's go to the coffee shop.' Mr Karpal Singh, Mr George John and Mr Fung Ket Wing then walked towards a nearby coffee shop. We wanted to follow Mr Karpal Singh to the coffee shop but we were prevented from going forward by about 10 to 15 policemen armed with batons and rattan shields. While we were waiting there, we were not allowed to move forward or go anywhere. After about five minutes a few police jeeps arrived and we were ordered to get into the jeeps. We were taken to the police station. At the police station we were told to sit in a room on the ground floor. About an hour later we were informed that we were arrested. We were not required by anybody to participate in a procession and we did not at any time intend to participate in a procession. Our only intention was to follow Mr Fung Ket Wing until he left the town proper.'

When Karpal learned the 18 supporters had been taken to the Alor Setar police station he and fellow DAP officials George John and Fung proceeded there immediately, where the metal gates were in the process of being closed on them as they approached. Given the earlier pushing and shoving, the police feared for their own safety as Karpal came nearer and in an ironic twist he had to push his way into the police station to arrange bail for the arrested men.

At the conclusion of the hearing Magistrate Radwan Ibrahim found all 21 defendants guilty of participating in an unlawful assembly during the 'Save Bukit China' walk of 1984. They were fined RM250 each or two weeks in jail. Eighteen of the defendants were also convicted of the second charge of disobeying a police order to disperse. On this second conviction they were fined a further RM250 with an alternative of two weeks in jail.

The prosecution appealed the decision and attempts to imprison Karpal on the assault charge were rejected by the Alor Setar High Court 12 years later in 1996 when Magistrate Radwan Ibrahim's decision on all 21 convicted persons was upheld on appeal. Under article 48 of the Constitution any MP convicted of a crime and sentenced to imprisonment of one year or more, or fined RM2,000 or more, is disqualified from standing for elections as a candidate for five years.

Karpal came away from this 12-year case thinking that maybe violence — in the court room at least — did pay after all. His 'small change' conviction had been a small price to pay for the opportunity to demonstrate his political beliefs.

Looking back on the unproven assault charge, Karpal found personal justification in the words of one of Sikhdom's best known gurus, Guru Gobind Singh, a religious teacher whose name had been passed on to the lawyer's second son.

"When all modes of redressing a wrong having failed, the raising of sword is pious and just," the warrior guru had taught. In this instance Karpal had to agree with him. The lawyer learned later from police friends that the Malaysian establishment very much wanted an assault conviction against him in the hope of seeing him sentenced to jail for 18 months, a punishment capable of ending his political career. The mistake, however, was putting the wrong policeman in the witness box.

There was satisfaction in the knowledge the 'Save Bukit China' campaign did actually save the Chinese hill cemetery from the bulldozers of development.

An aside to the case saw Karpal create a legal precedent in Malaysia when he was visited by Inspector Sudha of the Alor Setar police at his

Penang office on 1 December 1984. The inspector was investigating the events of 20 October 1984. At that time Karpal had not been arrested on any charges and he refused Inspector Sudha's request for him to make a cautioned statement on his activities on the day the 18 DAP supporters were arrested.

Following his refusal, the Attorney-General Tan Sri Abu Talib Othman wrote to Karpal saying it would be in his best interests to comply with the investigating officer's request. Karpal again refused and referred the matter to the High Court for a ruling, where Justice Mustapha Hussain found that the police could only take a cautioned statement from him *after* he had been arrested. The Attorney-General was ordered to pay costs in this case. The Attorney-General then appealed to the Supreme Court which dismissed his appeal with costs.

Increasingly over the years Karpal's role in the DAP had been one of defending political colleagues in trouble with the law. He assumed the mantle as DAP lawyer during the Official Secrets Act case against Lim Kit Siang, P Patto, who was editor of the DAP's *Rocket* newspaper at the time, and the *Far Eastern Economic Review* in 1978.

Lim faced five charges over the publication of secret government information relating to a RM157 million deal to purchase four Swedish-made fast strike craft for the Royal Malaysian Navy. Justice Tun Abdul Hamid Omar convicted him on all five charges in the High Court.

Karpal appealed on Lim's behalf to the Federal Court, where the total fine package was reduced from RM15,000 to RM6,500. The new fines imposed by the Federal Court were less than RM2,000 on each charge, meaning that Lim Kit Siang, the leader of the Federal Opposition, was able to retain his parliamentary seat.

Eighteen years after saving the opposition leader's job, Karpal began defending Lim Kit Siang's son Lim Guan Eng, the MP for Kota Melaka, on charges of sedition and maliciously printing false news. Lim Guan

Eng made a return to national politics in 2008 after being convicted and jailed on these charges.

Opposition politicians in Malaysia have often paid a heavy price for their disagreement with the government. A number of DAP politicians have simply cracked under the pressure or been wooed away to more profitable financial pastures by Malaysian Chinese Association (MCA) incentives.

Karpal's good friend, one-time employee and former Prai state assemblyman S Assamaley became another high-profile casualty in 1991. On 26 May that year the *Sunday Mail* carried as its lead front page article a story on allegations that a DAP state assemblyman was involved in an affair with a married woman. The paper quoted the assemblyman as saying he would rather 'give up the seat than the woman'.

Three days after the publication of the article, the body of Assamaley's wife Devi Saraswathi was found floating off the Batu Maung coast. Before she threw herself off the Penang Bridge she had left a note for her husband beneath the sacred *thali* (the string worn by married Hindu women around their neck) at the altar of their home. The note read: 'Sorry this has to end this way. I love you then, now and forever.'

On 30 May 1991 Assamaley issued a statement from the Penang General Hospital after he had identified his wife's body, resigning his position as the DAP's Prai state assemblyman. The statement read:

> I had been entrusted by the DAP with the responsibility of being the elected representative of the people. I deeply regret the embarrassment caused to the party. Having considered the position carefully in its entirety, I have decided to resign as state assemblyman. I have sent my resignation letter to Lim Kit Siang, the Secretary-General of the DAP. I leave it entirely in the hands of the party to decide what action

Lim Guan Eng (right) pictured with his wife Betty Chew Gek Chong and family when he was charged under the Sedition Act 1948 and the Printing Presses and Publications Act 1984 for printing a pamphlet containing false information involving an alleged rape victim. On Karpal's left and partially hidden is Lim Kit Siang, Lim Guan Eng's father.

Lim Guan Eng's appeal process against his conviction under the Sedition Act 1948 and the Printing Presses and Publications Act 1984 was fast running its course. The final appeal was heard in the Federal Court in Kuala Lumpur. Lim Kit Siang is pictured here addressing supporters outside the court during the Federal Court appeal hearing. Lim Guan Eng lost his final appeal and was sentenced to 18 months imprisonment in August 1998; he served 12 months behind bars.

ought to be taken under the circumstances. I will be writing
to the party to explain the regretful turn of events.

The party had no alternative but to accept Assamaley's resignation
letter. Devi Saraswathi and her husband had been a tower of strength to
Karpal's family during the 15 months of his Operation Lalang detention
at the Kamunting Detention Camp from 1988 to 1990.

A 'point-the-finger' opposition
politician in Malaysia cannot afford
to have any skeletons in his or her own
cupboard. Karpal had always known
he had to be beyond reproach. If he
was not, there were ways to get to a
politician, particularly an opposition
politician, and one way was to work
through his family. This was a lesson

Karpal's great Penang-based lawyer
friend S Assamaley, 1995.

driven home in the most forceful manner possible to Assamaley, the man
who helped Karpal defend Australian Kevin Barlow against the death
penalty for two years in the mid-1980s. Assamaley's name was high on
the shortlist of people Karpal, a man who understood loyalty, numbered
among his trusted friends and professional colleagues.

The Assamaley resignation saw Karpal contest the Prai by-election
on behalf of the DAP in July 1991, but he could not stem the Prai tide of
Hindu indignation and suffered his second State Assembly electoral loss
within a year. This loss was to Penang MIC chairman V Muthusamy by
862 votes. Muthusamy stood on a Barisan Nasional ticket and the victory
was a particularly sweet one for Karpal's old political foes in the MIC.

In the 1990 State Assembly elections Karpal also miscalculated
when he put himself on the line by moving away from his safe Bukit
Gelugor seat and contesting the Sungai Pinang constituency. The

Gerakan Party's Kang Chin Seng took the seat by a 1,698 vote majority in a go-for-broke state-wide contest, otherwise successful for the DAP. The DAP took 14 State Assembly seats in Penang in the 1990 election, up four from 1986, but still three short of the 17 seats required to achieve state control. The highlight for the DAP in 1990 was Lim Kit Siang's 706 vote knockout of political heavyweight Lim Chong Eu who, like Karpal, went down graciously.

Consolation for Karpal came a year after being released from his 15-month detention with a convincing 9,178 majority win in his Jelutong federal seat over Gerakan's Ooi Ean Kwong.

Among the mainly urban Chinese voters of Jelutong there had been great loyalty to their outspoken MP since 1978. Over the years the more trouble Karpal found himself in, the more his constituents voted for him. But in 1995, with the Malaysian economy booming, Chinese voters were not interested in what opposition politicians had to offer and the DAP faced its worst electoral defeat.

Karpal was one of just nine DAP MPs voted into parliament. He suffered a third defeat in his endeavour to return to the Penang State Assembly, once again at the hands of Gerakan party member Kang Chin Seng in the Padang Kota electorate. Residents in Penang referred to the victor as 'Wu Song', after a character from a Chinese novel who was reputed to have killed a tiger with his bare hands.

A trip down memory lane for Karpal occurred in June 1990, before the state and federal elections that year, when police armed with M16s crawled over the Penang State Assembly building in an endeavour to harass and intimidate the DAP opposition representatives. For once in his political career the man who holds the distinction for being evicted from state and federal parliaments more than any other Malaysian politician did not prompt the armed police callout by Penang State Assembly Speaker Ooi Ean Kwong.

On this occasion the riot squad was called in after the Speaker would not let Lim Kit Siang ask what criteria had been used by the state executive council for recommending the appointment of state senators, and whether the state government would agree to have such senators elected by voters. (At the time Chief Minister Lim Chong Eu was being criticised, even from within his own party, over the appointment of a senator.) In the ensuing exchange Lim Kit Siang was ejected from the chamber. Police were called in to remove the DAP member for Berapit, Chian Heng Kai from the Assembly when he, too, persisted with Lim Kit Siang's line of questioning.

The return of the police to the Assembly proved too much for Karpal, who entered the fray himself when a police officer tugged on Chian's arm in their efforts to force him to leave the chamber. Karpal grabbed the police officer by his arm and pulled him away from Chian, who in turn left the assembly quietly after being ordered to do so by the Speaker. Attention then turned to Karpal, who was thrown out after criticising the Speaker for inviting the police to invade the Assembly. As he left Karpal threw his copy of *Standing Orders* at the Speaker. The book hit him squarely on his left shoulder from a range of three metres. On this note, Karpal's tempestuous career in the Penang State Assembly ended for all time.

The incident resulted in the *New Straits Times* saying this of Karpal the following day: 'He has displayed such open tantrums in the past. When the throwing incident occurred, no one was in the least surprised. It was typical of the man... It speaks of his volatile character.' The paper also observed the suspension would free him 'to attend to his legal practice'.

For Karpal this 1990 eviction — his last from the Penang State Assembly under the armed gaze of police — held a special place among his political memories.

In a more sedate and controlled environment, the 1995 contest for the Jelutong seat was closely fought between Karpal and Penang lawyer Rhina Bhar, who made much of the fact Karpal was so busy with his law practice that he had little time for the concerns of his electorate.

But the Chinese of Jelutong appreciated the fact their man spoke his mind from the opposition front bench whenever the red light, signifying an active microphone, went on in the federal parliament. If something had to be said, Karpal would say it, in the name of justice and democracy. The Chinese small traders, hawkers and factory workers were impressed that the name of Jelutong had so often been associated with a challenge to the system. They loved the bearded Sikh fighter.

On election night 1995, Rhina Bhar's supporters were in victory mode at their Penang Free School headquarters. They were convinced a woman had finished off the Tiger of Jelutong.

But when all the votes were counted Karpal's total of 21,896 was still 283 ahead of Rhina Bhar. It would be four months, the time it took for the High Court to dismiss Rhina Bhar's election petition challenging the result, before Karpal was officially declared the winner. Those four months were a time of soul-searching for the DAP and Karpal, in particular, who resigned from his position as Penang state chairman after 19 years at the helm.

Four years later in 1999 Karpal did lose his Jelutong federal seat to an electorate disillusioned with the DAP policy approach of deciding to work closely with the Islamist-based PAS party. Many thought this would be the end of Karpal's political career but the Tiger pounced back into parliament in another Penang electorate, Bukit Gelugor, in the 2004 election.

Inevitably, it would only be a matter of time before he found himself outside the parliamentary fence looking in. Indeed, 24 years after first being banned for two years from the Penang Assembly, he was red-

Karpal retains his seat as MP for Jelutong following Rhina Bhar's electoral challenge, 1995. Pictured here with Karpal are sons (from left) Jagdeep and Gobind, wife Gurmit and sister Amar Kaur.

carded yet again, a further six-month ban, before he'd even had a chance to resume his seat in parliament after his one-term absence.

As MPs were being sworn in on 17 May 2004, Karpal objected to the fact that some MPs were not raising their right hand during the ceremony as he said they were required to do under the Statutory Declarations Act.

At the time the Speaker of the Dewan Rakyat Tun Dr Mohamed Zahir Ismail overruled the objection and simply referred the matter to the Privileges Committee. The committee found Karpal had been incorrect; the MP himself acknowledged in parliament he had been in error. Nevertheless the majority of committee members concluded Karpal had deliberately misled the House during his interruption at the swearing-in ceremony and recommended he should apologise and be suspended for ten days.

Needless to say no apology was forthcoming and Karpal was suspended from parliament.

During the suspension debate he turned the heat up on the Speaker. Speaking under parliamentary privilege he asked the Speaker what he had done wrong. Was his (Karpal's) offence in the same category as former US president Bill Clinton and his handling of the Monica Lewinsky affair? Was it like stealing the parliamentary mace or, indeed, was it like helping yourself, Mr Speaker, to a parliamentary fence?

From the moment Karpal suggested a certain fence may indeed have been perked by a key political figure to fence off an orchard his six-month ban was set in concrete in the minds of the ruling BN. The Geneva-based Inter-Parliamentary Union's committee on the human rights of parliamentarians subsequently looked into the issue of Karpal's 2004 ban. It circulated a confidential paper dated April 2005 stating the Malaysian parliament's 2004 decision to suspend him lacked well-founded arguments.

Despite yet another ban, the man referred to as 'the scum' by Lim Chong Eu decades earlier had solidified his political position and the outspoken Sikh was happy to be back outside the fence consigned once again to a life of political exile.

Karpal did, however, have occasion to return to parliament soon after the six-month ban was imposed upon him, in his capacity as the newly elected national chairman of the DAP. The purpose of this visit was a sad one. It was to pay his last respects to the Speaker Tun Dr Mohamed Zahir Ismail, who died during the period of Karpal's ban.

Karpal at his swearing-in session in Parliament, following the
25 April 1995 general election.

Karpal juggles his legal and political career. *Cartoon by Datuk Mohammad Nor Khalid, more commonly known as Lat, for the* New Straits Times.

7 INDIAN BLUES

It is not difficult to understand the speedy implementation of the 2004 ban against Karpal by the Malaysian parliament's Privileges Committee. Speaker Tun Mohamed Zahir Ismail was a former judge, who for many years had worked closely with the ruling UMNO political party in the running of the parliament. He was, therefore, keen to reassert his authority over a returning MP who had a reputation of rocking the political boat. The long-serving Speaker (he was the Dewan Rakyat's longest-serving Speaker ever) and a succession of his deputies had learned the hard way that here was a politician who knew how to use his knowledge of standing orders in pursuit of political objectives.

In his 21 years as the MP for Jelutong, Karpal conducted two major political crusades. One involved prominent members of the Malaysian Indian Congress (MIC) and the other, a successful campaign to subject Malaysia's nine hereditary sultanate rulers — who select one from among their ranks to be the reigning monarch every five years — to the rule of law. Along the way the lawyer used every political trick in the book to force through a political agenda that was often highly embarrassing to the ruling coalition.

In his first parliamentary term the lawyer locked horns with the influential and affable Works Minister and MIC boss Samy Vellu. At the heart of this early dispute with Samy Vellu, who retired from the MIC leadership in December 2010, was the metaphoric hand of a deceased Indian landowner Sangily reaching up from the grave.

Karpal specialised in the highly irritating (for his political foes) and strategically dangerous 'I'll see you in court and sue me if you dare' approach to politics.

One conspicuous example of the strategy involved Samy Vellu in October 1982 when Karpal stated, initially under the protection of parliamentary privilege, that Samy Vellu had obtained land from the deceased Sangily in an untoward fashion

In going for Samy Vellu, Karpal wanted to get the message out there that the DAP was not just a Chinese party. It, too, could look after the interests of Indian citizens in Malaysia, citizens like S Periasamy, son of Sangily. In his speech to parliament on 15 October 1982 Karpal went for Samy Vellu and expressed reservations about the Works Minister's fitness to occupy a cabinet role.

Elaborating on why he held that view, he told parliament Samy Vellu had wanted Sangily's land to build a private swimming pool. All hell broke loose in parliament when Karpal raised the issue of Lot No 6130 CT 18052, Mukim Batu, Daerah Kuala Lumpur with Samy Vellu.

The Works Minister described himself as a Hindu lion who would be quite prepared to take on 'the tiger' in court if Karpal cared to repeat his allegations outside parliament. Samy Vellu told parliament there had been absolutely nothing illegal in his handling of the land transfer.

Anyone who knew Karpal as a political opponent — as Lim Chong Eu certainly did at a state level in those days — knew a challenge to pick up the cudgels outside parliament would not be ignored. Suitable arrangements for round two of this dogfight were put in place and preparations made for the challenge to continue at Kuala Lumpur's venerable Chinese Assembly Hall on Monday 25 October 1982.

Samy Vellu wrote to Karpal Singh, via his lawyer, saying he would, of course, happily turn up if Karpal obtained a police permit for the meeting from the Home Ministry. The permit materialised.

In an entertaining and amusing build-up to the big day, Malaysia's then retired first Prime Minister Tunku Abdul Rahman expanded on the animal theme in his weekly column in *The Star* newspaper. He described the feud between the two men as a contest between a cat, Samy Vellu, and a dog, Karpal Singh. In referring to Karpal as the 'big dog' the former prime minister, with his tongue firmly in his cheek, said canines were loyal and faithful animals.

On the afternoon of the challenge about 2,000 highly vocal people crammed into the hall, closely watched over by riot police, to personally witness the 'law of the Malaysian jungle' confrontation between the MIC's Hindu 'lion' and the DAP's Sikh 'tiger'. The Malaysian press accorded the issue major coverage status.

Karpal was accompanied to the big showdown by fellow DAP leaders Lim Kit Siang, Lee Kaw, V David and Lee Lam Thye. He spent approximately 25 minutes repeating the speech he had made in parliament ten days earlier and then distributed 30 photocopies of his speech notes to the assembled media. Present as a key adviser in the Samy Vellu camp that day was lawyer DP Vijandran.

On 17 November 1982 Samy Vellu filed his promised retaliatory defamation proceedings against Karpal. Samy Vellu's defamation suit was finally dismissed for want of progress seven years later in July 1989.

While Samy Vellu's defamation suit never made it to a court hearing, a number of other cases involving DP Vijandran and Karpal most certainly did. The legal careers of both these men were flying high in the late 1970s. DP Vijandran's reputation received a major boost about that time when he defended eight Malaysian Indian temple guards charged with the beating and stabbing to death of four Muslims who broke into a Hindu temple in Kerling, just north of Kuala Lumpur.

Hindus provide round-the-clock security for their temples. The four Muslim men learned this the hard way when they were hacked and battered to death for attempting to destroy the Sri Subramaniam shrine in Kerling. Evidence accepted by the Sessions Court president revealed the four had been on a Hindu temple-bashing tour throughout the Kerling region before they were killed.

The 11-month trial concluded with DP Vijandran's clients being sentenced to relatively light jail terms following convictions being entered for culpable homicide not amounting to murder.

The outcome of the hard-won case provided DP Vijandran with a national profile upon which to build a powerful legal and MIC political career. He was subsequently appointed a senator and elected to the federal parliament in 1986 on an MIC ticket before being quickly elevated to the Deputy Speaker's chair.

Life went along reasonably smoothly for Deputy Speaker DP Vijandran until Karpal stood up in parliament on 6 December 1989. Speaking under privilege, he told parliament that a safe stolen from DP Vijandran's Kuala Lumpur home 18 months earlier had contained a number of videotapes that featured a prominent MIC politician in compromising positions.

In parliament again on Monday 11 December 1989 Karpal kept up the onslaught, on this occasion naming the Deputy Speaker for the first time as the MIC man involved in the blue movie tapes. Subsequent legal action involving the two Indian legal heavyweights was to continue for the next decade.

Karpal, with his political career still intact, emerged the winner, albeit with a bloodied nose, in a points decision after the lengthy legal standoff between the two men. After Karpal made his blue movie comments in parliament a decision was made to move DP Vijandran sideways out of the Deputy Speaker's chair soon afterwards.

As he was being moved DP Vijandran vociferously described Karpal's allegations as a load of rubbish unworthy of public comment. He accused Karpal of raking up things against him for years in retaliation against the times he had evicted his fellow lawyer from parliament.

On 28 December 1989 DP Vijandran, via his lawyers, filed a defamation suit against Karpal, with details published in the *New Straits Times* on 12 January 1990. After filing the defamation suit, DP Vijandran, who was also Chairman of Maika Holdings (the MIC political party's investment arm), revealed he was taking three months special leave to enable him to recharge his batteries before returning to his parliamentary duties in March 1990.

He also filed a second libel suit against Karpal soon afterwards for allegedly maligning him in statements published in *The Star*, *New Straits Times* and *Sunday Mail*.

On 11 January 1990 the Malaysian 'porngate' saga was back in the news when Attorney-General Tan Sri Abu Talib Othman released a statement saying he had ordered, in January 1989, the destruction of videotapes, 2,000 photographs and negatives recovered from the safe burglars.

Because of a lack of evidence, the Attorney-General did not order prosecutions against the burglars who were detained and questioned by police in October 1988. On 20 January 1989 the Attorney-General directed the police to close the case and release the four suspects.

MIC boss Samy Vellu, in the early months of 1990, was particularly outspoken in support of DP Vijandran.

Also in early 1990 Prime Minister Dr Mahathir went on the videotape saga offensive against Karpal during a speech in Ipoh. He observed that four categories of people knew what was on the tapes: DP Vijandran, the police, the Attorney-General and the burglars themselves. All of this, of course, begged the question, how did Karpal know what was on the tapes?

Karpal could have been charged with possession of the tape he subsequently tabled in parliament if police had evidence of him being in possession of it outside parliament.

Meanwhile, as the videotape furore continued on in the media, DP Vijandran returned from his extended leave in March 1990. He then resigned his positions as Deputy Speaker, MIC Secretary-General and Maika Holdings chairman but he did stay on as a Maika Holdings director. The resignations, however, were not going to be the last parliament heard of the videotape saga.

His lawyers wrote to Karpal on 23 June 1992 advising that the former Deputy Speaker was withdrawing a defamation action against Karpal and three Malaysian newspapers. DP Vijandran was ordered to pay Karpal costs of RM9,414.39 relating to the withdrawn defamation proceedings.

When there were problems surrounding the cheque Karpal issued a highly critical 3 March 1996 press release, which became the subject of yet another defamation action launched by DP Vijandran. The final saga in this defamation case saw the Court of Appeal on 3 August 2001 ordering Karpal to pay DP Vijandran RM100,000 (plus costs and interest) in damages. In its decision in this case the court described Karpal as a well-known lawyer and former politician (as he was in 2001 after having lost his Jelutong electorate seat in parliament in 1999).

The Court of Appeal found it was common knowledge that Karpal had been responsible for exposing DP Vijandran and thereby bringing about the latter's political downfall.

'The cheque incident gave him another opportunity to further ruin the respondent. He utilised it to the fullest' the court found.

'The fact that his press statement was typed on his MP letterhead with his party symbol and the fact that he signed the press statement as Deputy Chairman, DAP Malaysia and MP Malaysia shows his political motive.'

'He did not apologise and he stood his ground throughout' the court found in reaching its decision to award DP Vijandran the RM100,000.

Away from the world of court actions there can be no doubt Karpal was determined in his pursuit of DP Vijandran. Evidence of this was there for all to see on 20 July 1992 when the MP took one of the biggest risks of his political career by tabling a videotape in parliament during the debate on the Companies (Amendment) Bill. The object of the exercise, from Karpal's perspective, was to get the police to investigate the contents of this videotape.

It was risky business for if Deputy Speaker Ong Tee Keat had refused to allow the videotape to be tabled, Karpal could have been charged under the Films (Censorship) Act 1952 for possession of a lewd film. A conviction would have seen him automatically barred from practising as a lawyer and sacked from parliament.

The elaborate contingency arrangements — meticulously planned in the event the videotape could not be tabled — included bringing into parliament a small bottle of petrol and a specially constructed metal container that fitted neatly inside a large legal briefcase. The plan was to use the flameproof container to destroy the evidence inside the parliamentary debating chamber itself if the Deputy Speaker refused to allow the videotape to be tabled.

Getting a videotape into parliament was supposed to be the easy part, but even here there was an interesting moment as the lawyer travelled from Penang to parliament in Kuala Lumpur. As he walked through the airport terminal in Penang and approached a routine checkpoint, a security guard held his left arm and gently removed a videotape he was openly carrying. The guard explained he did not want to see it damaged in any way by the airport security equipment.

The stage was then set for the big parliamentary moment.

During the Companies Amendment Bill debate on 20 July 1992, Karpal told parliament how much he welcomed government moves to enhance penalties for white collar crime, particularly at the top level of companies. He referred to the ethics of company directors as being more important than the legal issues referred to in the legislation.

Continuing his speech he removed the videotape from his briefcase and began walking with it towards the Deputy Speaker's chair.

"But Mr Speaker, what is more interesting is this tape," he said as he walked towards the chair. He told parliament the tape was a gift from the MP for Jelutong for all of his colleagues in parliament and he was relieved when the Deputy Speaker accepted the videotape from him.

But the job was still only half done, for the videotape had to become part of the parliamentary proceedings. He asked the Deputy Speaker to mark the tape as an exhibit as he had accepted it. Ong Tee Keat obligingly complied with the request.

Karpal smiled in the direction of his colleagues when he resumed his seat following one of the biggest bluffs of his political career. As he looked down at the bottle of petrol and the cigarette lighter in his metal-lined briefcase he was more than happy on this particular day, and not only as a Sikh who viewed tobacco as taboo for religious reasons, to see parliament's no-smoking ban complied with.

The briefcase was to remain within the confines of parliament until the Speaker Tun Mohamed Zahir Ismail officially handed the videotape over to the police.

Throughout the videotape saga many people, including Prime Minister Dr Mahathir, asked Karpal where he had obtained the tape. The question was eventually answered from the witness box of a Sessions Court in Ipoh. Karpal told the court a person he did not know phoned him in Penang on 28 June 1992 to advise there was a videotape near his Green Hall office door.

The legal saga ended with a Court of Appeal judgement on 23 February 1999, which upheld a lower court finding that DP Vijandran was involved in the pornographic videotape. The Court of Appeal also acquitted and discharged the appellant DP Vijandran on a charge of fabricating false evidence. In its judgement the Court of Appeal also found in part:

> It is true that the appellant stated on oath that he had been made out as a person 'who has acted in pornographic tapes'. It is equally true that the prosecution had established beyond a reasonable doubt that the male actor appearing in the pornographic video was indeed the appellant.

Still on videos, in the past two years a video purportedly showing opposition leader Anwar Ibrahim in a compromising position with a woman had been doing the rounds. Karpal found the latest video, allegedly featuring Anwar, quite amusing, given the fact he had worked on achieving acquittals for Anwar in not one, but two lengthy sodomy High Court cases since 1998.

Anwar's wife Wan Azizah and his family vehemently denied their husband and father was the man in the latest video after watching it for themselves. Wan Azizah, a saintly-looking woman, described the latest tape as just another attempt by his political opponents to discredit her husband. It was part of the ongoing smear campaign, she said, which was designed to discredit him in the build-up to the 5 May 2013 election. Wan Azizah described the tape as 'vile, false and baseless'.

For Karpal the latest sex tape doing the rounds of Malaysian politics gave him a chance to take a trip down memory lane. He suggested on 4 April 2011 that all parliamentarians should be given an opportunity to view the latest tape in parliament albeit with two provisos.

One was that Anwar himself, who was under yet another ban from parliament for six months at the time, should be invited back to view the tape alongside his colleagues. The second was that the tape should be marked as an exhibit so that it became part of the proceedings of the parliament, just as the DP Vijandran tape had been treated in 1992.

Neither of Karpal's suggestions was taken up by Anwar's parliamentary colleagues.

Reflecting on the 1992 videotape tabling episode, Karpal recalled an attempt by police to charge him for possession of the videotape outside parliament. "It was contended that I could only have brought the pornographic videotape into the House from outside. It was further contended by the police that there was parliamentary immunity attached to my handling the pornographic videotape only in the course of proceedings in the House."

The police had told him he was not protected for having possession of the videotape outside parliament. Karpal stood his ground and was never charged for possession of a pornographic videotape outside parliament in 1992.

(*above left*) DP Vijandran's legal career received a major boost when he very
capably defended eight Indian security guards charged with beating and stabbing
to death four Muslims who vandalised the Hindu temple in Kerling. Pictured
here are the replacement icons for the ones damaged in the attack; (*right*) Works
Minister Samy Vellu (in white jacket) and his MIC lawyer-politican DP Vijandran
(in suit and tie) arrive at the Chinese Assembly Hall in Kuala Lumpur to hear
Karpal's allegations against Samy Vellu, 25 October 1982.

In the MIC corner, Samy Vellu is laid back as he listens to Karpal re-read
his statement. Seated on his right is DP Vijandran, and seated on his left is
another lawyer, Robert Chelliah.

(*above*) In the Rocket corner, the
DAP faction, Karpal re-reads the
statement made in Parliament at the
Chinese Assembly Hall surrounded
by his DAP supporters. Among them
are his long-term bodyguard Master
Kam (seated on his left) and Lim Kit
Siang (seated on his right); (*right*)
Karpal leaving the Chinese Assembly
Hall in Kuala Lumpur after re-
reading a statement involving Works
Minister Samy Vellu. Lim Kit Siang
is on the right of Karpal's right hand.
Photo courtesy of The Star, *Malaysia.*

8 ONE LAW FOR ALL

Running parallel with the campaign against the MIC leadership of the 1980s and 1990s was Karpal's quest to have Malaysia's royals subjected to the rule of law. Under Malaysia's founding Constitution the rulers of the states of Selangor, Perlis, Kedah, Pahang, Kelantan, Terengganu, Johor, Negeri Sembilan and Perak had long enjoyed immunity from prosecution.

It was a situation Karpal found legally abhorrent. One man, in particular, did not help the immunity cause of the royal families. The late Sultan of Johor was notorious throughout the country as a man who allegedly beat to death a caddy on a golf course as well as carrying out a number of other acts against private citizens.

In 1984 Karpal was suspended from parliament for two years when he asked a question relating to a 1982 court case relating to the sultans of Pahang and Johor.

In April 1982 Karpal represented two brothers who were cousins of the Sultan of Pahang, who heads the state on the east coast of peninsular Malaysia, against charges of cheating at a Johor disco. He was invited to handle the case by the father of the boys, Tunku Temenggong Pahang, who was the uncle of the Sultan of Pahang and at that time head of the Kerabat (royal council) of the state. In receiving instructions from Tunku Temenggong Pahang, Karpal was told the Kerabat regarded the Pahang royal household's honour as having been brought into disrepute by the treatment of his two sons and their two friends in Johor.

The court subsequently heard how the young men from Pahang — Tunku Muiz Shah, his brother Tunku Bongsu Putra and their two friends Shaikh Shazalan and Mohamad Hassan — visited the Goldmine Discotheque in Johor on the night of 22 April 1982. Tunku Muiz Shah was subsequently charged with passing himself off at the disco as the Regent of the State of Pahang to obtain free drinks and a RM2,000 loan. The remaining three were charged with aiding and abetting him on the impersonation charge. All four were found not guilty.

The hearing of the case was transferred from Johor Bahru to Kuala Lumpur where the former supervisor of the disco Seah Boon Huat testified how he had provided the four men with free drinks after Tunku Muiz Shah 'passed himself off as the Regent of Pahang'. The four men left the disco at 3:00 a.m. Later that day Seah received a call at his home from Tunku Muiz Shah requesting a RM2,000 loan to go shopping in Singapore. He would be at the disco at 11:00 p.m. that night to pick up the money.

Seah decided to check the so-called 'Regent of Pahang' out and phoned the Sultan of Johor's residence. He was surprised when the Sultan (now deceased) himself picked up the phone.

That night eight policemen in three patrol cars picked up the four men from the Straits View Hotel in Johor Bahru and drove them to the Sultan's residence. There they were welcomed by the late Sultan and another 14 police officers. They were allegedly assaulted and at one stage whisky was poured down the throat of one of the men after he had been grabbed by the hair.

The court heard in evidence how they were whipped, kicked, made to roll on the ground and do hundreds of squats before being taken away, locked up and charged by the police. They were released on bail on 24 April 1982 and advised by police under no circumstances to mention the role the royal household had played in the somewhat unusual arrest proceedings.

Honour was restored to the Royal House of Pahang by Karpal and his co-counsel Abbas Rowlands when court President Haji Halim Mohamed ruled there was no need for the defence to be called. The four men had no case to answer.

Chaos reigned in parliament on 5 November 1984 when Karpal began asking questions about this case. The line of questioning focused on the behaviour of the late Sultan of Johor, who also happened to be the Agong at the time.

In asking his questions Karpal committed an 'unforgiveable sin' in the eyes of the Malays. He had directly challenged the ideology of Malaysia's dominant UMNO political party, rooted as it is in its *bumiputra* sons of the soil philosophy, with the rulers symbolising Malay dominance. It was a dangerous excursion into a political no-go zone, and being highly contentious, Karpal walked very much alone among the opposition MPs.

In the fortnight before his formal suspension from parliament on 22 November 1984, Speaker Tun Mohamed Zahir Ismail struggled with how to handle a man who was steadfastly refusing to apologise for his questioning in parliament. He sent a staff member to the DAP MP's Kuala Lumpur office suggesting a retraction.

Twenty-eight years later, on 9 January 2012, Karpal, Dr Chen Man Hin (with hat) and Lim Kit Siang are at the Lake Club, Kuala Lumpur, celebrating Anwar Ibrahim's acquittal on his second sodomy charge. Anwar's High Court acquittal was subsequently overturned by the Court of Appeal on 7 March 2014.

Senior DAP leaders Dr Chen Man Hin and Lim Kit Siang suggested similar strategic outs for their colleague but Karpal would not budge.

There would be no retraction or apology.

For three hours on 22 November 1984 parliament debated Deputy Home Minister Dato' Seri Radzi Sheikh Ahmad's motion calling for the suspension of the Member for Jelutong for contempt of parliament. A majority voted to suspend him from parliament indefinitely until he apologised for his remarks — or until the parliamentary term ended.

In response Karpal advised parliament what he had said was factual. He did, however, offer to resign to enable a by-election to take place in Jelutong if the Deputy Home Minister was prepared to withdraw his motion. In a Sikh impersonation of General MacArthur's return to the Philippines, Karpal said dramatically as he left parliament: "This Honourable House can take whatever action it wishes. However, in the coming elections, I will stand for re-election once again and I will return to this Honourable House. I give that assurance."

In the two years following this suspension the Barisan Nasional's coalition tactic was to endeavour to turn the parliamentary suspension issue into a Karpal behavioural problem. This concerted approach was an attempt to undermine the MP's credibility and deflect attention away from what the lawyer MP had actually said.

From the time of the 1984 suspension onwards, Malaysians regularly read in their newspapers how the bad boy of politics was held in contempt of parliament yet again for another egregious breach of standing orders.

Instead of destroying Karpal's political credibility, the ban actually enhanced his standing, although in some quarters he was demonised. Many Malaysians, on later encounters with the lawyer-politician, had been genuinely surprised to come across a softly spoken, very-much-in-control wheelchair-bound man when they met him.

If anything he became an ever bigger nuisance to the ruling Barisan Nasional during his two-year suspension. As the first MP ever to be suspended for contempt of Malaysia's parliament, a certain novelty value surrounded him and a curious media relished reporting his every anti-establishment move.

In October 1986 he was returned to parliament with an almost doubled majority of 10,099 votes over the establishment candidate Lim Boo Chang. The Chinese voters of Jelutong liked what their man had achieved from his world of political isolation.

His return to parliament did present his DAP masters with the problem of how to handle the 'disloyal' subject at the official opening of Malaysia's seventh parliament which was to be presided over by the Agong who, at the time, was the Sultan of Johor. The monarch had not set eyes upon the Jelutong MP since the latter's much-publicised suspension.

For his part, Karpal was ready for any eventuality as officers and men from the First Battalion of the Royal Malay Regiment fired off a 21-cannon salute coinciding with the arrival at parliament of the king and queen of Malaysia.

The red carpet reunion was to take place amidst the pomp and pageantry in the senate lobby of parliament buildings. Karpal considered it wise to ask his wife to remain at home in Penang on this day. He did not want her to suffer any embarrassment should a scene develop.

At the function the Agong, followed by his loyal retinue, moved along the line from group to group, making polite small talk. Finally the royal party moved towards Karpal and the two men just looked at each other. Nothing was said, not even a mention of the fact the monarch had recently named one of his dogs 'Karpal Singh'. A pin-drop hush had come over the assembled gathering of parliamentarians, diplomats, foreign dignitaries and loyal subjects. The unofficial silence reflected genuine concern over the rift between the two men.

Finally the monarch broke the ice by extending his hand. Karpal reciprocated and there were smiles all round from bystanders, particularly from DAP party leader Lim Kit Siang. Hushed polite conversation resumed among the relieved members of Kuala Lumpur's elite cocktail set. There had been no apology and the MP for Jelutong had officially made good his promise to return to the parliamentary fold.

Throughout the suspension Karpal often thought the impasse might end in bloodshed — his own. He took security precautions against this unhappy prospect, even investing in special vehicles with bulletproof windows.

If the late Sultan of Johor thought Karpal's return to parliament was to be the end of the feud between the two men, he was mistaken. In April 1986 Karpal sued the Agong, in his own name, on behalf of businessman Daeng Baha Ismail bin Daeng Ahmad.

(*above left*) Karpal and the then Agong, Sultan Mahmud Iskandar of Johor, at the official opening of the 1986 session of parliament. Looking on are Lim Guan Eng and Lim Kit Siang. *Photo courtesy of Bernama*; (*right*) The front cover of *Asiaweek* (6 January 1993) previews the impending 1993 change to the Constitution allowing court proceedings to be brought against rulers.

In his brief of evidence, Daeng said he had been subjected to a protracted and brutal physical attack, including a whipping with the *rotan*, on 4 June 1983 at the hands of the man who was at that time (i.e. April 1986) the Agong. The alleged assault took place in the king's palace in Johor.

The case was thrown out by the Supreme Court on 5 December 1986. If nothing else, Daeng's case confirmed that Karpal would take on any case — even sue a king — no matter what political odds might be stacked against him.

Karpal often looked back in wonder at how he personally survived those difficult days. The thought occurred to him on more than one occasion that he managed to live through those days of challenging the royals because his political opponents knew many of the people he defended in court had impeccable underworld credentials.

Karpal was left in no doubt as to what some members of the royal household thought of him when he received a phone call from a Kuala

Lumpur lawyer friend Robert Chelliah at the time when he was banned from parliament.

Chelliah urged him to stay away from the state of Johor and relayed a story to back up his concerns. He had been set upon by a group of Malays in Johor Bahru when they mistakenly identified him as Karpal, the Sultan of Johor's 'public enemy number one'. Chelliah understandably quickly and wisely disowned his colleague. In the subsequent phone call he advised Karpal to be very, very careful whenever he entered the state of Johor.

The late Sultan of Johor was a curious paradox in Malaysia during his long life. On the one hand he had a reputation for ruthlessness, on the other he could be incredibly generous. There are numerous stories in Johor of the Sultan lavishly entertaining, on the spur of the moment, large gatherings of poor people off the street and giving away personal items of jewellery.

But for Karpal, the assault cases clearly illustrated why Malaysia's Constitution needed amending to ensure the members of its royal family became subject to the rule of law.

Some of Karpal's clashes with royalty were quite humorous. In the early 1980s when the then Sultan of Perak Sultan Idris Shah indicated he wanted to expand his empire to take in a portion of the southern Penang state, Karpal told him he should stay within the boundaries constituted at the time of independence in 1957. The Sultan did not appreciate him saying he would defend Penang's territorial rights, right to the end! On a lighter note, Karpal later heard that the word that went out from the Sultan of Perak's residence was that this "bullock carter's son" needed to be taught a lesson.

Another far more serious tussle with a ruler featured a Malay *bomoh* (shaman) in an interesting sideshow. *Bomohs* are widely regarded, particularly among rural Malays, as possessing supernatural powers capable of bringing good or evil upon friend or foe. Well-intentioned Malays delight in taking their mixtures of orange betel nuts and big dark green *sireh* leaves to their *bomoh* and much faith is placed on the soothsaying qualities of the message they receive. They consult *bomohs* to obtain lucky lotto numbers or to ascertain thought patterns of influential people; teachers and parents even threaten to visit a *bomoh* to get their misbehaving children into line.

Karpal had never come face to face with a *bomoh* before and the meeting in September 1987 with *bomoh* Kiai Arshad Mohamad Gamat was certainly not by appointment. Rather it was the result of divine intervention for, in the *bomoh*'s words, a divine hand guided him to the Kuala Lumpur High Court. The same guiding power evidently inspired the father of 16 to tell anyone at the courthouse who would listen he was there to 'fix' Karpal up.

Karpal had incurred this divine wrath of the *bomoh* and of members of the Selangor UMNO Youth group over a decision to sue Sultan Salahuddin Abdul Aziz, the then Sultan of Selangor, a man who would go on to become the eleventh Agong. The Sultan, as reported in newspapers, had stated on Sunday 26 July 1987 in his speech to the Selangor branch of the Ex-Serviceman's Association that he would not pardon convicted drug traffickers in his state. Karpal's subsequent court action against him for this statement was one of the first occasions a sultan had been taken to court in Malaysia.

So incensed in fact with Karpal were the UMNO Youth members of Selangor that they wanted the lawyer banned completely from the state. They also filed a report with police in the state capital in Shah Alam alleging sedition against Karpal for his 'outrageous' decision to sue their beloved sultan.

Karpal first set eyes on Kiai Arshad through a High Court window. Looking up from his files, he recalled seeing a large Malay man with a round face repeatedly pointing in his direction through a window. Believing the man must have been impressed with his advocacy, he waved at him and thought nothing further of it until leaving the courtroom for the day.

Outside the court he was greeted by a worried-looking Special Branch police contingent headed by Mervyn Fernandez. The policeman suggested it would be in the best interests of all if Karpal left the court building via a rear entrance. Inquiring as to why he should skulk away and use the back door for the first time in his life, Fernandez told Karpal not to argue the point, that a 'dangerous' man at the front entrance had been telling everybody he wanted to attack him.

A man making violent threats of this nature deserved to be arrested and Karpal lightheartedly reminded the police they should do their duty and protect him. Never before had the lawyer-politician slunk out the back door of a courtroom and 'by my beard' he was not about to make life easy for his police minders in this instance. He did, however, agree to wait briefly while Fernandez noted details of the *bomoh*'s identity card. As this was being conducted, Karpal walked out the front door in the direction of Kiai Arshad and Fernandez.

Unexpectedly presented with a willing quarry, the *bomoh* walked smilingly towards Karpal and the latter felt confident enough to hold out his hand in a gesture of friendship. Kiai Arshad seemed willing to reciprocate the gesture saying, *Yang Berhormat* (honourable sir), but he withdrew his hand at the last minute and slapped Karpal's face, informing him he had placed a curse upon him. This powerful curse would result in his inevitable early death, Karpal was told.

Most Malaysians generally respect the logic behind criminal law books but on this day the printed word, contained in the swinging form of a hefty legal briefcase, proved rather too much for the shaman.

With the *bomoh* grounded and winded following the blow, Karpal was quite content to shrug off the attack. His superstitious DAP minders were taking no chances, however. They believed a religious curse had been placed on his head and firm action had to be taken to remove this otherworldly hex. They told the lawyer he would most certainly die if he did not agree to undergo a purification ritual.

"That man has got you. You'll be dead," one political advisor told him. After lodging an official police report they packed him in a car and, ignoring the lawyer's protests, headed for the nearest Sikh temple where water and flowers were poured over his head.

The following morning the lawyer was grateful for the concern accorded him by his political allies

Karpal at the Privy Council in London, 1986, where he appeared six times in his career since 1976.

when the *bomoh* thoughtfully proclaimed to a Malay newspaper that the man whom the spirit had moved him to attack would soon 'go deaf, dumb and blind before meeting with a premature death'.

In his subsequent appearance in the Magistrate's Court Kiai Arshad made much of saying he could hurt people from afar. Karpal responded to this remark that he would outlive the *bomoh*. Sadly for Kiai Arshad, his supernatural powers could not keep him out of Pudu Jail where he was sent for two days in April 1988 for his unprovoked assault.

As *bomohs* go, Kiai Arshad was tame in comparison to *bomoh* couple Mona Fandey and Mohd Affandi Abdul Rahman. Along with their assistant Juraimi bin Husin, Karpal's client, the trio planned for weeks how they intended to rob and kill the Talam state assemblyman Datuk Mazlan Idris.

Hours before he was killed on 2 July 1993 Mazlan withdrew RM260,000 from a number of banks. The *bomoh* couple had earlier told him they would double his money for him once he had completed a *mandi bunga* (purification bath) at their Ulu Dong home in Pahang. But unbeknown to Mazlan, plans were being hatched for his murder. He was beheaded by Juraimi with a sharp axe in Mona and Affandi's home. The couple then headed to Kuala Lumpur, where they went on a two-week spending spree which included the purchase of a Mercedes-Benz car and plastic surgery for Mona.

In the subsequent 69-day trial the Temerloh High Court heard how the three defendants participated in the gruesome ritual of cutting Mazlan's body up into 18 pieces. Juraimi used his axe while Mona and Affandi used knives they had sharpened days before the murder. The body parts were dumped into a 1.8-metre hole dug earlier by Juraimi at the couple's homestead.

The three were found guilty and sentenced to hang by the High Court in Kuala Lumpur. Their final appeals against their death sentences were dismissed in 1998 and they were executed at Kajang Prison outside Kuala Lumpur in 2001.

Meanwhile, the Sultan of Selangor — a man who conducted himself with dignity during the widespread 1992–93 community debate on the possibility of removing constitutional immunity from the ruling families — did not need the sort of help offered by Kiai Arshad in defending himself against Karpal. Nor did the future Agong need the type of assistance being offered by other religious Malay nationalists who threatened Karpal with death in the build-up to the 16 September 1987 hearing of his suit against the Sultan of Selangor.

Death threats were nothing new to Karpal. In 1982 he received bullets through the mail predicting his imminent demise from a group calling itself the Sungai Golak Peace Brigade. His activities in the Penang State Assembly as the member for Bukit Gelugor had upset this group, who wrote their threatening letters to him in a potpourri of unintelligible English and Malay.

These threats were shrugged off as being the work of misguided youths, yet Karpal did not take any chances when he took the Sultan of Selangor to court over the royal's statement on not pardoning drug traffickers in his state; for the one and only time in his legal career he decided to wear his MP's holster and gun when he took the Sultan to court. For weeks before the case he had received the 'Don't you touch Malay royalty or we'll kill you' phone calls. Then one night when he was driving back from Ipoh to Kuala Lumpur, a group of young hoodlums in a car endeavoured to ram him off the road. The incident with the *bomoh* had reminded him of the passionate respect and devotion Malays held for their rulers, and maybe somebody out there was upset enough to be prepared to kill a man perceived as a legal nuisance.

Malays generally regarded Karpal's action in this suit as a scandalous, frivolous and vexatious exploitation of a sensitive racial issue. They saw it as an abuse of the court process and in the eyes of many, the shaman Kiai Arshad was a crusading hero who had come to the aid of their much respected sultan.

In deciding to take court action against the Sultan of Selangor, Karpal's point was that no matter how heinous a crime a person may have committed, they were still entitled to proper consideration at the clemency stage, under their constitutional rights.

When Karpal advised the High Court registrar he was carrying a gun, a deal was struck with Chief Justice Tun Abdul Hamid Omar. The lawyer had to surrender his gun to a policeman who would sit near him in court and keep a close watch on the public gallery. He was specifically assigned to protect the lawyer throughout the proceedings. At the end of the hearing the gun would be returned. As far as Karpal was aware, he was the only lawyer in Malaysia who was granted permission to bring a gun into a courtroom.

Such was the atmosphere surrounding the hearing, Karpal quietly told his family in Penang before he flew to Kuala Lumpur that it might well be the last time they saw him alive.

The High Court case was held in Kuala Lumpur's Supreme Court and the courtroom was packed to capacity. The public gallery was filled mainly by UMNO Youth supporters.

Tun Abdul Hamid Omar ruled that Karpal did not have the *locus standi* to take the case. He said the newspaper clippings the case was based on provided insufficient evidence of what the Sultan had actually said in his speech to the Selangor branch of the Ex-Servicemen's Association.

Karpal said that justice should from time to time be tempered by a ruler exercising mercy, rather than simply taking a pre-judged uncompromising approach of rubber-stamping drug-trafficking convictions. The very Constitution keeping Malay rulers in power, Karpal argued, required them at the same time to accord legitimate constitutional rights to those in danger of death by execution.

Tun Abdul Hamid Omar dismissed the suit on 17 September 1987 in favour of the submissions made by Attorney-General Tan Sri Abu Talib Othman on the Sultan's behalf that: 'the originating summons discloses no reasonable cause of action in that the issue raised therein is not justiciable; the originating summons is barred by reason of the provision of Article 181(2) of the Constitution; and Mr Karpal Singh the plaintiff has no *locus standi* to maintain the proceedings he has brought.'

An interesting sequel to the decision in this case was that the cheque for costs diligently sent to the Sultan of Selangor was never presented at the bank. This was perhaps an honourable and privileged royal's way of letting a lawyer-politician know his views had been noted. Karpal was very impressed.

When Prime Minister Dr Mahathir finally decided to move against the rulers in 1992 it was once again the late Sultan of Johor who provided the Prime Minister with all the ammunition he needed to begin the formal process of constitutional change. Ironically, Dr Mahathir had had a strong working relationship with the late Sultan of Johor when he was Agong between 1984 and 1989.

The final straw for the rulers' immunity from prosecution, however, occurred when the hockey coach of the Maktab Sultan Abu Bakar (English College) in Johor required medical attention for facial cuts and bruising after being summoned to the former Sultan of Johor's residence one afternoon in November 1992. Arriving at the official residence Douglas Gomez was surrounded by six men wearing jeans and T-shirt. Some ten to 12 others from the Sultan's now disbanded private army, the Johor Military Force, were looking on.

Earlier Gomez had had the audacity to go public on the reason why Johor teams had been withdrawn suddenly from a prestigious Malaysian Hockey Federation secondary school tournament. A member of the Johor royal household had been disciplined by the federation after assaulting a Perak goalkeeper.

The subsequent constitutional change of 1993, making all persons including sultans accountable before the law, highlights Karpal's role in changing Malaysian law. In helping deliver Dr Mahathir the 20 DAP votes on the issue, Karpal showed himself as an opposition lawyer-politician capable of political expediency.

When the 1993 constitutional debate was all over, he allowed himself the luxury, with the incense from the shrine of Guru Nanak wafting sweetly through his Penang office, of looking back on a memorable achievement. He thought of the unexpected assistance he had received from Dr Mahathir and realised better than anyone the personal risk the prime minister had opened himself to by taking on the Malay rulers.

The prime minister and the lawyer, long-haul politicians both, had used each other and Karpal recalled how Dr Mahathir had been strangely quiet when everyone else was baying for his blood before his suspension from parliament in 1984. Some had even suggested at the time he should be charged with treason.

Then there was the late Sultan of Johor Sultan Mahmud Iskandar himself. During his term as Agong the Sultan played an active role in the dismissal of Tun Salleh Abas on 8 August 1988 as Lord President of the Judiciary. Tun Salleh Abas had prosecuted the late Sultan in the case involving the 1977 manslaughter conviction relating to the shooting to death of Teo Ah Bah near His Majesty's helicopter.

Dr Mahathir in 1993 was able to confidently tell the royals that if their assent was not forthcoming on the need for them to be accountable, he would simply enact the legislation and hand the matter over to the courts.

Karpal remembered his own two-year suspension and the attitude of prominent people who publicly opposed him when he took the Sultan of Selangor to court in 1987 — people like former Deputy Prime Minister Ghafar Baba; UMNO Vice-President Datuk Abdullah Badawi (a future prime minister following Anwar Ibrahim's 1998 dumping by Dr Mahathir); and former MCA Youth leader Datuk Yap Pian Hon, who said Karpal did not comprehend history.

The wheel of Karpal's political life had seen some strange turns but he believed there had been none more unusual than Dr Mahathir publicly backing him on the need to remove legal immunity from Malay royalty. The two men became unusual bedfellows on this issue, coming as they did from totally different perspectives, with Karpal prepared to back Dr Mahathir to the hilt amidst rumours he had sold out and was going to be appointed a judge.

Dr Mahathir, a man with a long memory, arrived at his desire to curb the power of the rulers in part from a position of political pragmatism. He was also genuinely concerned by the anti-social behaviour of the then Sultan of Johor.

Karpal had set himself the goal of making Malay royalty accountable before the courts way back in 1982. In pursuing this through to its logical conclusion he was granted latitude by DAP leader Lim Kit Siang.

How the wheel of fortune had turned. Everybody, it seemed in 1993, with the exception of Tengku Razaleigh Hamzah's Semangat 46 party and some PAS (Parti Islam Se-Malaysia) MPs, wanted to 'forgive' Karpal for his consistent belief the royals should be subject to the law.

Karpal believed there was one good reason motivating the ruling Barisan Nasional's decision to sway public opinion against the royals by allowing newspapers to publish unflattering stories involving the sultans. The then Sultan of Kelantan Sultan Ismail Petra had delved into politics and actively campaigned on behalf of family member Tengku Razaleigh Hamzah's Semangat 46 party during the 1990 elections. At that time Semangat 46 competed directly for Malay votes against Dr Mahathir's UMNO grouping

By seeking to make the rulers more accountable before the courts Dr Mahathir would also have remembered problems he experienced in 1983 when the Agong refused to sign the Constitution Amendment Act. This legislation proposed to give the prime minister power to declare a state of emergency — a power remaining to this day with the Agong.

For public consumption, however, the 1993 proposal to remove immunity was an acknowledgment on the part of Dr Mahathir that educated modern Malaysians had had enough of royals who did not know how to behave themselves.

It also presented the prime minister with a rare opportunity to provide more power for his own executive by clipping the wings of two birds with one action — the rulers and Tengku Razaleigh Hamzah, a one-time opponent within UMNO.

In December 1992, as the constitutional debate was heating up, Karpal was quite happy to help the prime minister handle Tengku Razaleigh Hamzah when he observed that the Semangat 46 leader should not consider the immunity issue from a princely point of view.

Bad law in the constitutional area was bad law whichever way Karpal looked at it and he wanted it changed. He had long and unsuccessfully been placing on record before the courts cases reflecting his belief that the government was bound to protect the life and property of every Malaysian, even when they were assaulted by royals — one royal in particular.

Under the 1993 changes to the Constitution the clause preventing personal court proceedings against rulers was removed, and a new one establishing the Special Court for the monarchy to be presided over by the Lord President was introduced. A proviso was also inserted that no action could be taken against the Agong or the rulers of Selangor, Perlis, Kedah, Pahang, Kelantan, Terengganu, Johor, Negeri Sembilan and Perak unless the Attorney-General specifically authorised such a move himself.

It had been 36 years since Independence but the 1993 changes meant everybody in Malaysia was now equal before the law and entitled to the protection of that law. The mere existence of the Special Court for royals has indeed helped to curb the behaviour of the monarchy. Lawyer and publisher Sahadevan Nadchatiram was able to testify to this as a result of a land dispute he had with Malaysia's tenth Agong, Tuanku Ja'afar.

On 16 November 1979 the Agong had signed a trust deed with

Sahadevan, a close friend. (In a 2005 address to the West Australian Bar Association in Perth, Karpal said the deed related to ten plots of land in the district of Rantau near the popular resort town of Port Dickson in the Agong's state of Negeri Sembilan.) Signed by both men in the presence of a solicitor, it assigned 70 per cent of the land to Tuanku Ja'afar and 30 per cent to Sahadevan. Tuanku Ja'afar agreed to get the consent of Sahadevan before selling any part of the land.

In April 1995 the late Sahadevan wrote to the Agong that he had heard the Agong was selling 560 acres of the land for RM2,145 per acre. Sahadevan thought the price was too low and wrote that he was unable to accept the price. Eventually the final selling price was far higher but Sahadevan was not given his share.

When he met the Agong at the palace, the monarch no longer recognised the validity of the trust deed. Sahadevan told the Agong he would sue him. The Agong responded that he had no objection to Sahadevan taking him to the Special Court. Sahadevan later wrote to the Agong to say he was going to do just that and to advise him he had engaged Karpal as counsel.

Karpal had agreed to sue the Agong on Sahadevan's behalf as he felt the rule of law had to be defended above all.

"I took this statement by the Agong as an affront to the rule of law," Karpal said. "I immediately wrote to the Agong asking for details of Sahadevan's share of the land and noted there could be an element of criminality in what has transpired."

Karpal said the king's lawyers phoned him to say they would probably contest the case. The royal cudgel having been thrown down, he willingly accepted the challenge and wrote to the Attorney-General for his written consent — a pre-requisite if one wanted to sue the king.

In the event, the monarch reached an out-of-court settlement with Sahadevan.

Karpal's legal and political battles with the rulers over the years showed his basic philosophy on life. If something needed to be done he would focus on the principle rather than worry about the consequences and be committed to the cause. The Constitution in Malaysia also allows Muslims, whose Islamic religion is the country's main religion, to impose their own system of sharia law.

The offence of *khalwat* (involving people of the opposite sex in close proximity to each other) is one area of sharia law where Muslims are treated more harshly than their non-Muslim Chinese or Indian partners.

Officers from state religious departments can force entry into dwellings where they believe the crime of *khalwat* is being committed. There have been a number of instances of people leaping out of windows to their death as a result of these raids.

If both parties to the offence are Muslims both are liable to be found guilty of *khalwat*, generally punishable by way of a fine in a Sharia Court. If one participant is Muslim he or she can be found guilty of *khalwat* under state law; the non-Muslim participant, regardless of sex, cannot be charged.

There are occasions when the country's religious and secular criminal systems do clash. Muhiyaludin Jidun, a state religious officer, was a member of a *khalwat* raid team on a Sungai Petani house in northern peninsular Malaysia on 16 November 1995.

A police inspector was one of the parties involved in the alleged offence. In his efforts to elude the raiding party he jumped from the roof of his 27-year-old companion's home. A struggle ensued between the policeman and villagers (including Muhiyaludin). During the struggle Muhiyaludin was shot in the stomach by the inspector. Forty-one days later, on 26 December 1995, he died from his wounds.

Muhiyaludin's wife Sepiah Shaari, mother of the couple's two children, was wheelchair-bound. She commissioned Karpal to keep a watching brief on the outcome of the police investigation and prosecution of her husband's killer.

The police inspector was acquitted and discharged on a charge of murder by the Alor Setar High Court. However, the Court of Appeal overturned the acquittal and in a 1999 judgement found him guilty of manslaughter. The inspector was sentenced to imprisonment for two years from the date of his conviction. The Court of Appeal took his clean and long-serving police record into account when passing sentence.

Karpal saw this incident as reflecting the rising influence of sharia law in Malaysia. The Islamic PAS party's policy of Malaysia becoming an Islamic state remains a contentious political issue.

As part of this objective the Terengganu state assembly passed the Syariah Criminal Offences (Hudud and Qisas) Bill in 2002. For Karpal this legislation was draconian and riddled with serious implications for the judicial system and the public and national interest, and he was incredulous that PAS members passed state legislation prescribing amputation for theft and death by stoning for adultery.

People facing punishment for a *hudud* offence, which include theft, robbery, illicit sex, consumption of alcohol and apostasy, have to be medically fit before the punishment can be inflicted. The legislation also provides for whipping between 40 and 80 lashes, depending on whether the person is a repeat offender, and a prison term if the court deems it fit, for consumption of liquor or intoxicating drinks.

For *zina* (unlawful intercourse) it is stoning to death by medium-sized stones. A man who has anal sex with another man or woman other than his wife is liable to be stoned to death by medium-sized stones. For incest the punishment is also stoning to death using medium-sized stones. For theft it is amputation of the right hand for the first offence and left foot for the second offence. The offender faces jail, for a period at the discretion of the judge, for the third and subsequent theft offences.

For robbery (theft with violence or threats of violence) it is death followed by crucifixion if the victim of the robbery is killed and his property is taken away; amputation of the right hand and left foot if the victim is uninjured; amputation and payment of compensation if the victim is injured and jail if only threats are issued.

There are, however, 'tender mercies' in the legislation which prohibits a pregnant female offender from being stoned until after she has delivered her child. There is also provision for a mother's death by stoning to be stayed for two years if she is breast-feeding, unless a wet nurse can be found to suckle the child in that period. A whipping sentence imposed on a pregnant woman is also stayed until after she has delivered her child and thereafter becomes clean of blood and is fit again to undergo the punishment without hazard.

Finally, said Karpal, those renouncing Islam were given three days to repent. If they did not, punishment was death and confiscation of property.

He pointed out that while the legislation was on the books, it was not used. Enforcement of such sharia legislation lies completely in the hands of state religious authorities. The country's state policemen are under instructions from central government to provide no assistance whatsoever to state religious sharia law enforcement officers.

Karpal described the PAS politicians who passed such state legislation as being very cunning. "They pass this nonsense [sharia legislation] but don't use it. It's there ready for the day, if ever these fanatics get their Islamic state," he said.

Following the passage of this sharia legislation Karpal said there was no way PAS and the DAP could ever work together.

"As far as the DAP is concerned, we have passed the brink. There is no way back now," the DAP Deputy Chairman said in an 11 July 2002 interview with *The Star* newspaper.

However, since the 2008 election Karpal, in his capacity as DAP national chairman, had softened his position against PAS politicians.

The issue was one that both sides appeared happy to park until the day voters handed both parties a coalition government mandate.

The 2008 elections resulted in opposition leader Anwar Ibrahim's Parti Keadilan Rakyat bringing the DAP and PAS together to produce a DAP-led state government in Penang.

Karpal worked with PAS on the hustings in Penang, as evidenced by the fact he delivered food parcels to Malay flood victims on 20 November 2010. But PAS' avowed aim of turning the country into an Islamic state, headed by an Islamic government, was always a no-go zone for him.

"That is not going to happen on my watch," he said.

9 PAYBACK

In 1987 Malaysian Prime Minister Dr Mahathir was struggling to achieve the rock-solid control of his ruling UMNO political party that would inevitably come his way over the next decade. He was confronting major problems on many fronts, particularly from within the UMNO establishment via a strong challenge to his leadership from Trade and Industry Minister Tengku Razaleigh Hamzah. At one point, in the dispute between the two political heavyweights, UMNO was actually declared an illegal political entity by a High Court decision in February 1988.

The opposition DAP party, with its leader Lim Kit Siang and Karpal at the fore, was not making life easy for Dr Mahathir either by challenging his plans for a massive North-South highway project through the courts. The RM3.4 billion, 504-kilometre long North-South highway project had been let to an UMNO subsidiary company — United Engineers

Malaysia (UEM) — and the DAP made a very strong point the contract should not have been let in-house.

Lim Kit Siang, with Karpal as his lawyer, successfully obtained an injunction temporarily blocking the highway project from proceeding. For the first time in his political career, Karpal had used his legal skills to go after the prime minister at a time when he was fighting for his own political survival. While opposing the highway project Karpal said Dr Mahathir and his fellow cabinet ministers should be held accountable for the decision to let the contract in-house to an UMNO subsidiary.

These allegations of impropriety from Lim Kit Siang and Karpal drew a predictably strong response from Dr Mahathir who totally rejected suggestions he would benefit personally from the highway project.

In March 1988 a bench of five Supreme Court judges in a 3:2 decision dissolved Lim Kit Siang's earlier interim injunction, thus allowing the UEM highway deal to proceed.

Lord President Tun Salleh Abas, who would be dismissed from office in August 1988 after writing a letter to the Agong complaining about Dr Mahathir's public criticism of the judiciary, gave his deciding judgement in favour of the government. The then Agong may have involved himself quietly behind the scenes in assisting Dr Mahathir to dismiss the Lord President from office; he certainly had a motive to do so. This was because Tun Salleh Abas prosecuted the future Agong (Tunku Mahmud Iskandar as he was then) in the case involving a 1977 manslaughter conviction relating to the shooting death of an alleged smuggler Teo Ah Bah. Tunku Mahmud was pardoned by his father, the earlier Sultan of Johor, for his role in this alleged shooting.

In Karpal's view the sacking of Salleh Abas was part of a wider campaign to provide UMNO with a more user-friendly compliant judiciary. Against this troubled background Karpal expected some form of retaliation from the Government for his role as Lim Kit Siang's counsel in a number of cases. He also knew he was inviting trouble when he had earlier sued Dr Mahathir, once again on behalf of Lim Kit Siang, alleging contempt of court against him for comments the prime minister made in a *Time* magazine article published on 24 November 1986, where Dr Mahathir had criticised the way the Malaysian judiciary went about its business.

The courtroom sequel in the civil appeal in the DAP's *Time* magazine case was eventually thrown out by Salleh Abas in an 11 December 1986 Supreme Court decision.

Karpal respected Dr Mahathir as a hardball politician and knew it was only a matter of time before the hammer descended upon the man whom those in power viewed as a stirring vexatious DAP litigant. However, he did not expect the severity of the retaliation which came like a thunderbolt out of a dark Kuala Lumpur sky on 27 October 1987. That was the day the lawyer was swept up, along with 106 others in the following week, and detained indefinitely without trial under the ISA.

The widespread ISA operation, dubbed Operation Lalang (wild grass), began with the arrest of all the detainees and their subsequent incarceration at the Police Remand Centre (PRC), a mere stone's throw from the popular Batu Caves tourist spot in Kuala Lumpur. The exercise was masterminded by the then head of the Special Branch Abdul Rahim Noor, a man who would go on to make a name for himself as a controversial Inspector General of Police a decade later.

As soon as possible following his arrest and first 60-day detention period in strict isolation at the PRC, Karpal embarked on a campaign of action to obtain his own freedom from Kamunting Detention Camp via a writ of *habeas corpus*. He was imprisoned at Kamunting Detention Camp for allegedly inciting racial violence.

On 9 March 1988, five months after being detained, Karpal managed to successfully argue for his own release in front of Justice Peh

(*above*) Kamunting Detention Camp where Karpal was incarcerated, following his detention under the ISA, October 1987 to January 1989. DAP MPs detained during Operation Lalang were Karpal (top right and centre left), Lim Kit Siang (top left), P Patto (centre right), Lau Dak Kee (bottom left) and Lim Guan Eng (bottom right).

Swee Chin in the Ipoh High Court. All his problems were temporarily forgotten as he heard the judge say, "It is ordered the application for writ of *habeas corpus* be issued and it is ordered the applicant be released." ISA detainee T1636/87 (Karpal Singh) had successfully argued for what would be his own short-lived freedom.

Outside the court during a press conference Karpal told the assembled Malaysian and international journalists that 'all detainees under this draconian legislation should be freed'.

Justice Peh's decision meant Karpal was now free to visit the Sikh temple in Pusing with his wife and four of their five children — Jagdeep, Gobind, Ramkarpal and Sangeet — who would all go on to become British-educated lawyers themselves. After giving thanks at the temple Karpal was more than happy to have a celebratory drink with his brothers, friends and family. His family had suffered along with him throughout the imprisonment and now, briefly, they were all able to rejoice in his release.

Arguably the happiest three hours of his professional life as a lawyer were spent in the Long Bar of the Ipoh Club on that day. His fellow counsel were not men to think of their own rice bowls in this situation. His late brother Manjit Singh, A Mariadas (his old mate from university days in Singapore), S Assamaley, Oh Choong Ghee and Kartar Singh were among them. They ushered Karpal into the Long Bar, once the colonial meeting place of wealthy British Perak planters. For three hours he was the toast of the Ipoh Club as martial arts expert Master Kam, lawyer Xavier and many other friends offered him liquid congratulations. Karpal was expecting a prompt re-arrest after his release, but in the meantime he was determined to enjoy these precious moments of freedom with friends and family.

With six grounds given for his detention when he was served with the warrant at the PRC outside Kuala Lumpur in December 1987, the plan to achieve freedom focused on ground number six, which read:

> On October 10, 1987 at a gathering in front of Bangunan Tuanku Syed Putra, Lebuh Downing, Penang, you used the issue of appointing non-Mandarin qualified headmasters and senior assistants in the national-type Chinese primary schools to incite racial sentiments of the Chinese community.

The education dispute arose over an Education Ministry decision to send teachers who could not speak Mandarin to Chinese primary schools as senior administrators. The move was seen by Chinese as a threat to education in their own language.

The lawyers who were getting progressively merrier in the Long Bar beneath a large portrait of the Deputy Agong Sultan Azlan Shah knew their client had the perfect alibi to this charge. On 10 October 1987, at the time he was supposed to have been inciting racial tension and enmity among Chinese, Indian and Malay communities in Penang, Karpal was, in fact, appearing before Malaysia's then Chief Justice Tun Abdul Hamid Omar.

Justice Peh Swee Chin found Karpal's argument for being elsewhere on that day compelling and he concluded:

> ... viewed objectively and not subjectively, the error in all the circumstances, would squarely amount to the detention order being made without care, caution and a proper sense and responsibility and that such circumstances had gone beyond a mere matter of form.

Free, but for how long? That was the question on Karpal's mind as he and his family left the Ipoh Club at about 6:00 p.m. for the two-hour drive to Penang, with driver Jeffrey at the wheel of their 300d Mercedes.

Many of their friends in the club were in no fit state to drive anywhere and the party continued with Karpal's brothers Manjit and Santokh enjoying the whisky provided by the latter's absent (overseas) son Jaswant Singh. The revelry came to an abrupt halt, however, when a phone call came through from Assamaley's wife Devi about 9:00 p.m. to say Karpal had been re-arrested outside the Nibong Tebal police station south of the Penang Bridge.

As they were driving past St Michael's Institution located just across the road from the Ipoh Club, 14-year-old Gobind was the first to spot a car following the family. He had seen the same car shadowing his father on the drive to the Sikh temple in Pusing earlier in the day.

Karpal knew the cat-and-mouse Special Branch tactics of handing over the chase by radio to another vehicle further up the road. But what he did not know at the time was that the Deputy Agong Sultan Azlan Shah, who was also Sultan of Perak, was possibly not keen on an immediate re-arrest taking place in his state.

As Jeffrey drove towards Penang there was no sign of a pursuit vehicle and Gurmit clung to her man, hoping against hope the welcome home party organised by their respective mothers Puran Kaur and Kartar Kaur in Penang would go ahead. Then Gurmit saw it — a police roadblock ahead. Her husband had said, "Don't worry, there're often roadblocks on this road." But he knew in his heart that his wife's and family's agony was about to begin again, for the UMNO establishment could not allow the DAP lawyer to go free in such troubled political times. If Karpal was permitted to remain on the outside the problems he would cause representing the likes of Lim Kit Siang and his son Lim Guan Eng — residents of units five and six at Kamunting Detention Camp — did not bear thinking about, from a Barisan Nasional perspective.

A terrible scene ensued at the Nibong Tebal Police Station as the well-fortified Sikh, in front of his children, vented the frustrations of five months of ISA incarceration upon the head of a humble country cop. This policeman said with genuine sympathy and concern, as many other policemen did during those days, "Look here, Mr Karpal, I'm only doing my duty."

The real action started when Special Branch police officer Khor Bah Chik formally re-arrested Karpal by stating that Karpal had acted in a manner prejudicial to the security of the nation. As had been the case five months earlier, one of the nation's most wanted men never had time to bid farewell to his wife and family before he was whisked across the Penang Bridge to the Penang Police Station.

In the back of a police car surrounded by Special Branch officers and

Gurmit and Ramkarpal with Di Parsons in Melbourne, 1989.

their motorcycle outriders, all with sirens blaring, Karpal reflected on the events of the day, which brought elation and then despair for his family. The lawyer had just about had enough of Malaysia and its hardball politics on that evening. But amidst all the anxiety he was grateful that Di Parsons, who provided his oldest son Jagdeep with board and lodging in Melbourne, and Australian education authorities in Melbourne were doing everything possible to get Jagdeep into a college there for his final year of secondary education.

At the family home in Penang another painful scene was played out when Puran, the woman who had moved in with her daughter's family from day one of her son-in-law's detention, had to be tranquilized on hearing the news of the re-arrest. Gurmit stood outside the gates of the Penang Police Station that night with Jagdeep and brother-in-law Dr Nirmal Singh, displaying a toughness and a disgust for the authorities as she supported her husband throughout his ordeal. Surrounded by about 200 well-wishers she shouted out many times 'He needs a doctor' through the metal picket fence surrounding the police station.

Indeed he did, for after Karpal's first 57 days of solitary confinement at the remand centre he had developed a condition diagnosed by a specialist at Kuala Lumpur Hospital as 'severe backache caused by the degenerative process of the spine and disc prolapse'. This had been brought on by having to sleep on a concrete floor for 57 nights. It was all part of the ISA solitary confinement treatment, perfected originally by the British to break communist terrorists and now carried on by Abdul Rahim Noor and his Special Branch underlings on Ipoh Road, near Batu Caves.

The family members waiting outside Penang Police Station on the night of Karpal's re-arrest could take some slight consolation from a nearby blind man making a living by selling toilet paper to passing tourists at 30 sen a roll. There is always someone worse off than yourself, Gurmit tried to tell herself.

The family group kept up a three-hour vigil, hoping for any snippet of news. They expected Karpal to be sent back to the remand centre. Officially, according to the Ministry of Home Affairs, his ISA detention without trial was to begin again and this automatically meant another two months of solitary confinement. Karpal would pay a painful price, via severe back problems for many years caused by sleeping on a concrete floor in the remand centre, for those nine hours of freedom on 9 March 1988.

Early the next morning he was taken back to Kuala Lumpur and Gurmit knew she and her family were not alone when an anonymous caller rang to say Karpal had been admitted to an isolation room at Kuala Lumpur Hospital.

She knew that her role now was to get a battered family back on track. The major problem confronting her, apart from the obvious financial ones, was what to do with Jagdeep. He was simply refusing to catch his 12 March flight to Australia (which he had earlier delayed), saying he would go only on condition his father was at the airport to bid him farewell.

Fortunately, Puran had recovered from the previous evening. She called a meeting of her Penang-based daughters where the decision was made for Jagdeep to go to Australia, even if it meant family members having to physically carry him onto the plane. Gurmit's role in getting Jagdeep to board the plane was to arrange a meeting between father and son before the latter departed, which required the permission of Malaysia's IGP.

The farewell meeting, another absolute low point of the detention period for the family, took place at the hospital in the presence of Special Branch officers. As he departed Jagdeep said nothing to his father but embraced him before kneeling and touching his feet in the ultimate Sikh gesture of respect. The father turned away, and the young man, who eight years later would head the Penang branch of Karpal Singh & Co., managed to contain himself until the doors of the hospital lift closed. Such was the level of support surrounding the family in 1988 that Gurmit still has no idea who it was who paid for her oldest son's airfare to Melbourne.

For Karpal the worst was still to come when he was returned blindfolded to the PRC after being released from hospital and greeted by three Malay warders whose role in life, in conjunction with his visiting Special Branch interrogators, was to break him.

This time he knew what to expect and was not as shocked when the reception committee once again told him to remove all his clothes. Taking his clothes off garment by garment, he stopped when he got down to his underpants at which point he shot his jailors a look that said enough. This evoked a stern 'Underpants off!' order. Competely naked in front of his warders, Karpal recalled they looked somewhat puzzled when he asked them, "Is there anything else you might like?"

The lawyer did his best to look on the bright side of his predicament. It was not easy, particularly as most detainees went through solitary confinement just once in their lifetime before being issued with their standard two-year Kamunting Detention Camp imprisonment orders.

In the general prisons Karpal knew of a number of former clients who had been broken after being subjected to beatings at the hands of other prisoners. At least in the PRC he had a cell to himself where he could pace the floor, even if it was only three metres long and two metres wide. He had two sets of loose-fitting clothes, a plastic cup and pail, a bucket, toothpaste, soap, blanket and a towel with the cheerful words 'Good Morning' printed on it in English and Mandarin.

The main human contact he had was with the warders who brought his food. He also had twice-weekly visits from Special Branch interrogators. Their suits contrasted starkly with Karpal's unwashed blue cotton Vietcong-like apparel.

The interrogators did not like Karpal's attitude perhaps because they could not break him the way they had already broken some others, among them politicians, Islamic fundamentalists, trade unionists, academics, rubber workers and religious teachers who were also incarcerated under the ISA operation in October 1987. The one thing it seemed they all had in common, which had drawn the attention of Special Branch head Abdul Rahim Noor, was their criticism of the government and its policies. While Karpal could understand why he had been imprisoned, the DAP lawyer found it hard to believe how many of the people who were in prison alongside him could possibly be a threat to the security of Malaysia.

While the Special Branch did not try to physically harm Karpal, their approach seemed aimed at slowly destroying his mind by depriving him of such basic comforts as a pillow and a mattress. They kept a naked light bulb turned on in his cell around the clock, made sure

Karpal suffered major back problems after sleeping on a concrete floor at the Police Remand Centre for 57 nights at the end of 1987. He is pictured here being brought into the Federal Court in Kuala Lumpur in a wheelchair from the Kamunting Detention Camp to argue the UEM appeal on Lim Kit Siang's behalf in January 1988.

plenty of mosquitoes were available to feast on a once healthy body and organised a version of the old Chinese water torture via dysfunctional toilet water cisterns.

Usually, once their handcuffs and blindfolds had been removed, detainees were shocked to discover a real-life horror movie set comprising cobwebs, thriving colonies of insects, geckos, soot on the concrete bed and faecal mud on the mosquito breeding-ground floor. As a special treat the floor was also home to an ensuite squat toilet and tap. If that was not enough, room service was provided by rats and cockroaches. Sleep was further interrupted by gecko droppings, barking dogs and the mating calls of a number of cats who frequented the complex at night.

The whole process is designed to remove all self-respect and dignity of those incarcerated. Yet even in such conditions some could still see the funny side. Tan Seng Giaw, the DAP MP for Kepong, aroused much mirth at Kamunting later when he swore the geckos at the PRC had been trained by the authorities to perform a specialist role, namely aiming their droppings at the heads of ISA detainees. In the 13th general election, Tan retained his Kepong seat with a massive 40,000-vote majority.

At least during his second period of isolation Karpal knew why the authorities wanted him put away. In between the interrogations, he mulled over his response to the charges. Apart from the charge upon which his earlier *habeas corpus* Ipoh High Court case had been won on — where he was said to be inciting racial tension on 10 October 1987 but was actually appearing before the Chief Justice on that day — the other charges were:

> [1] That since the year 1980 until the date of arrest on October 27, 1987 you Karpal Singh have [been] involved in activities that would incite racial sentiments among the multi-racial community of this country. These activities of yours could lead to an atmosphere of tension and enmity among the races of this country and endanger the security of the country;

Karpal wondered why he had not been picked up earlier since he was accused of inciting race problems from as far back as 1980.

> [2] On January 11, 1982 at an emergency meeting of the DAP, Penang state which was held at No 123-D Jalan Batu Lancang, Penang, you alleged that rights of studying the mother tongue of non-Malays is obstructed by the government by implementing the 3M curriculum. At the same meeting you also alleged that the interest and fundamental rights of Chinese and Indians are not safeguarded and requested the public especially the parents

to oppose the implementation of 3M curriculum in the Chinese and Indian primary schools;

Was not mother-tongue education guaranteed under the provisions of the Malaysian constitution? Karpal asked himself.

[3] On March 2, 1986 at a gathering in the compound of the Kuan Im Temple, Pitt St, Penang, you quoted the case of Sim Kie Chon and Datuk Mokhtar Hashim to incite a clash between the Malays and Chinese;

Sim Kie Chon was executed for possession of a revolver and five rounds of ammunition. They had not been proven to have been used to inflict death or injury. By contrast the Minister of Culture, Youth and Sports Datuk Mokhtar Hashim was charged and convicted for murder but his sentence of death was commuted to one of life imprisonment. Karpal considered the inconsistency in the way these two cases were dealt with to be unjust.

[4] On August 16, 1986 at a forum organised by the DAP, Penang, which was held at Kelab Ilham No 225, Jalan Macalister, Penang, you accused that the new economic policy is only in favour of one race, i.e. the bumiputras;

Karpal said this charge was taken completely out of context. He did not question the New Economic Policy although he did dwell on the plight of the non-Malays by urging the government to assist all citizens.

[5] On September 5, 1987 while speaking at the Arumugam Pillai Hall, Jalan Kulim, Bukit Mertajam, Penang you

alleged that the Malaysian Chinese Association (MCA party) and the Gerakan Rakyat Malaysia had sold the fundamental rights of non-Malays to UMNO.

Karpal considered he had every right to criticise rival political parties such as the MCA and Gerakan parties. To his thinking they had more than once shown cowardice when the issue of the fundamental rights of non-Malays had been raised in parliament.

With little to occupy his mind apart from the injustice of it all, Karpal found the remand centre a long, lonely, back-breaking experience. He was aware of a number of long-term communist internees who had the freedom of the cellblocks. They would cheerfully greet him as he was led to and from interrogation sessions. But because of the opaque glasses he was compelled to wear that were designed to disorientate, there was no chance of making eye contact.

Without his watch the only way to remain aware of the time and the outside world as the days and nights rolled slowly by came from the *imam* at a nearby mosque. Karpal grew to love the sound of those calls to prayer: the Azan Subuh (5:50 a.m.), Azan Zohor (1:15 p.m.), Azan Asar (4:25 p.m.), Azan Maghrib (7:30 p.m.) and Azan Isyak (8:25 p.m.). They provided a reassuring contact with reality and reminded him of home life in the fourth-floor apartment on top of his Jalan Pudu Lama building in Kuala Lumpur. Similar calls to prayer would emanate from the national mosque near Merdeka Square.

The lawyer bade farewell once again to the PRC on 17 April 1988 and was transported to the Kamunting Detention Camp where he took up residence in unit 6 and shared a room with DAP MP for Pasir Pinji in Perak Lau Dak Kee, and Chinese educationalist Kua Kia Soong. Kamunting resembles a World War II German prison camp with its watchtowers and surrounding barbed wire but it was good to be able to

Karpal in contemplative mood at Kamunting Detention
Camp, January 1989.

talk to people again, even if it was behind roll upon roll of barbed wire, and to be able to see Maxwell Hill and the sky at night.

For Karpal, Kamunting threw up unexpected bonuses, in particular a reunion with a former client and committed member of the Malayan National Liberation Front Heng Choon Teng, whom he had earlier represented in an ESCAR case.

Provisions at Kamunting were relatively better. Mosquito nets and a thin foam mattress to cover the concrete bed base were made available. Karpal was also able to make use of medical facilities at the nearby Taiping hospital for his back problems. A downside to the Kamunting luxuries were the bed bugs and the incessant march of red and black ants which invaded everything.

There is a special bond among those who have been through the Police Remand Centre and Kamunting isolation process. For Karpal, knowing that he and his family were not alone and undergoing this process with a number of new-found friends and their families made the ordeal easier to bear.

He just wanted freedom and economic security for himself, Gurmit, his five children — his youngest son Mankarpal was born a few months before he was arrested — and the employees in his Kuala Lumpur and Penang law offices. Without freedom he could not contribute, financially or in any other way. The highlight of his life during this period was the weekly visit from Gurmit and family members who faithfully made the 90-minute drive from Penang.

Nobody said much on these trips. Occasionally the children, in an effort to cheer their mother up, would break into a song they'd written called 'We're going to bring the old man home'. Every week the visitors would have to justify their presence to Superintendent Rama Das' employees at the front gates before being allowed into the visiting area.

Gurmit was a wife visiting her imprisoned husband, yet also a mother wondering where the next meal for her children would come from. In addition, she was his freedom campaign manager and the tough business lessons she learned during those difficult days would ensure the continued viability of Karpal Singh & Co. once her husband was released, whenever that might be.

Outside the wire the Special Branch employed subtle psychological tactics on the family to place pressure on Karpal. Gurmit was told on more than one occasion that her husband no longer belonged to her. He was exclusive government property, they said. Before each meeting at Kamunting she would be instructed to speak in English and confine the conversation to family matters.

The Special Branch officers should have saved their breath for during the visits Karpal's five-month-old son contributed to the cause by generally making so much noise that nobody could hear what was being said, except the person speaking directly with Karpal across the prison divider. After waiting for hours to see his father, the baby was often irritable when the meetings finally took place. Special Branch officers kept their distance from irritable babies and they disliked the baby Mankarpal almost as much as they disliked his father.

Away from the prison environment Mankarpal, nicknamed Ju-Ju, was a godsend for family morale. He was a happy baby and during the family's low moments his grandmother Puran had a knack of getting the baby to turn on the laughter. Soon everybody in the house would be laughing along with Ju-Ju. Puran referred to him as the lucky baby, and she took a dim view of the superstitious knockers who claimed the fifth child had brought the family bad luck.

His birth coincided with the family law firm making some major decisions such as mortgaging everything they

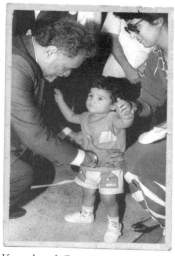

Karpal and Gurmit with youngest son Mankarpal at the Federal Court in Kuala Lumpur after being brought from Kamunting to argue his *habeas corpus* appeal in 1988.

had to purchase a Jalan Pudu Lama four-storey office building in Kuala Lumpur for RM880,000 and the Penang office building for RM500,000. There were three lawyers on the staff to be paid when Karpal was detained and basic business running costs of approximately RM50,000 per month to cover, all of which were very much dependent on the Sikh's advocacy ability. Clients were attracted to the firm of Karpal Singh & Co. largely because of its principal who had a reputation of getting acquittals in difficult cases other lawyers declined to take on.

The firm suffered a further setback when lawyer Nimal de Silva resigned soon after Karpal's detention. He had been offered a partnership with another firm early in 1988 but continued to help Gurmit wherever possible from his new position.

When she sat down with her financial advisers, brother Prakash Singh, brother-in-law Dr Nirmal Singh and Francis Ooi in June 1988, the picture was far from rosy. It was obvious there would have to be a meeting with Alex Lee at the Development & Commercial Bank. Gurmit and Prakash met with him, and Lee could not have been more helpful, agreeing to reduce loan repayment levels during the detention period. There would be two further demoralising meetings for Gurmit with Lee before her husband was finally freed. She will always be grateful for the understanding displayed by her Chinese bankers during those difficult days.

With the first anniversary of Operation Lalang approaching on 27 October 1988, the detainees decided to stage a week-long hunger strike inside Kamunting to protest their continued detention. Everything proceeded smoothly with the hunger strike until the Deputy Home Minister Megat Junid told parliament Karpal and Lim Guan Eng had been caught eating in the dead of night.

So incensed were the families of the detainees, many of whom were also fasting on the outside, that they staged a demonstration in parliament grounds and surrounded Megat Junid himself. Second son Gobind acted as the spokesman for the group and began questioning the politician who, clearly frustrated at being held to ransom by a tall youth and the other supporters asked, "Who is this boy?"

"I am Karpal Singh's son," the youngster replied, before being restrained by Jagdeep, who was home from his studies in Australia at the time.

A solidarity picnic staged in the Lake Gardens by the families of the fasting detainees on Sunday 30 October 1988 had earlier been broken up by Special Branch police wielding tear-gas canisters. The wives of detainees Dr Mohamed Nasir Hashim and Dr Kua Kia Soong lodged police reports following this picnic stating they had been manhandled

Karpal and Gurmit enjoying a meal with Dr Nirmal Singh
(second from right) and his wife Manjit Kaur (left) in a
photo taken in happier times in Penang, July 1982.

by the police while in the act of releasing balloons. These balloons had
the names of the imprisoned detainees inscribed upon them.

When news of Megat Junid's comments reached Kamunting on the
fourth day of the hunger strike Karpal noticed Lim Guan Eng looking
particularly downcast.

"What's the matter with you, man?" he asked.

Lim Guan Eng said he had heard of media reports claiming they
had been caught eating and drinking in their cells. Karpal's reaction to
the news was immediate. Lim Guan Eng was ordered onto a typewriter
while Karpal dictated to him writs against Megat Junid and the Malaysian
prison authorities.

Towards the end of their hunger strike Karpal, Lim Guan Eng
and Lau Dak Kee were charged by Kamunting camp Superintendent
Das with refusing to eat food without reasonable excuse in a place of
detention. The hearing was quite a heated affair and when Das asked
Karpal how he pleaded to the charge, the latter advised he needed to give
the issue further consideration before making a plea.

The faces say it all. Kartar Kaur reassures her son after losing his second High Court application for a writ of *habeas corpus* in July 1988. Among the relatives present are (*from left*) son Gobind, daughter Sangeet (behind Gobind), Karpal, son Ramkarpal (partially hidden), wife Gurmit (seated) and mother Kartar. *Photo courtesy of* The Star, *Malaysia.*

At this point Das proclaimed the three men guilty but forgot to pass sentence. As they were being ushered out of the room, Karpal reminded Das that he had forgotten to pass sentence.

"Come back in here," Das called out and advised them their privileges would be removed for seven days. They were sentenced to seven days deprivation, meaning their families could not make their weekly visits to the camp.

At that point the camp commandant was told, "We'll see you in court, Das."

On 29 April 1989 the disciplinary order was quashed in the Ipoh High Court on the grounds that Superintendent Das had failed to observe the rules of natural justice in arriving at his decision to remove privileges for a week from the hunger strikers.

Karpal and Gurmit, during their meetings at the Kamunting Detention Camp in those days, were a young couple facing an uncertain future. When they whispered to each other there was a lot they did not say. Karpal spared his wife the details of how detainees released from the Police Remand Centre or Kamunting had had their spirits broken.

Gurmit was under strict instructions from her mother to ensure she looked her best every time she made the trip to Kamunting. She would concentrate on briefing her husband on family and business matters, not going into too much detail about her meetings with their bankers, while another group of frequent visitors focused their efforts on the lawyer's initially successful bid for freedom via the *habeas corpus* legal process.

This group was headed by Karpal's now deceased brother Manjit, an Alor Setar lawyer practising in his own right. The year 1988 was payback time for Manjit who ensured the security prisoner — a man who had helped put him through law school at Buckingham University in England — was supplied with all the law books and *habeas corpus* precedents he required. Manjit coordinated the legal efforts of many people outside Kamunting, and following Karpal's arrest on 9 March 1988, filed another writ of *habeas corpus* with the Ipoh High Court on the grounds the arrest had been unlawful.

The issue was put to rest by the Supreme Court in Kuala Lumpur on 20 July 1988, following an appeal against Justice Peh Swee Chin's decision by Dr Mahathir himself.

The Supreme Court, headed by the acting Lord President Tun Abdul Hamid Omar (Tun Salleh Abas had by then been suspended as Lord President on grounds of misconduct), ruled that the flawed allegation referred to in the March 9 decision was an error of no consequence. Tun Abdul Hamid Omar said the courts had come to accept the best judge of national security was the body with authority for security, namely the government. The court found Dr Mahathir (as Minister of Home Affairs at the time) alone had the power to decide whether there was reasonable cause to detain and this could be challenged only if it were shown he 'does not hold the opinion which he professes to hold'.

In sum, the appeal court found Justice Peh Swee Chin had erred in applying an objective rather than a subjective test. On 26 July 1988 the High Court in Ipoh dismissed Karpal's second *habeas corpus* application. In a short judgement, Justice Datuk Haji Abdul Malek Ahmad said the court had no alternative but to dismiss the application in view of the Supreme Court's earlier decision.

Justice Abdul Malek received an unusual letter after arriving at his decision to defer his judgement on the April 1988 hearing until after the result of Dr Mahathir's appeal to the Supreme Court was known. It came from Karpal's oldest son Jagdeep in Australia who asked why the decision on his father's second *habeas corpus* case had been delayed. Jagdeep did not need the judge to provide him with the answer to this question.

Down, but not entirely out, Karpal filed notice of appeal against the Supreme Court decision. On 16 December 1988 he was informed the Supreme Court in Kuala Lumpur had thrown out his final legal avenue in the second freedom bid via a writ of *habeas corpus*.

The quest to free Karpal was very much a family effort.

Gobind and his uncle Santokh played key support roles as couriers on behalf of Gurmit and her lawyer brother-in-law Manjit. On many early mornings in 1988, Gobind could be found sleeping on the stone bench beside the ticket box of the Taiping Railway Station from 3:00 a.m. until daybreak, after coming off an overnight train from Kuala Lumpur. When the gates opened at the Kamunting Detention Camp at 8:00 a.m. Gobind would be there arguing and advising Special Branch personnel he had important business documents for his father to sign.

Fifteen-year-old Gobind lost three months of school because of his 'courier' role during the detention period. For him, even at his impressionable age, it was a personal crusade; his father was in trouble and he would play his part to help his family. It was also the time when he decided to become a lawyer, which was a relief to his father in more ways than one. Early on in life, Gobind thought he might become a mechanical engineer and would dismantle the family's Mitsubishi Lancer on weekends in an effort to see what made it tick. There were Monday mornings when Karpal would prepare to drive his car to the Penang court only to find the radiator or another essential part leaning up against the wall of the garage. Gobind graduated with an LLB from the University of Warwick, England in 1995.

Karpal's detention left his many clients in a bind, particularly the death row inmates who were relying on him to conduct their appeals. After Australian Kevin Barlow went to the Pudu gallows in July 1986 the dubious title of Karpal's most high-profile clients went to New Zealand mother and son Lorraine and Aaron Cohen.

Lorraine Cohen, a pleasant person, was a one-time prostitute and drug addict. She was condemned to death by the man known in Australia as the 'hanging judge', Justice Tun Mohamed Dzaiddin Abdullah on 1 September 1987 for trafficking in 140.78 grams of heroin at Penang International Airport on 9 February 1985. Her son Aaron was sentenced to life imprisonment and six strokes of the *rotan* after being found guilty of possessing 34.61 grams of heroin in the mother and son joint High Court trial.

In February 1988 Lorraine Cohen wrote to Karpal who by then had been in detention for four months. She asked in her letter whether he considered his political activities worthwhile and accentuated the fears she and her fellow death row prisoners felt about having their own lawyer in detention. Cohen told Karpal many prisoners who had retained him were anxiously awaiting his release. The situation was not so bad for Aaron and herself. At least they had had their day in court. She wrote:

But I really feel for those who are still waiting for dates and even worse for the ones who have already got them. They will now have to get postponements or another lawyer.

At the time of her letter Lorraine and Aaron Cohen were awaiting a Supreme Court appeal date in Kuala Lumpur. The New Zealand mother and son had been visited by Karpal's Alor Setar-based brother Manjit, who had told them that if a date for the appeal was set they may have to engage another lawyer as the Supreme Court did not like adjourning cases.

New Zealand's High Commissioner to Malaysia Ray Jermyn entered the letter-writing fray on the Cohens' behalf when he wrote to Attorney-General Tan Sri Abu Talib Othman on 29 July 1988 inquiring whether Karpal could be released from detention to represent the Cohens during the appeal stage. The letter apparently went into a bureaucratic limbo for four months, for it was not until 4 November 1988 that he received a reply.

> ... I am afraid it would be difficult to make any arrangements for the Cohens to have access to Mr Karpal Singh in his capacity as their solicitor and counsel. You may perhaps wish to advise the Cohens to engage another lawyer.

To sack or not to sack Karpal was an uncomfortable question facing his clients. Many of them did, but Lorraine and Aaron Cohen made the decision to stick with him even after receiving advice to the contrary from prominent lawyers in Malaysia and Australia.

On 12 December 1988 Karpal wrote to the Cohens advising them of his failure to win his own freedom via the *habeas corpus* appeal route. He was exhibiting the type of spirit his parents had been called upon to demonstrate when their home was destroyed by an American B-29 bomber in Penang 43 years earlier. He wrote optimistically:

Do not fear. There is no doubt I will be allowed to appear for you and Aaron at the hearing of the appeal. I was allowed to argue the UEM appeal in January this year. There is provision in the Internal Security Act to allow a detainee to appear in court. The Minister of Home Affairs invoked the provision in the ISA for me to appear before the Supreme Court and argue in the UEM appeal. Rest assured I will do my best in your appeal. The rest I leave in the hands of God. Yours is a criminal appeal involving the death penalty... All is not lost. It cannot be. Both Aaron and you are always in my thoughts. Take heart. We must not lose heart. Every cloud has a silver lining. That lining will enlighten that which has been plunged into darkness.

Lorraine and Aaron Cohen made a brave decision to stand behind bars with their Sikh lawyer. Lorraine Cohen knew how hard Karpal had worked for Aaron and herself. In a letter to a friend she had observed:

A lawyer has to feel right and Karpal felt right to Aaron and myself. No matter how much advice I got about sacking Karpal I felt deep down it wasn't the right move. It was something I could not have done as impersonally as by writing him a letter, as it would have been like kicking a dog when it is down.

Lorraine Cohen's loyalty was later to be rewarded.

While some Malaysian lawyers were clearly enjoying and benefitting from the business opportunities provided by Karpal's absence, the

Operation Lalang saw Karpal's family support him at every step of the way during his 15 months of detention from 1987 to 1989. These photos tell the story of a battling united family during those difficult days.

majority did everything possible to assist Gurmit on the occasions she picked up the phone seeking assistance.

Karpal Singh & Co. was hit hard by the tactics of a few members of the bar who sent out distress signals, particularly to prisoners of Penang Jail, saying Karpal was a government target and anyone who engaged his firm or kept him on as counsel would be doomed. Such people would visit the prison and advise inmates like Hong Kong Chinese Tam Tak Wai, who was facing the death penalty on a government appeal after being sentenced to life imprisonment for drugs trafficking. "You'd better get yourself another lawyer because he is going to be inside for the rest of his life," Tam was told.

When Tam approached Gurmit expressing concerns about Karpal's future ability to represent him, the lawyer's wife jolted him into reality. "If he is forever inside, you are forever alive. If you want to rush to the gallows, get yourself another lawyer now."

After that remark Tam Tak Wai and the other Hong Kong Chinese in the prison never again hassled Gurmit about the unavailability of her husband to represent them.

By December 1988 just 16 of the Operation Lalang detainees remained in custody, Karpal being one of them. He managed to retain his sense of humour with light-hearted talk with his brother Santokh about a mass breakout from Kamunting. To his amazement he later found out it could be done — two of his Indian clients Sukdev Singh and Shahid Akthar Ran Abdul Majid escaped in the boot of a car early one morning in August 1990. They made their escape while wardens watched a telecast of a World Cup soccer match between England and Italy. The two men, last heard of from Canada, had told the lawyer their escape plans but he did not believe they would go through with the attempt.

Shortly before Christmas 1988 eight-year-old daughter Sangeet played her part in the family campaign to win her father's freedom. She wrote a personal letter to Prime Minister Dr Mahathir asking him how he could be so cruel by separating her from her father. 'You are not fair. This is a very big sin. God hates this. Please don't do this because God will soon punish you,' she wrote.

There were no 1989 New Year celebrations at the family's Penang home; far from it, in fact. On New Year's Day Gurmit was down, so down she locked herself in her upstairs room. Following her Friday visits to Kamunting, where she would brief her husband on business developments and have him co-sign the cheques, Gurmit always made a point to visit the Pusing temple, where she would confide in the priest there.

"I am hanging onto a cliff by one finger," she told him on Friday 20 January 1989.

The priest told her, "Don't worry, your prayers have been answered."

Five days later the High Court granted Karpal permission to argue a third *habeas corpus* writ before it in Penang at a hearing set down for Tuesday 31 January 1989. It was all to be academic really, because on Friday 27 January 1989 — after 15 months of detention — Karpal was among five ISA detainees freed from the Kamunting Detention Camp.

Gurmit knew something strange was going on when her husband came on the phone from Kamunting and asked her to come and pick him up. She called his mother and then her own mother. The three Punjabi women drove to Kamunting where they collected him and went once again to the Sikh temple in Pusing.

This time no policemen shadowed them as the family offered prayers of thanksgiving. It was supposed to be a conditional release but Karpal refused to sign the release forms. He then presided over an open house for the weekend at his Jalan Utama home in Penang.

Fifteen months of legal footwork, anxiety, pain, emotional trauma and being treated as common criminals had come to an end for all family

Freedom! Karpal on 27 January 1989 shortly after being released from Kamunting Detention Camp surrounded by family and friends. From left are brother Balwinder Singh, fellow incarcerated DAP MP P Patto, Karpal, daughter Sangeet, Gurmit and sons Mankarpal (in his mother's arms), Gobind and Jagdeep.

Safe at home at last. Celebrating Karpal's release from detention are (from left to right) Manjit, brother-in-law Gurbak Singh, Santokh, Karpal, Balwinder and their mother Kartar at Karpal's Penang home.

members. Dr Mahathir had unwittingly done Karpal's extended family a favour for, with the exception of one person, they had all emerged from their ordeal physically, morally and mentally tougher.

In jail Karpal had become Malaysia's leading authority on *habeas corpus* law. He was subsequently able to convert this experience into revenue for his law firm when he obtained freedom court orders for approximately 100 clients detained indefinitely under the ISA and Dangerous Drugs (Special Preventive Measures) Act 1985 in centres such as Simpang Renggam Jail in Johor.

In hindsight Karpal admitted to actually having enjoyed the cut and thrust of his detention days. He had expected to spend six years behind bars, enough time for his practice to be destroyed, and was surprised when the Special Branch notification came through for his release.

His family will not forget what they went through and survived together. Soon after it was all over and her job of helping to hold the family together completed, Gurmit's mother Puran Kaur died. For the first time in their lives the family saw a husband and father cry. Karpal knew just how important this woman, along with his own mother, had been in guiding his wife and children through their time of trial.

It would be another three months before Operation Lalang officially ended when Lim Kit Siang — the man who had also been held for 17 months under the ISA following the May 1969 race riots — and his son Lim Guan Eng were released from Kamunting on 20 April 1989.

The tough lesson Karpal learned during Operation Lalang in 1988 and 1989 was that when there are major problems within the ruling UMNO party, it is wise to keep your head down. But, as shown by his student activities at the University of Singapore, Karpal was a slow learner when he chose to be.

Thirteen years after his release from detention, High Court Judge Datuk Abdul Hamid Said finally agreed with the lawyer's submissions.

Karpal with then Prime Minister Dr Mahathir Mohamad (right) at the latter's Sri Perdana home in Kuala Lumpur, 1986. In the centre is Dato' Sulaiman Daud, now deceased, who was the then education minister in the Mahathir administration. *Photo courtesy of* Thina Kural.

He declared that the detention order dated 18 December 1987 had been issued legally but became unconstitutional when an advisory board heard the lawyer's representations against the order on 2 August 1988. The court, in awarding costs and damages against the government, ruled the advisory board should in fact have considered the issue on or before 31 March 1988.

Victory in this case meant Karpal could finally put Operation Lalang behind him. He was awarded an agreed and confidential sum for damages on 20 February 2002.

There was a certain inevitability about Karpal's non-compromising decision to sue his political nemesis Dr Mahathir and his government, in alleging they had acted unconstitutionally over the handling of his detention orders. The wrong in this very personal case had, at long last, been put right.

Of all the Operation Lalang detainees, Karpal was the only one to take Dr Mahathir on in court and win. The result of this case went further than this, however. It also left him in a one-man club of his own, as the only Malaysian citizen to successfully sue Dr Mahathir over a human rights issue during his prime ministership.

During his ISA detention another top-level spat was going on behind the scenes involving Dr Mahathir and Karpal with the 1988 removal from office of three senior judges for alleged misconduct: Tun Salleh Abas, Tan Sri Wan Suleiman Pawanteh and Datuk George Seah. Karpal had always believed the judges were unfairly removed from office.

He wrote to the former prime minister on 27 March 2007 stating the judiciary had never regained its hitherto superiority as one of the finest judiciaries in Asia. He called upon Dr Mahathir to make an unqualified and unconditional personal apology to the three judges and their families.

There would be no apology from Dr Mahathir; nor did Karpal expect one. The former prime minister did, however, respond in a letter dated 3 April 2008 saying Karpal would never believe him no matter what he said. Dr Mahathir wrote:

> *You are moved by pure hatred and I cannot respond to people who can never accept reality... My conscience is clear. I have done what was my duty and I owe nobody any apology. I am sure you will make use of this letter to dirty my name further. That is your right. I think you are the most contemptible of politicians and individuals.*

Karpal and Lim Kit Siang (right), with Malaysia's first Prime Minister Tunku Abdul Rahman, attending a human rights seminar in Kuala Lumpur following their release from Kamunting Detention Camp in 1989.

10 EAST VS WEST

Karpal defended a number of clients he believed did not deserve to die on Malaysian gallows. High in this category is Australian Kevin Barlow. Right to the very end, Barlow told his lawyer, "Karpal, I did not do it."

The main reason Karpal said Barlow should not have gone to the gallows on 7 July 1986 related to the fact that the 179 grams of heroin that led to his execution and that of his travelling companion Geoffrey Chambers were found in the latter's bag.

Barlow was hanged alongside Chambers largely because he was carrying the bag when apprehended by Assistant Superintendent of Police Abu Shahriman at Penang International Airport on 9 November 1983. When asked to open the bag during the airport search, Barlow could not because he did not know the combination lock number of the bag Chambers had purchased earlier in the day.

Another significant reason Barlow was executed, said Karpal, was because of the evidence given in court by Abu Shahriman, led by Chambers' counsel Rasiah Rajasingam, of an attempted airport bribe.

Kevin Barlow may have come to Malaysia for the express purpose of trafficking in drugs, but the picture Karpal painted of his client was that of a young man who got cold feet, thought better of the drug run and opted out of the deal at the eleventh hour in Penang. This view is backed by an article written by a British journalist Andrew Drummond shortly before another Briton Derrick Gregory was executed at Kajang Jail outside Kuala Lumpur on drug trafficking charges in July 1989. In this article Drummond quoted Gregory as saying Chambers himself had told him, while they were on death row together in Penang, that Barlow was innocent and that all the heroin found on Barlow had belonged to him (Chambers). Gregory was executed three years after Chambers and Barlow died on the Pudu Jail gallows. Not surprisingly the memory of Barlow continued to haunt Karpal who, till the end, descibed him as an 'unwilling partner in the whole affair'.

The major sideshows in the Chambers and Barlow case involved the bitter public confrontations between Karpal and two other lawyers involved in the case: Chambers' Penang-based lawyer Rajasingam, and Barlow's Melbourne-based lawyer Frank Galbally.

The dispute between Karpal and Rajasingam arose when, according to Karpal, the latter introduced bribe evidence against Barlow in the Penang High Court while cross-examining him. Until the introduction of the bribe evidence Karpal's approach had been to shepherd both men away from the gallows by creating real doubt as to who exactly was the trafficker in the minds of Supreme Court judges who would later hear the appeal. When the bribe evidence was introduced the trial became a dogfight between two Malaysian lawyers before death sentences were handed down by the judge. In the trial Rajasingam also submitted

Barlow had placed the heroin in Chambers' bag and his client knew nothing of its existence.

The relationship between Frank Galbally and Karpal, to put it mildly, was also strained. Galbally became part of the Barlow defence team after the High Court in Penang had found both Chambers and Barlow guilty of drug trafficking under section 39B of the Dangerous Drugs Act and sentenced both men to death. The clash between the lawyers turned into a heavyweight contest between two larger-than-life characters, undoubtedly leading legal figures in Australia and Malaysia respectively. For 20 years, until Galbally's death in Melbourne in 2005, both men traded blows in the media.

Galbally was of Irish Catholic origin and was a legal legend among the Australian criminal law fraternity. He was involved in the defence of about 300 murder cases and was described by a former chief justice of Victoria John Harber Phillips as a 'lionhearted man and one of Australia's greatest advocates'.

With Chambers and Barlow well set up on death row in Penang Jail, Galbally sent Karpal an introductory matter-of-fact telegram on 2 December 1985, which read:

> Barlow requests that you apply to High Court for permission for me to appear with you on his appeal. I am a barrister and solicitor of the High Court of Australia and other states Supreme Courts. Please act accordingly. Regards. Frank Galbally.

Karpal and Galbally first met when Galbally called into Karpal's Penang office before the Chambers/Barlow 17 December 1985 appeal hearing. They exchanged pleasantries but with his waiting room full of clients, Karpal suggested that he visit the Australian at his hotel in Batu Ferringhi once the morning's business had been completed. Accompanied by his assistant S Assamaley, the two drove to the hotel to discuss the case. When they arrived, the Galbally party was having lunch. Karpal and Assamaley made an assessment of the situation and, speaking in Malay, they both agreed to curtail the meeting. From Karpal's perspective, second impressions of the tall silver-haired Australian were not good ones. The two men were destined not to get on together.

Before his death in May 2000 Assamaley recalled that, for some reason, Karpal did not appreciate Galbally's 'demeanour' during the meeting at the hotel.

At the time Galbally and Karpal had built for themselves similar reputations, in their respective countries, as lawyers who were not shy about taking on difficult cases. But clearly when it came to Kevin Barlow's defence the two men were unable to work together, in the manner Karpal was able to work with New Zealand lawyers Peter Williams QC and David Hagar, for instance, during the defence of Lorraine and Aaron Cohen from 1986 to 1990.

Galbally and Karpal clashed bitterly during the Supreme Court appeal hearing in Kuala Lumpur on 17 December 1985. Karpal later told journalists he had the distinct impression the Australian was trying to take over the case completely and required 'the third world man to sit down quietly and do as he was told'.

Karpal had some sympathy for Galbally. He believed the problem was created in part through Galbally's unfamiliarity with the Malaysian judicial and penal systems. Living and working around the death penalty was at that stage of Karpal's career a routine everyday event. For Galbally, according to the Malaysian, it was something quite different.

On the eve of the Chambers/Barlow appeal hearing in Kuala Lumpur, Galbally rang Karpal at his office from the Shangri-La Hotel and invited Karpal to join him. Karpal explained he and his assistant

Oh Chong Ghee were busy working on the appeal and could not meet up. He invited Galbally to come to his office instead to discuss the appeal there, if he wanted to, but Galbally declined.

The disagreement with Galbally reached its lowest point at the beginning of the second day of the hearing when Karpal complained to the court how the Australian had uttered the words 'blame it on your bloody system', referring to the Malaysian judicial system. He went for broke, asking the court to cite Galbally for contempt for the flippant remarks made the previous afternoon.

It was Justice Tan Sri Eusoffe Abdoolcader who took the lead in questioning Frank Galbally on the matter from the three-man bench the following morning. The bench also comprised the Lord President Tun Salleh Abas and Justice Datuk George Seah. By way of explanation to the appeal court Galbally said he had not been referring to the Malaysian judicial system but rather the prison system when he used those words.

Soon afterwards Galbally left the court, checked out of the Shangri-La Hotel and returned to Melbourne. There he embarked upon a barrage of abuse in the Australian media over Karpal's handling of the appeal.

For his part, at the end of the appeal hearing, Karpal tore into Galbally via the media pack assembled for the appeal. He told the press:

> I want to make it very clear I will not take any nonsense from Mr Galbally. Let that be understood. I have got a job to perform and I intend to do it to the best of my ability. We do not require people… who have no respect for our judicial system to come here and scandalise and insult our court in the courtroom itself — this is the highest court in the country, the Supreme Court. Tell Mr Galbally this: he doesn't breathe down my neck. We in this country are not living in trees; he may think we are. We can think, you

know — tell him that. You think that we Malaysians don't even know how to talk English. No white man or otherwise is going to come here and just insult us. We will not accept it. Let that be understood. Whether he is a great criminal lawyer in Australia or not is not the point. I will take him on if necessary. He can sue me for defamation if he wants.

Events took a new twist when a telegram arrived on 22 December 1985 from Kevin Barlow's mother Barbara Barlow. It instructed Karpal:

Do not proceed until you hear from Galbally. Most urgent.

When he received the telegram Karpal knew he may have been sacked in the mind of the very caring loving mother Barbara Barlow, but he also knew that her views and those of the Australian lawyer doing his best for her son differed totally from those held by the man who was a resident on Pudu Jail's death row. Barlow retained confidence in his Kuala Lumpur lawyer. He and his fellow prisoners on death row knew from bitter experience Karpal was not the type of man to walk out on a client at a time when they needed him most.

Following his return to Australia, Galbally was also scathing in his criticism of Karpal in a Perth newspaper. He was reported as saying Barlow wanted to sack Karpal (after the Penang High Court trial) and have Galbally represent him instead (although this would not have been possible as Galbally was not a member of the Malaysian Bar). The Perth newspaper article in part read:

In hindsight he [Galbally] admits to one regret that he didn't persuade Barlow to sack Singh immediately after his initial trial in August 1985 and then appoint another lawyer.

The report continued by quoting Galbally:

> The defence of Barlow by Singh can only be described as pathetic and one which here would certainly result in a retrial on the ground of negligence. I mean can you believe that at the trial Karpal Singh did not know that the death sentence for drug trafficking was mandatory? That's true.

In other comments back in Australia, Galbally said Karpal had not followed his instructions and a further statement said the Malaysian 'was obeying the instructions of neither myself nor his client'. Galbally also said Karpal failed to deal adequately with a conflict of interest that Rajasingam had found himself in during the High Court trial. Rajasingam had earlier represented Kevin Barlow for a brief period and Galbally felt this should have been pointed out to the High Court at an early stage of the trial.

Karpal viewed Galbally's use of the words 'obey' and 'instruct' in this context as an indication of the Australian's mindset. He believed Galbally may have had difficulty realising he was in Malaysia purely in a support role. He did not take his instructions from Galbally, but from Kevin Barlow. Reacting to Galbally's accusations of negligence, incompetence, inefficiency and arrogance, Karpal said he did everything in his power to help Barlow and his conscience was clear. "To me that counts and not Galbally's antics."

From the earliest days Karpal's Penang-based assistant Assamaley was under no illusions about the likely outcome of the Chambers/Barlow case. He told Barbara Barlow he believed the Malaysian government wanted to make an example of the men to prove to the world its tough new anti-drugs legislation would be implemented even-handedly.

In this respect Chambers and Barlow were very much a 1986

Malaysian general election campaign issue. How else could one explain the young Australians were frog-marched to the gallows a mere 32 months after their arrest? The process of law in most section 39B cases under the Dangerous Drugs Act in Malaysia takes at least a decade to take its final and irrevocable course.

Responding to Galbally's criticism that he should have objected to Rajasingam representing Chambers at the High Court trial, Karpal said Barlow had told him nothing before the trial that indicated Rajasingam could have been in a conflict of interest. The situation only arose during the trial when a police witness referred to an alleged bribe Barlow was supposed to have offered him when he was arrested at Penang International Airport in November 1983.

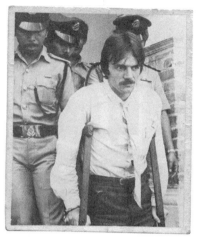

Kevin Barlow during his Penang High Court trial. *Photo by Chan Looi Tat and featured in the 20 July 1986 issue of* Asiaweek.

Karpal was adamant the police witness told the court 'something which actually did not happen'. Trial judge Justice Tun Mohamed Dzaiddin Abdullah accepted the bribe evidence and said in his judgement that he found the policeman to be a truthful witness.

Before the trial began Barlow briefed Karpal fully on what he had told Rajasingam. There was nothing about any bribe to an airport police officer in that briefing. Karpal understood Barlow had not divulged anything incriminating to Rajasingam. "Kevin Barlow told me himself there was no bribe. I believe him," he said.

For Karpal, Rajasingam's decision to question the bribe evidence ended the healthy friendship between the two Penang-based lawyers.

Early in 1984 Rajasingam withdrew his services from Barlow.

Following an approach from Barlow in Penang Jail before the High Court trial, Karpal agreed to take over his defence. In court he left Rajasingam in no doubt what he thought of him as he led the bribe evidence.

Galbally, upon his return to Australia, also said Karpal failed to lead relevant medical evidence that could have explained Barlow's shivering at the time of his arrest. Karpal did not place as much importance on police evidence that Barlow was shivering when apprehended at the airport as Galbally did. In his view, completely innocent travellers, realising the existence of the death penalty, understandably shiver in fear when spoken to by police during routine spot checks at Singapore and Malaysian airports.

In his written judgement on the High Court case Justice Tun Mohamed Dzaiddin Abdullah rejected the medical evidence, led by Karpal, referring to Barlow's shivering at the airport as being the result of his pelvic injury. The judge was referring to evidence given by Dato' Dr Nadason Arumugasamy, the Head of the Department of Neurosurgery at Kuala Lumpur General Hospital, who said it was possible Barlow might have shivered at the airport because of pain. Karpal said he placed Dr Arumugasamy's medical evidence before the High Court, after Justice Tun Mohamed Dzaiddin Abdullah had made his decision to convict Barlow, primarily for the benefit of the Pardons Board.

Galbally made his 'blame it on your bloody system' comment as an aside at the end of the first day's appeal hearing when Karpal advised him it would be inappropriate to submit new medical evidence from Australian forensic psychiatrist Dr Allen Bartholomew at the appeal stage. The Malaysian advised the Australian that fresh evidence could be led only in exceptional circumstances in the Supreme Court at the appeal stage.

As for Galbally's statement that Karpal was ignorant of his own country's law, this allegation was ludicrous, he believed. It related to the Malaysian lawyer's submission to 'bind Kevin Barlow over' under section 294 of the Malaysian Criminal Procedure Code. Even in a death penalty case there is provision within Malaysian law to convict and free a person on a sponsored good behaviour bond for a set period of time.

For Karpal, the comment highlighted Galbally's lack of knowledge of Malaysian law. He could not have been expected to know that Malaysian law required defence counsel to make a plea in mitigation to ensure the Pardons Board has all relevant information before it, in the event of an appeal being lost.

One week before Barlow and Chambers went to the gallows in July 1986, former Australian Foreign Minister Bill Hayden said efforts to save the two men had been 'set back' by Galbally. Hayden had earlier been accused by Galbally of making little effort to save the lives of Barlow and Chambers. Hayden retaliated that the Australian High Commission in Kuala Lumpur had confirmed the two men received a fair and just trial and that one of the 'less flamboyant' Australian lawyers involved had disassociated himself from Galbally's 'bloody system' comments.

The less flamboyant Australian referred to by Hayden was Perth-based lawyer Ron Cannon, who was a back-up member of the Chambers defence team. Cannon observed the build-up to the December 1985 Supreme Court spat between Karpal and Galbally and in its aftermath sided firmly with the former.

There has to be a trace of the actor and the vain in all good criminal lawyers, according to Cannon. In a 1999 interview in Perth, Cannon told me that both Karpal and Galbally had these characteristics as they were at the top of the advocacy profession in their respective countries. From Cannon's perspective, however, Galbally chose the wrong man to set his sights upon on this occasion. Cannon said it was obvious for all to see that Karpal did not get along with Galbally.

Cannon said he knew, when sitting in the Kuala Lumpur appeal court, that Chambers and Barlow would never leave Malaysia alive. As he waited for the hearing to begin he had pondered the hopeless situation of two young men having to beg for their lives following the inevitable failed appeal and clemency petition to the Governor of Penang Dr Haji Awang bin Hassan. He knew there would be no point in the Chambers and Barlow families, when all else had failed, appealing in a last desperate effort for clemency from the Agong.

According to Karpal, Galbally never fully appreciated the pre-1986 general election 'scapegoat' political considerations. Chambers and Barlow were the first westerners to be tried in Malaysia for drug trafficking under a 1983 amendment to the Dangerous Drugs Act making the death penalty compulsory.

In February 1987 Karpal complained to the Victorian Bar Council over the contents of the Perth newspaper article, saying Galbally's remarks constituted an insult to the Malaysian judiciary.

In the article Galbally was quoted as saying: 'The whole affair was shameful for the Malaysian authorities and the lawyers involved in the case. It was incompetent, arrogant, inefficient.' He was also further quoted as saying: 'Certainly it was very sad but a wonderful experience, in many ways, to see how some other countries get on, rough justice to the extreme and little concern for human life.'

In the complaint to the Victorian Bar Council Karpal said Galbally's apology to the Malaysian Supreme Court in December 1985 was obviously insincere and he called upon the Council to bring Galbally to heel for ignoring the usual dictates of legal decency and propriety. The council responded that it was powerless to act as it had no mechanism to deal with a complaint from a foreign lawyer.

The one aspect on which Karpal did agree with Galbally was that

Gurmit and Karpal greeting the Governor of Penang Dr Haji
Awang bin Hassan. The figurehead leader of the Penang Pardons
Board had it within his power to spare the lives of many of
Karpal's clients, including Kevin Barlow. To the governor's left
in this 1985 photo is Lim Chong Eu.

Barlow's guilt was less than Chambers' even though the two men died as
equals, side by side, on the Pudu Jail gallows.

Later, in his autobiography, Galbally launched another scathing
attack on Karpal over the Malaysian's handling of the Barlow defence.
Clearly the slug-out between the two was always going to be a fight to
the death. Both Frank Galbally and Karpal Singh are now dead. Both
men involved in this all-in over-the-top legal brawl would have had it
no other way.

Chambers and Barlow were not the first white men to face the
gallows in Malaysia. In 1951 Australian Jeffrey Watts-Carter was
charged under Emergency Regulations for having consorted with
armed communists at a Perak rubber plantation. He was successfully
defended by David Marshall, an outstanding criminal lawyer of Iraqi
origin who accompanied Tunku Abdul Rahman, the Chief Minister of

the Federation of Malaya at the time, for the Baling talks with Chin Peng and the communists in 1956.

Significantly, coinciding with the Chambers and Barlow death sentence on 1 August 1985 was a nationwide political campaign in Malaysia, backed by the Chinese community, to save the life of former factory worker Sim Kie Chon. Sim was convicted and sentenced to death by the Kuala Lumpur High Court in 1983 for possession of a .38 Smith and Wesson revolver and five rounds of ammunition in Kuala Lumpur.

His appeal to the Federal Court was turned down and he was first scheduled to go to the Pudu gallows in July 1985, but managed to obtain a stay of execution pending the hearing of a suit filed by him against the Pudu Jail superintendent, the Pardons Board and the government. Sim claimed the Pardons Board had violated his rights under article eight of the Federal Constitution by not commuting his death sentence to life imprisonment as was done for former Minister of Culture, Youth and Sports Datuk Mokhtar Hashim.

Karpal was in no doubt that Sim had a good point.

A Malay cabinet minister could use a gun for murder on 14 April 1982 and escape the gallows via a Pardons Board reprieve yet Sim Kie Chon could get no joy from a Pardons Board for mere possession of a revolver and five rounds of ammunition.

Sim Kie Chon created legal history in Malaysia when he obtained a second eleventh-hour stay of execution on 14 August 1985, thereby becoming the first man condemned under the ISA to temporarily escape the hangman's noose twice.

There were other eleventh-hour desperate legal moves brought before the High Court by Karpal and other lawyers. In 1982 Chow Thiam Guan obtained a stay of execution pending the outcome of his suit questioning the legality and constitutionality of the mandatory death sentence under the ISA. He was later hanged. On 17 January 1983

Liew Weng Seng obtained a stay of execution from the Agong. He had questioned the constitutionality of the Federal Territory (covering Kuala Lumpur) forming part of the Federation of Malaysia. He lost in the end and had to take the journey through the gallows doors. These cases accentuated the Chinese community's view that the administration of the prerogative of mercy by the Malay rulers was biased.

On 27 August 1985 Sim told the Kuala Lumpur High Court he wanted Justice Tun Mohamed Dzaiddin Abdullah to submit a supplementary report to the Penang Pardons Board highlighting certain mitigating factors. On 17 October 1985 Justice Tan Sri Harun Hashim ruled there were triable issues in Sim Kie Chon's suit. The High Court struck out his suit and on 4 February 1986 the Supreme Court struck out Sim's appeal on the grounds it had no merit. He was executed on 5 March 1986 after the Agong turned down a third appeal for clemency.

With a general election scheduled for the following year the Sim Kie Chon saga created for the Malaysian government a credibility issue where the Chinese community was concerned. One way it could possibly restore some credibility back into its Pardons Board clemency system would be to hang two white men before the 1986 election.

Chambers and Barlow were in the wrong place at the wrong time. Barlow spent his last night on earth in the *bilik akhir* beneath Pudu's guard tower number four. Directly opposite Barlow was Chambers, who was similarly housed in a small cell.

In those dreadful final days, members of the Barlow family worked closely with Karpal to deal out every possible appeal card in a forlorn quest to stop the hangings. He did his best for Kevin Barlow, but he knew it was not enough and could never be when he broke the news of the execution to Barlow's mother Barbara and sister Michelle in room 2011 of the Hilton Hotel.

At least the members of the Barlow family gathered in Kuala Lumpur for the execution on 7 July 1986 had the consolation of knowing that, with Karpal as a final advocate, they all went down fighting to the last. There were last-minute appeals to Queen Elizabeth II, United Nations Secretary-General Pérez de Cuellar, former Malaysian Prime Minister Tunku Abdul Rahman, the Agong and the Australian Council of Trade Unions. Such was the drama of the whole Chambers/Barlow saga that a TV mini-series was made, with Julie Christie playing Barbara Barlow and Victor Banerjee playing Karpal.

Karpal outside Pudu Jail on the morning Geoffrey Chambers and Kevin Barlow were hanged, 7 July 1986.

Right until the eve of his death, Barlow expressed a desire to pay Karpal the little money he had. The lawyer refused to accept it. He insisted the money Barlow received from an AUD4,500 accident claim payout should be paid to his brother Christopher, who eventually did receive it. Earlier in 1984 Kevin Barlow had paid RM500 to Karpal for handling the case.

The third Australian to be hanged for drug trafficking in Malaysia was Michael McAuliffe at Kajang Jail in 1993. McAuliffe's tour of Asia came to an abrupt halt in 1985 when he was arrested at Penang International Airport while trying to board a plane for Manila. He was charged with trafficking in 142 grams of heroin found in 14 condoms in a pouch bag attached to his belt.

There was not much for Karpal to work with in this case, what with McAuliffe carrying the material in his waist pouch. The Australian required a miracle, such as prosecution chemists botching the drug analysis job as had occurred in the 1983–85 case of Australian Bob Pavone. There would be no miracle for McAuliffe, who described the substance in the condoms as 'bang bang powder' sold to him for AUD450 by a Thai dancer Lung Noi, with whom he had had sex in Bangkok.

McAuliffe waited six years in Penang Jail before his case came to trial. During this period he bade farewell to Chambers, Barlow and Englishman Derrick Gregory before being condemned to death himself in the Penang High Court by Judicial Commissioner Abdul Hamid Mohamed on 17 August 1991.

McAuliffe was told he would be taken from the court to a prison and later to a place of execution where he would be hanged by the neck until dead. Reacting stoically to the sentence he turned to the French Catholic nun seated beside him, Sister Nicole, and said, "Don't sweat, worse things happen at sea."

Sister Nicole made it her life's work to look after foreigners facing the death penalty in Malaysian jails, and went out of her way to assist the 36-year-old McAuliffe on the day he was condemned to death.

McAuliffe lost his Supreme Court appeal against the death sentence in May 1992. He kept his early morning appointment with the hangman 13 months later at Kajang Jail, just outside Kuala Lumpur. On many occasions during his imprisonment at Penang and Kajang jails, the former Sydney barman would ask Karpal the same question: "If you were a betting man, Mr Karpal, what odds would you give me on escaping the noose?"

It was a question the lawyer dreaded having to answer for he knew McAuliffe's odds with the Penang Pardons Board would not be good.

"Don't worry, McAuliffe, we'll see what we can do," he would answer.

McAuliffe would remind Karpal how he managed to get Australian Bob Pavone off on a trafficking charge in 1985 involving 402 grams of heroin. "If you can get him off a 400 gram rap, you can do it again for me with 140 grams." Sadly for McAuliffe, Malaysian prosecution chemists had learned the difference between opium and opiate by the time he shuffled into Penang International Airport with his 14 condoms full of 'bang bang powder'.

On the eve of McAuliffe's execution Karpal left his client nibbling peanuts in the company of a Catholic nun. Soon after the condemned man had been weighed and measured by the hangman, McAuliffe could still raise a smile with his lawyer and the nun. "What a way to be remembered, by eating peanuts," he joked.

The lawyer's standard eleventh-hour plea to the Agong fell upon deaf ears, as did the personal appeals from Australian Prime Minister Paul Keating and Foreign Minister Gareth Evans.

In the early hours of Saturday 19 June 1993 McAuliffe became the fourth western drug trafficker to be executed in Malaysia.

The day before, Khoo Hi Chiang and other inmates on Kajang Jail's death row saw McAuliffe being led away by prison guards for what they thought would be just another lawyer's meeting or a meeting with Australian High Commission staff. Because of language differences, McAuliffe was effectively in his own solitary confinement in Kajang Jail. He never did get to say goodbye to the Chinese men around him on death row.

Khoo Hi Chiang told me, following his own release after McAuliffe's hanging, the first he and the other men on death row at Kajang Jail knew of the Australian's execution was when they were informed by prison authorities it had taken place. He said the death row inmates at Kajang were all shocked and impressed by the calm gentlemanly manner in which McAuliffe had quietly left them.

The restrained political reaction in Australia to the hanging of McAuliffe contrasted starkly to the events of July 1986 involving the executions of Chambers and Barlow. Public reaction to the McAuliffe hanging in Australia reflected the generally accepted notion, by that time, that those who broke the law in Southeast Asia should expect to pay the penalty. Gone were the days when Caucasian traffickers would escape the gallows primarily because of their white skin. This was part of the 'one law for all' policy Malaysia's fourth Inspector General of Police Tun Mohammed Hanif bin Omar implemented from behind his desk in his 20 years in the role from 1974 to 1994.

The gallows at Kajang jail where Michael McAuliffe was executed in the early hours of Saturday 19 June 1993.

Lorraine and Aaron Cohen's case, like Bob Pavone's, turned out to be a Karpal success story. Aaron Cohen was 18 years old when desk clerk Tan Kian Wah checked him and his mother into the New China Hotel in Penang on 15 December 1984; the former backpacker hotel building still stands today but has been converted into a chocolate boutique retail outlet. He was arrested for possession of 34.61 grams of heroin at Penang International Airport on 9 February 1985.

Two years later the then 20-year-old created a legal precedent in Malaysia when Justice Tun Mohamed Dzaiddin Abdullah agreed with Karpal's submission that the heroin in Aaron Cohen's possession was for his own use as an addict.

The prosecution lodged a cross-appeal seeking the death penalty against the younger Cohen on the grounds that the judge had erred in law and fact in the High Court by finding Aaron Cohen had rebutted the presumption of trafficking under section 37 of Malaysia's Dangerous Drugs Act and accepting Aaron Cohen's contention the heroin in his possession was for his personal consumption.

The Supreme Court noted the precedent-setting significance of the earlier High Court decision by assembling a five-member bench to hear the appeal comprising Lord President Tun Abdul Hamid Omar, Justice Tan Sri Hashim Yeop Abdullah Sani, Justice Tan Sri Lee Hun Hoe, Justice Tan Sri Eusoffe Abdoolcader and Justice Dato' Mohamed Yusof Abdul Rashid. An ironic touch occurred when the Lord President postponed the hearing of the Cohen appeal by two days to accommodate a visit to the Supreme Court by the then Sultan of Selangor — the man Karpal had sued in 1987 for publicly stating he would not grant clemency to any convicted drug traffickers.

The Sultan's visit did nothing for Lorraine Cohen's confidence but it provided a reminder of just where clemency power lay in Malaysia. As it turned out, Lorraine Cohen would not have to throw herself at the mercy of the Sultan's brother ruler, the Governor of Penang.

The prosecution appeal against her son was rejected and Aaron Cohen's sentence of life imprisonment and six strokes of the *rotan* was upheld. Lorraine Cohen was sentenced to death in the High Court for trafficking in 140.78 grams of heroin but she benefitted from the precedent established in her son's case when the five-member bench of the Supreme Court found Justice Tun Mohamed Dzaiddin Abdullah had made a mistake when dealing with the mother.

The appeal court disagreed with the judge's statement in his notes of proceedings which said the needle marks on Lorraine Cohen's arms had been caused by bashings from her de facto husband Don. The court unanimously agreed with the defence contention that the marks on her arms were those of a multiple intravenous drug user. Because of this the court felt it necessary to give Lorraine Cohen the benefit of the doubt and reduced her sentence from death to life for possession of heroin under Section 39A of the Dangerous Drugs Act.

The Cohens had lived under the threat of death for four and a half years, and cheating the hangman meant they would spend 11 and a half years in Penang Jail before finally being freed by way of a royal pardon. Life imprisonment in Malaysia is defined as 20 years, with one-third remission for good behaviour.

Aaron Cohen's six-stroke whipping with the *rotan* — a cane over a metre long and a centimetre thick — on 12 December 1991 came after appeals against the whipping to the Governor of Penang and the Agong were turned down. It took Aaron Cohen by surprise, as Karpal had managed to stall it for two years by raising the issue in parliament, lodging formal appeals and, when these failed, filing a suit against the decisions in the Penang High Court. Furthermore on 1 April 1991 Deputy Home Affairs Minister Datuk Megat Junid had given Aaron Cohen some hope of escaping the *rotan* when he said the government did not propose to whip addicts as they were sick people who ought to be rehabilitated. The then young New Zealander certainly came within that category and when Karpal heard his client had been caned, he once again went for a ruler.

This time his target was the Sultan of Perak Sultan Azlan Shah, a former Chief Justice and Lord President who went on to become the ninth Agong of Malaysia in 1989. The Sultan should have ensured justice was done in Aaron Cohen's case, Karpal said.

"Aaron Cohen was an addict and, therefore, in the words of the government, a sick person. We have whipped a sick person. The magnitude of the shame astounds me," Karpal said.

Caning has been widely used in Malaysia as a supplementary punishment to about 40 crimes ranging from robbery, rape, kidnapping and causing grievous hurt. Children, females, males sentenced to death and males over the age of 50 are not caned.

Aaron Cohen did not come within any of those exemption categories. His prison shorts and white T-shirt, with its blue collar signifying more than 18 months spent behind bars, were removed and in the presence of a doctor he was strapped to an A-frame. His hands, ankles and calves were tied and padding strategically placed on either side of his naked buttocks. The six blows opened up flesh wounds on his buttocks and it was two weeks before he was able to sit comfortably again.

Unlike McAuliffe, the Cohens were fortunate they had people in New Zealand and Australia with financial resources and ability to support their defence. New Zealand lawyers Peter Williams QC and David Hagar, representing the Howard League for Penal Reform in New Zealand which concerns itself with prisoner welfare, helped Karpal coordinate the Cohens' medical defence. Auckland doctor Fraser McDonald and his Sydney counterpart Stella Dalton flew to Penang to give evidence on behalf of their former patient Lorraine Cohen, who had the added burden of suffering from cancer during her time in Penang Jail.

Dr McDonald's evidence on Aaron Cohen having been born addicted to drugs obviously impacted upon Justice Tun Mohamed Dzaiddin Abdullah who, in sentencing the young man to life imprisonment and six strokes of the *rotan*, observed, "You have escaped the gallows by the skin of your teeth."

In Karpal's discussions with Peter Williams and David Hagar, the name of a New Zealand farmer Arthur Allan Thomas was mentioned. Thomas was convicted of double murder in two High Court jury trials, with the conviction being further upheld by the Court of Appeal and the Privy Council. Thomas would possibly have been hanged if there was capital punishment in New Zealand in the 1970s. His subsequent innocence was established by a Royal Commission of Inquiry.

The briefing on this case from Peter Williams and David Hagar reinforced Karpal's main opposition to the death penalty — that mistakes could be made during the judicial process and innocent people, especially those unable to pay for their defence, could be executed as a result.

Before the mother and son eventually left Malaysia, Karpal was unable to arrange for Lorraine Cohen's final wish. She wanted to visit the grave of Sister Nicole, the French nun regarded as an angel of mercy by the Caucasian inmates of Penang Jail. Sister Nicole had been run over by a car while crossing a Penang street on her way to mass early one morning in 1996.

When he said goodbye to the Auckland-bound Cohens from Kuala Lumpur International Airport at the end of June 1996 the lawyer thought he had seen the last of his foreign clients. But they kept coming and are hoping one day to leave.

Liberian Nobies Weah Ezike is one man who did not go anywhere in a hurry. He has faced two section 39B trafficking charges. Karpal got him off one; his 1997 death penalty conviction for trafficking in 327.3 grams of heroin was reduced to a sentence of 18 years imprisonment and 15 strokes of the *rotan* when Karpal argued his case before the Court of Appeal in November 1997. He was not so fortunate on his second 39B charge however. The Federal Court unanimously dismissed his appeal in May 2010 for trafficking 412.8 grams of heroin at the United Parcel Service office in Petaling Jaya in 1996. His life then rested in the hands of the then Sultan of Selangor.

Peruvian university student Jorge Enrique Tellon, 20, from Lima, Peru was more fortunate. He was apprehended at Gate 13 of Kuala Lumpur's Sultan Abdul Aziz Shah Airport on the morning of 26 November 1996 while carrying 2261.2 grams of cocaine. The cocaine was found in nine packages strapped to the inside of his underpants. He faced the death penalty when charged with trafficking under section 39B of the Dangerous Drugs Act. At the time Tellon was a transit passenger on a flight from Buenos Aires bound for Bali.

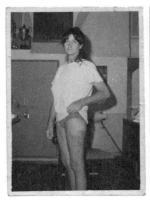
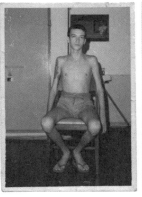
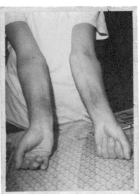

(*above left and middle*) Lorraine and Aaron Cohen soon after their arrest in Penang on 9 February 1985; (*above right*) Lorraine Cohen's 1987 death sentence was reduced to life imprisonment on appeal, largely because of the needle marks on her arms; (*right*) Aaron Cohen was strapped to one of these A-frames for his six-stroke whipping.

Karpal responding to media questions outside Penang Jail prior to Lorraine and Aaron Cohen's release and departure for New Zealand in June 1996. To his left is lawyer-son Ramkarpal.

Gurmit and Karpal speaking with the late, former New Zealand Prime Minister David Lange at a restaurant in Wellington after attending the Commonwealth Law Conference in Auckland, 1990.

In his August 1997 High Court trial, the court acknowledged Karpal's submission of Tellon's status as a cocaine-carrying transit passenger. In a legal precedent Justice Faiza Tamby Chik reduced the charges from trafficking in cocaine to bringing cocaine into Malaysia while in transit, under section 21 of the Dangerous Drugs Act, and sentenced the Peruvian to three years jail.

The prosecution appealed the decision, which meant Tellon lived in the shadow of death until 21 July 1998 when the Court of Appeal upheld the High Court decision. Tellon happily flew home with his lawyer's blessings in time for Christmas 1998.

About the time Tellon flew home, Englishman David Chell would provide the next difficult life-and-death challenge for Karpal. He was grateful that Chell, whom he described emphatically as a 'good, innocent man', was the last of the Caucasian clients he had to represent.

Chell, a psychiatric nurse from Stoke-on-Trent and one of Britain's first male graduate nurses, was arrested at Penang International Airport in October 1998. He was literally following in Kevin Barlow's footsteps when he was stopped in 1998 while attempting to board a flight for Perth. He spent two and a half years in jail during which time he was sentenced to death by hanging for possession of 190 grams of heroin in 133 condoms. He professed his innocence vigorously throughout and said crooked officials had set him up. With Karpal advocating, his innocence was upheld in an appeal court when he won his appeal against his death sentence on the basis of inadequate forensic prosecution evidence.

After winning his appeal, Chell was quoted in Britain's *Telegraph* newspaper as saying: 'All I can say is it's not before time. I know it sounds clichéd but the whole thing has been a living nightmare and should not have happened to anyone.'

There was no shortage of work for Karpal in the capital punishment drug-running stakes with plenty of international drug mules still prepared to risk all for a fast dollar. The Caucasian traffickers have been replaced by Iraqi, Iranian, Nigerian and Indian alleged traffickers all facing death in Malaysian jails on section 39B drug trafficking charges.

While the death penalty still remains in place Karpal noted in early May 2013 it seemed to be losing its appeal with the authorities in Kuala Lumpur.

"I have not had a client executed for about three years now," he said.

11 ON THE RUN

As he stood outside Taiping Jail on the afternoon of 29 May 1990 Karpal had genocide and the World War II German 'Beasts of Belsen' on his mind. He was struggling to come to grips with the fact that eight of nine Hong Kong Chinese nationals would hang under section 39B of the Dangerous Drugs Act (DDA) the following morning. They had been members of a tour party when they were caught smuggling 12,759 grams of heroin out of Malaysia.

The lawyer tried to think of a comparable situation to the one he found himself in on the eve of their hangings. All he could think of at the time was famous British executioner Albert Pierrepoint's post-World War II role in hanging 13 former Belsen concentration camp staff members all in one day. He could think of no other situation in modern times outside wartime to compare with the eight judicial killings on track to take place the following morning.

Four of the nine Hong Kong nationals were at one time or another his clients. Li Chi Ping had been convicted of trafficking in 2,530 grams of heroin while Au King Chor had been convicted of trafficking in 2,525 grams at Penang International Airport on 30 October 1982. He also handled Chow Sing's unsuccessful appeal against his death penalty for abetment, while his fourth client in the case Tam Tak Wai provided the only good news to emerge for the defence from the massive drugs bust by Penang authorities. Tam was freed on appeal after the charge of abetment against him was dropped by the Supreme Court in Kuala Lumpur.

Karpal never forgot the gut-wrenching helplessness he experienced when Tam Tak Wai went down on his knees after the Penang High Court trial and pleaded with his lawyer, "Master, master, I am innocent. Please help me"

Li, Au, Yuen Kwok Kuan (2,575 grams), Chan Yiu Tin (2,594 grams), Ip Tak Ming (abetment) and Ng Yiu Kwok (abetment) were executed at Taiping Jail in two batches of three on the morning of 30 May 1990. At Kajang Jail approximately 300 kilometres to the south of Taiping, nightclub hostess Hau Tsui Ling (2,535 grams) and car dealer Chow Sing (abetment) simultaneously went to their deaths.

In the days prior to their execution Karpal helped Hau Tsui Ling and Chow Sing fulfil a final wish. They wanted to be married so as to be together forever in the afterlife. The authorities, formally acknowledging there is no discrimination when it comes to the gallows, duly obliged the pair by marrying them and then executing them alongside each other. Hau became the first foreign woman to be executed on drug charges in Malaysia when she stepped up to the mark on the gallows trapdoor.

The build-up to the hangings was particularly difficult as relatives of all the condemned flew in from Hong Kong in late May 1990 looking for a miracle. Karpal sought to solicit such a miracle via an application to the High Court for judicial review of the Governor of Penang's decision to reject their pleas for clemency. This was based on the fact that neither the condemned nor their legal representatives were permitted to appear before the Pardons Board during the clemency proceedings.

Lawyers K Kumaraendran (for Ng Yiu Kwok and Chow Sing) Rasiah Rajasingam (for Chan Yiu Tin, Yuen Kwok Kuan and Ip Tak Ming) and V Sithambaram (for Hau Tsui Ling) acted for the seven condemned men and one woman throughout the proceedings.

The final visitations for the relatives, who had travelled from Penang to Taiping in a Salvation Army van, took place in a compound near the prison superintendent's office. It was such a tense time for the condemned, their families and the lawyers that during the day Karpal had to remove himself from it all by taking a walk in the nearby Lake Gardens.

Taiping Jail, where six Hong Kong Chinese drug traffickers were executed in two batches of three early in the morning of 30 May 1990.

The lawyer said there was no task on earth more difficult than seeing family members having to prise apart a distraught mother from her condemned offspring as the time allowed for the final visit comes to a close. When he said goodbye to his client Li in Taiping Jail, the Hong Kong Chinese simply said, "Do you mean that's it? We are all going to die tomorrow? There's nothing more we can do?"

When Karpal responded that it appeared likely, the man just shrugged his shoulders and asked the warders to return him to his cell. In the case of the Hong Kong Chinese Karpal did not create any false expectations, for he remembered only too well the 1986 Barlow and

Chambers case when he incorrectly advised them there might be an eleventh-hour reprieve.

As he left his clients for the last time he reminded them of the British prime minister's personal appeal to Dr Mahathir, seeking clemency on humanitarian grounds. Margaret Thatcher had suggested to Dr Mahathir that he commute the death sentence to life imprisonment as the Hong Kong eight had been arrested six months before hanging became a mandatory punishment for drug trafficking in Malaysia. Karpal also reminded Li and Au that he had earlier personally delivered an appeal to the Agong on their behalf.

Thirteen hours after the first of the Hong Kong Chinese had their arms strapped behind their backs in preparation for the hanging process, the lawyer received his answer by post from the Agong. Ambassador Dato' Yeop Adlan Che Rose wrote:

> Your appeal letter dated May 28 1990 has been duly brought to the attention of his Majesty Yang di-Pertuan Agong IX, Sultan Azlan Shah. With deep regret I have been commanded to convey that His Majesty Yang di-Pertuan Agong is in no position to usurp the powers of the state Pardons Board of Penang.

The Penang Pardons Board had sat on 29 March 1990, but news of the decision declining the appeal for mercy for the eight only reached the British High Commission in Kuala Lumpur informally when First Secretary Ashe Windham travelled to Kajang Jail on 17 May 1990 to visit the newlyweds Chow Sing and Hau Tsui Ling. The British diplomat was not allowed to meet the couple and was told he could gain access to them on 29 May 1990 — the same day their relatives in Hong Kong were advised to make their final visit.

Windham was unhappy with the delay in notification of the Pardons Board decision, which he described as being one of great interest to the Home Office and the administration in Hong Kong. Following representations to the Director-General of Prisons for access, he was finally allowed to see the pair, but the visits took place through barred glass and an intercom system. Chow and Hau discussed their funeral arrangements and the last-minute appeal tactics of their lawyers with Windham, while prison staff of all ranks positioned on both sides of the glass listened in to every word.

The Hong Kong Chinese case highlighted a basic philosophical difference in drug running between Caucasian and Chinese traffickers. If a Chinese is going to run the risk of death as a drug runner, he or she generally carries substantial quantities rather than go to the gallows for trafficking in a comparatively small amount such as those carried by the executed Australians Chambers and Barlow.

At no stage during the four-month joint trial of the nine Hong Kong Chinese in the Penang High Court did any one of them admit to knowing of the 12,759 grams of heroin secreted into similarly constructed lined compartments of five suitcases. The five traffickers carrying the false-bottomed suitcases — Au King Chor, Hau Tsui Ling, Chan Yiu Tin, Yuen Kwok Kuan and Li Chi Ping — all told the court they were innocent carriers provided with suitcases by their Hong Kong-based travel agency.

The movements of the nine were closely monitored by the international drug enforcement authorities in the British colony, Thailand and Malaysia before they attempted to board their Singapore Airlines flight to Brussels via Singapore at Penang International Airport.

Malaysia's death penalty for trafficking in dangerous drugs, even though it was not mandatory at the time of the 30 October 1982 arrest, was presumably the reason the international authorities decided to make an example of the Hong Kong Chinese by making the bust in Penang. The mandatory death sentence for drug trafficking came into force in Malaysia on 14 April 1983, when anyone apprehended with more than 15 grams of heroin was automatically assumed to be a trafficker.

The High Court heard detailed evidence of how the Hong Kong residents had flown to Bangkok and separately converged on Penang via different methods of transportation.

Ip Tak Ming had purchased the tickets for the convicted traffickers to fly to Brussels from Sharma Travels & Tours on 29 October 1982 in Penang. He had specifically requested Tam Tak Wai's name to be removed from the trafficking party. This request by a former gambling friend turned out to be a lifesaver for Tam, who had visited Malaysia from Hong Kong on four occasions in 1982. Tam's ticket to Brussels from Penang was earlier paid for by Ng Yiu Kwok, who also paid for the tickets of the three men who went to the gallows for jointly abetting the five traffickers. Tam's final visit to the country in 1982 lasted an unscheduled six years and seven months in Penang Jail before he was set free.

Tam Tak Wai, a cook from the New Territories in Hong Kong, left the former British colony for Thailand on 22 October 1982 with a friend Lai Yuen Tim. In Bangkok Tam checked into the New Imperial Hotel before meeting Ip Tak Ming, whom he knew in Hong Kong, while having a meal at the Canton Restaurant in Bangkok. The following day he and Lai Yuen Tim went to the Mandarin Hotel in Bangkok where they joined Li Chi Ping, Ip Tak Ming and Chow Sing in a gambling game.

While in Bangkok, Tam told the Penang High Court, he had given Ip Tak Ming HKD4,000 for him to purchase an airline ticket to Holland where he wanted to get a job as a cook. On 29 October Tam travelled from Haadyai to Penang in the same taxi as Au King Chor and Hau Tsui Ling where all three stayed in the Golden Sands Hotel in Batu Ferringhi.

Ip paid for Tam's hotel bill, the latter told the court, out of the HKD4,000 he had given Ip in Bangkok. When Tam was arrested at Penang International Airport at 5:10 p.m. on 30 October 1982 his soft brown suitcase was found to contain no drugs.

In the Penang High Court, Justice Tun Mohamed Dzaiddin Abdullah considered there to be enough circumstantial evidence against Tam Tak Wai to sentence him to life imprisonment and eight strokes of the *rotan*. The prosecution sought the death sentence against him on appeal before his conviction was dismissed by the Supreme Court in Kuala Lumpur. Chief Justice Tan Sri Hashim Yeop Abdullah Sani found insufficient evidence of abetment against Tam and he was freed on appeal.

The execution of the eight Hong Kong Chinese contrasts rather sharply to the appeal court decisions handed down to an attractive 22-year-old French trafficker Beatrice Saubin and Australian Bob Pavone. The Frenchwoman and the Australian man were both arrested when the death penalty for drug trafficking was optional. But unlike the eight Hong Kong Chinese, Saubin and Pavone got away with their lives.

Beatrice Saubin — a popular prison inmate who taught herself new Asian languages and was generally a model prisoner — wrote a book on her ten years in Malaysian jails entitled *My Ordeal*. It told a story of a young woman who realised a dream of visiting exotic places by travelling to Malaysia, among other countries. In Malaysia, she fell in love with a Chinese man and the couple made plans to meet and later marry in Europe. As she made her way through Penang International Airport in 1980 her suitcase, a gift from her Chinese boyfriend, was ripped apart and found to contain 534 grams of heroin hidden in secret compartments. She was horrified when she learned she had been 'set up' at the airport.

(*above*) Li Chi Ping, Tam Tak Wai, Ip Tak Ming and Chow Sing engage in a spot of gambling in their hotel room in Bangkok enroute to Penang. Tam was the only one to escape the hangman's noose; (*right top*) Tam Tak Wai after his arrest; (*right middle and bottom*) Li Chi Ping and his suitcase.

A relieved Tam Tak Wai after being freed on a drug trafficking abetment charge by the KL Supreme Court on 7 July 1989. Photo courtesy of *Nanyang Siang Pau.*

In the Penang High Court in 1982 she was condemned to death by Justice Datuk Bigley Lee Tian Huat. The following year the sentence was overturned by the Federal Court on appeal and commuted to life imprisonment. The court did not give any reasons for the decision except to say there were extenuating circumstances in the case. The Federal Court went one step further by saying the decision was not to be cited as a precedent.

Karpal said the Federal Court was inconsistent with the Saubin decision. Saubin was represented by Kumaraendran, who was fortunate his client was young, very attractive and white. Karpal's cynicism over the Saubin decision seemed to have been backed up by Malaysia's then Chief Justice Raja Azlan Shah who said while delivering judgement in another drug trafficking appeal:

Beatrice Saubin during her High Court trial in Penang. *Photo by Chan Looi Tat and featured in the 20 July 1986 issue of* Asiaweek.

We have been referred to the case of Beatrice Saubin, a 22-year-old French girl who was convicted for trafficking in heroin and sentenced to death by the High Court which on appeal to this court was altered to imprisonment for life on the grounds that there were extenuating circumstances in that case.

As no reasons have been given, either oral or written, in that case we do not know what the extenuating circumstances found were and we can therefore only consider that case as one on its own particular facts and circumstances.

We would however make it absolutely clear that a 22-year-old foreign female courier who traffics in heroin takes the same risk and does so at the same peril as a 52-year-old local male counterpart, and the sex, age and origin of the offender would appropriately be more a matter for consideration in any application for clemency.

The man Karpal referred to as the 'luckiest client of them all' was Australian Bob Pavone. A would-be transit passenger en route to Sydney via Singapore, Pavone was detected with 402 grams of heroin tied to his waist as he endeavoured to pass through Penang on 7 August 1982.

Pavone was arrested eight months before the mandatory death penalty for drug trafficking was introduced and in this regard he, too, was fortunate.

He was doubly lucky when the Attorney-General Tan Sri Abu Talib Othman used his discretion to press charges against him in the Sessions Court. Sessions Court President Ho Mooi Ching did not have the power to condemn Pavone, who chose to remain completely silent when asked to make his defence. In that lower court on 27 March 1983 the Australian was convicted and sentenced to life imprisonment.

On appeal to the High Court the Australian was given a retrial by Justice Tan Sri Edgar Joseph Jr because of 'misdirection' by Sessions Court President Ho Mooi Ching. The one significant statement made by Pavone in his defence was when he told Auxilliary Police Officer Wan Mohamed bin Wan Ismail at the airport search room that the material found round his waist was 'fertiliser for his plants'.

At the trial Karpal picked up the fact there had been a discrepancy involving the description of the substance found on Pavone in the Sessions Court. The investigating officer described it as opium whereas the government chemist described it as heroin. Court President Ho Mooi Ching had rejected the evidence of the investigating officer and accepted the government chemist's report without calling him to give evidence.

In ordering the retrial Justice Tan Sri Edgar Joseph Jr said he could not discharge the Australian as 'the unchallenged and uncontradicted evidence against the appellant was absolutely overwhelming'.

Pavone returned to Penang Jail and was there till April 1985 when his drug trafficking retrial began, presided over by Sessions Court President Tengku Baharudin Shah Tengku Mahmud.

On 23 May 1985, the Australian was once again jailed for life and this time an additional sentence of eight strokes of the *rotan* was imposed on him.

In August 1985 the Penang High Court, presided over by Justice Dato' VC George, heard Pavone's second High Court appeal against his life sentence. Justice George said although Pavone was caught red-handed there was a gap in the prosecution's case. The prosecution did not explain the difference in the findings of the investigating officer and the government chemist on what exactly was in the package found on Pavone.

"Was it opium, opiate or heroin?" Justice George asked. "If indeed there was a nexus between opium, an opiate and heroin, then expert testimony should have been adduced to show just that. The absence of such testimony has resulted in a significant gap in the prosecution case." Justice George then dismissed the charge against him.

Five weeks after Chambers and Barlow had been condemned to death by the Penang High Court, Pavone left Malaysia. When he flew home to Australia via Singapore that night, he must have reflected on the fact he would never be able to repay Malaysia's Attorney-General and

Karpal. In their respective ways, by charging Pavone in a Sessions Court, thus keeping him away from a High Court trial, and highlighting the conflicting prosecution versions of the contents of the package removed from his waist, the Attorney-General and the lawyer had saved his life.

Two weeks after Chambers and Barlow were hanged — an act described by Australia's Prime Minister Bob Hawke as barbaric — Malaysia's Ministry of Foreign Affairs diplomatically referred to the Pavone case in a very polite note sent to the Australian High Commission. The note read:

> The Ministry of Foreign Affairs, Malaysia presents its compliments to the Australian High Commission and has the honour to forward herewith an Australian passport… issued in Sydney on 30 July 1992 belonging to Mr Pavone, Bob. The Ministry of Foreign Affairs, Malaysia has further the honour to inform that Mr Pavone, Bob was arrested at the Penang International Airport on 7 August 1982 for possessing 402 grams of heroin. He was charged in Sessions Court, Penang on 23 May 1985. Subject was found guilty under section 39B of the DDA 1952 and was sentenced to life imprisonment and given eight strokes of caning. Mr Pavone, Bob appealed against the sentence and was freed by the High Court, Kuala Lumpur on 3 September 1985. He was issued with an Australian passport by the Australian High Commission in Kuala Lumpur and was deported to Singapore the same day. The Ministry of Foreign Affairs, Malaysia avails itself of this opportunity to renew to the Australian High Commission the assurances of its highest consideration.

The note concerning 'Mr Pavone, Bob' was perhaps the Malaysian ministry's way of diplomatically letting Australian High Commission staff in Kuala Lumpur know Malaysians were not that 'barbaric' after all.

Karpal shuddered at the memory of how Bob Pavone flew out of Malaysia five weeks after Chambers and Barlow were condemned to death. Pavone could easily have gone down that road if the Attorney-General had decided to prosecute him at any stage of his imprisonment in the Penang High Court, the lawyer recalled. He also recalled how Mary Pavone had been an absolute tower of strength to her partner and members of the Chambers and Barlow families.

Karpal, who liked the Pavones a lot, was pleased to be able to wish them very best wishes for their future after sharing a restaurant meal with them before they headed to the airport. He certainly was not going to suggest 'Mr Pavone, Bob' should remain in Malaysia to pick up a passport issued in Sydney on 30 July 1992.

The Saubin and Pavone prosecution experiences indicated the Malaysian government felt comfortable about hanging Asians of all nationalities when the death penalty was optional for trafficking in drugs between 1975 and 1983. Hanging for drug traffickers became the norm, rather than the exception, during this period.

Western drug couriers, as distinct from Asian couriers, remained largely immune until after the death penalty became mandatory. The one exception was Briton Derrick Gregory, who was arrested at Penang International Airport in 1982.

Gregory was charged for trafficking in 576 grams of heroin but, unlike Pavone, his case was prosecuted in the High Court for reasons known only to Malaysia's Attorney-General, whose life-and-death discretion to initiate prosecutions is constitutionally protected.

Gregory, from Surrey in Southern England, was making his way through Penang International Airport on 7 October 1982 but he never did get to board his SQ191 Singapore Airlines connecting flight to Singapore with plans to fly to San Francisco on the same day. When he arrived at the airport in a taxi from the Lone Pine Hotel beach resort in Batu Ferringhi, he was asked to remove his boots by Assistant Superintendent of Police Abu Shahriman. Abu Shahriman, who was also the arresting officer in the Chambers and Barlow case, described the boots as being too big for his feet. He found 14 packets of heroin in the boots and a further four packets of heroin in Gregory's underpants.

Gregory told the High Court he was forced, under threat of death, to carry the drugs by an international smuggling ring. British consultant psychiatrist Dr Colin Brewer, a director of the Stapleford Unit in Essex, told the court Gregory suffered from an organic brain disease. But Justice Tun Mohamed Dzaiddin Abdullah rejected this evidence. He described Gregory, 39 at the time of his death, as a courier involved in trafficking heroin from Penang to the United States. Justice Tun Mohamed Dzaiddin was in a position to sentence Gregory to life imprisonment and a whipping, as the death penalty for trafficking did not become mandatory in Malaysia until April 1983, but he imposed the death penalty to mark the gravity of the offence and to 'protect the public'.

Gregory's final desperate plea to Queen Elizabeth II for help went unanswered and he was hanged on 21 July 1989 at Kajang Jail.

Throughout the 1970s and into the early 1980s Malaysia, along with India and Hong Kong, had a reputation among international drug trafficking syndicates as being something of a soft-touch transit point for Golden Triangle suppliers. The Hong Kong Chinese case certainly made the 'Mr Bigs' in the British colony stand up and take notice of Malaysia's changed attitude. This case was interesting as it was one of the few to have gone through the Malaysian court system involving a well-organised major international syndicate.

It is hardly surprising Malaysia was also scoring points with such bodies as the United Nations International Narcotics Control Board praising Dr Mahathir's government (in its 1985 report) for its efforts to curb drug trafficking. Buoyed by the success in the international political arena, Malaysian drug enforcement authorities worked closely on a number of cases with the United States Drug Enforcement Agency.

The 35 condemned drug traffickers on death row whose appeals had been rejected by the Pardons Boards before February 1985 obviously did not share the Malaysian government's enthusiasm for eradicating traffickers and the drug menace generally. They received an unpleasant surprise when Deputy Home Minister Dato' Seri Radzi Sheikh Ahmad, in February 1985, revealed Malaysia was proceeding with plans to hang at least one drug trafficker a week. As part of the campaign he also encouraged state prosecution authorities to quickly finalise the Pardons Board clemency petitions from 35 other drug traffickers who had lost their final legal appeals in the Federal and Supreme Courts.

(In 1985 all appeals to the Privy Council from Malaysia were abolished. The newly constituted Supreme Court became the final appeal court for all constitutional, civil and criminal matters. This remained the case until the Supreme Court was abolished in 1994 and a three-tiered system involving the High Court, the Court of Appeal and the Federal Court, as the highest court in the land, was introduced.)

Karpal genuinely sympathised with his government in its stringent efforts to clamp down on the illegal drugs trade, but he did not see well-publicised weekly hangings as the answer to the problem. He believed the solution to the heart of the problem lay in tightening security at the border between Thailand and Malaysia.

To Karpal hanging was an act that went against the United Nations Declaration of Human Rights, and thinking back to his own faint childhood memories he recalled the public executions carried out by the occupiers of Malaya as having done nothing to bring honour to the Japanese. Furthermore there had been an increase in section 39B DDA prosecutions since the death penalty became mandatory, he argued, so clearly capital punishment was not a deterrent to drug trafficking.

Tougher penalties also caused major problems in Malaysian jails, such as the six-day Pudu Jail hostage drama in October 1986. During this incident six inmates stormed the prison medical clinic and overpowered Dr Radzi Jaafar and laboratory technologist Abdul Aziz Abdul Majid.

Four of the prisoners — Chua Chap Seng, Ng Lai Huat, Sin Ah Lau and Lam Hock Seng — were facing charges under the Firearms (Increased Penalties) Act 1971. This legislation incorporated penalty provisions of death and natural life.

Chua, the ringleader, was already facing death for the murder of a policeman in 1984 and, in fact, was later executed for this crime in 1989. He demanded a getaway vehicle for himself and the other five prisoners and their hostages. The request fell on deaf ears. Chua and his cohorts were overpowered by the Police Special Task Unit on the evening of 22 October 1986.

Karpal represented the other two inmates, Yap Chee Keong and Ng Lai Huat, in the subsequent August 1990 court appearance on abduction charges. They were sentenced to concurrent jail terms of three and five years respectively by Judicial Commissioner Dato' Faiza Tamby Chik, who took the view that Chua had been the ringleader, thus reducing the charges against them from kidnapping to abduction.

In October 1986, 7,113 prisoners out of a total Malaysian prison population of 23,000 were in jail on drug-related offences. The tough enforcement of anti-drug legislation in the mid-1980s saw Malaysia's then 13 prisons bursting at the seams. For Karpal the overcrowding at Pudu was the significant reason behind the hostage drama. At the time it

(*above and left*) The hospital inside Pudu Jail which was at the centre of the hostage drama in 1986. Karpal represented two of the four prisoners involved in the subsequent court case.

occurred, Chua was in an overcrowded remand cell after being returned to jail following six months' freedom as an escaper on the run.

Pudu was built to accommodate 800 prisoners and in 1985, when the sardine-can existence reached its absolute peak, 6,550 prisoners were crammed inside 900 cells. In the Pudu remand wing between ten to 14 prisoners were regularly housed overnight in a single cell. This not only meant inmates often did not have enough room to lie down on the concrete floor to sleep, it created potential male rape problems. Prisoners were locked in from 4:00 p.m. to 6:00 a.m. the next day. The toilet system was a common bucket in the corner.

The building of large new modern prisons at Simpang Renggam in Johor and Sungai Buloh outside Kuala Lumpur, to replace the British-built Pudu, has gone a long way to solve the housing problem for the Malaysian prison population. When the move was made to the new Sungai Buloh Prison in October 1996, there were 1,769 prisoners in Pudu Jail. Few among them were sad to learn the 100-year-old Malaysian institution would be consigned to a death row of its own in the future mid-city development.

The passing of the Dangerous Drugs (Special Preventive Measures) Act 1985 (SPMA) contributed to the overflowing quota of inmates in Malaysia's jails. The legislation was designed to place those suspected of being involved in drugs, particularly the masterminds, behind bars without trial. It proved to be a *habeas corpus* growth industry for lawyers in the early 1990s, but the approximately 100 court orders Karpal obtained — providing freedom for detainees during this period — did have their downside.

Karpal would often arrive at the gates of the Muar and Simpang Renggam drug detention centres in Johor with his court orders authorising the release of particular prisoners only to see police promptly re-arrest the detainees once they were outside the prison gate.

There had been some terrible scenes in these re-arrest situations, one of the more spectacular being the re-arrest of Madam He Ken Kiok outside the Kuala Lumpur High Court on 7 March 1991. She had been acquitted and discharged on a drug trafficking charge. The mother of three, who had been in jail since 11 May 1989, was re-arrested under the SPMA. Police overlooked the earlier courtroom events when Madam He's husband Tan Kim Guan pleaded guilty to a drug trafficking charge and was sentenced to death. In an act of bravery Tan had elected to take the noose for his wife so their three children, aged from six to 11, would at least have a mother to take care of them. Madam He was acquitted on the joint charge of trafficking with her taxi-driver husband immediately after he was sentenced to death. When Tan saw police move in to re-arrest the woman he had literally just given his life for, he understandably went berserk and had to be held down by prison officers. On 17 March 1993 Tan Kim Guan lost his appeal against the death sentence.

Confirming the sentence in the Supreme Court Justice Tan Sri Harun Hashim said, "We are of the view the learned trial judge had complied with the principle set out by the court when dealing whether the plea of guilt should be accepted or not. The judge in this case was extremely careful. If we go out against the principle, then no court would ever accept a guilty plea."

All was not yet lost for Tan Kim Guan, however. He was to be rewarded later in a most unusual and unexpected way in what was to be a landmark in Karpal's career.

The Malaysian police have often used the SPMA to lock people up on renewable two-year detention warrants because it saves them having to go through the long and difficult process of proving a prisoner's guilt in an open court. Lawyers have seen the re-arrest procedure as an abuse of the judiciary, court decisions and individual rights. Under this legislation alleged offenders are not given an opportunity to prove their innocence in a court of law. Karpal spoke from bitter experience about detention without trial being a most painful form of punishment.

So common did re-arrests happen under the SPMA that prisoners are very reluctant to seek writs of *habeas corpus*. Drug detainees obtaining freedom via *habeas corpus* are often made examples of by the authorities, who routinely reissue two-year detention warrants against them.

Karpal vividly remembered the reaction of one family who had second thoughts about obtaining such a writ for their son for whom he had successfully argued for a court order. 'Oh no, we've won. We're in real trouble now,' was their reaction.

Similarly, the October 1994 day in the Ipoh High Court was going wonderfully well for Karpal and his son Jagdeep when Judicial Commissioner Dato' Kang Hwee Gee spared Manokaran the gallows on a drug trafficking charge. However the tears of joy were short-lived as the man was re-arrested under the SMPA as soon as he walked down the steps of the Ipoh High Court. The sight of a husband, who had just escaped the gallows, being torn apart from his wife was a little too close to home for the father and son legal team as they recalled Karpal's own re-arrest from the same courtroom six years earlier.

Watching people like Kuala Lumpur hotel captain Loh Soon Hwa, mechanics Law Kien Tat and Ngin Seng Fatt, traders Wong Sai Hin and Soo Mau Kok arrested again after being freed by courts made Karpal wonder whether he was in the right profession at times. The trend in Malaysia's war against drugs in the 1990s was to detain prisoners without trial rather than hang them. Little wonder that many times in this situation he felt he just could not win.

One of Malaysia's major problems in endeavouring to clean up its drug problem involves corruption in the police and prison systems. Within the prison system Karpal had noticed, over the years, a few of the very people responsible for caring for death row and mainstream prisoners were happy to make money out of feeding the addiction habits of the inmates.

A death row inmate at Kajang Prison highlighted the problem on 3 November 1995. This man wrote advising Karpal:

I am in danger, facing torture and stabbing from a drug towkay's [Chinese drug boss] bodyguards after I saw a... prison officer handing two pounds of heroin to the drug towkay. I accidentally went to his room when this happened. The towkay warned me if I were to tell anyone what I saw, his bodyguards would stab me. On

1 November 1995 one informer was stabbed and is still in hospital in a serious condition. The officer, too, warned me to shut up. Sir, drugs brought in by officers and warders and sold to death row prisoners are common. I have proof with me to show who the prison drug suppliers are. Before I am hanged I want to expose everything from A to Z on how drugs are brought in and who are the regular suppliers. It is brought in through the main gate by prison staff. I myself have bought from them and I have proof with me to identify the culprits. I do not leave my cell at the moment. Sir, please help me as I am doing this in the nation's interest.

According to Karpal, there was something fundamentally wrong about a system which was capable of executing hundreds of people but did not have the ability to keep drugs out of its own death row cells, in particular.

Spot checks are often made on wardens entering prisons, and those apprehended are mainly dealt with under the SPMA, which allows for detention without trial. On 29 March 1993 a number of prison officers were detained at Pudu Jail for ferrying drugs into a drug-addicted prison population. These people were clearly in a position of being able to capitalise on their captive market as prisoners pay more to feed their drug habits inside prison than they do on the outside.

A major problem affecting the police and prison services is the poor standard of recruitment, allowing entry of riff-raff into the services, and the payment of low salaries. Until these root problems are addressed there will always be serious corruption in both agencies, with policemen confirming that females suspected of drug trafficking are often taken advantage of.

While not wishing arrest upon anybody, Karpal enjoyed his dealings with his foreign clients, most of whom he found to be highly anxious and at the point of breaking down when he first met them. He would try to put them at ease; it was not always easy in the stressful environment of an Asian jail.

Karpal's first appearance at the Privy Council in London was on behalf of two Americans and a Dutchman. The men were detained without trial at the Pulau Jerejak detention centre in 1975 because of their alleged involvement with an international drug ring.

Attempts by fellow lawyers Rasiah Rajasingam, K Kumaraendran and himself to gain freedom for the three foreigners via applications for writs of *habeas corpus* in the Penang High Court failed. The Judicial Committee of the Privy Council declined Karpal's application for special leave to appeal the case. The trip to London on behalf of the three men was not wasted, however, as it gave him valuable insight into the protocol and procedures required in the British Commonwealth's foremost legal tribunal.

Nineteen months later, in December 1978, the Privy Council was to be the scene of one of his most short-lived but satisfying legal victories when it ruled the Essential (Security Cases) Regulations 1975 (ESCAR) were invalid and unconstitutional in the Teh Cheng Poh case.

There have been a number of drug cases coming before Malaysian courts where the accused has been sentenced to a jail term shorter than the remand period for which he or she has already been jailed. But, Karpal said, this 'injustice' could not compare with the fate of some prisoners who have waited in crowded remand cells for up to nine years before finally being acquitted of the charges by the High Court. The question of reimbursement from the government in such cases never arises because a prisoner must prove malicious prosecution against him.

A former captain of an Iranian soccer team Reza Kajabi came to Karpal's attention in 1992 when he was apprehended carrying 202.5 grams of raw opium at Kuala Lumpur International Airport as he prepared to board a flight to Japan. Kajabi was charged with possession of the drug under section 39A of the DDA (under section 39B a trafficker risks the death penalty if apprehended with 1,000 grams or more of raw opium). He was subsequently sentenced to two years jail and three strokes of the *rotan* in 1993 by Magistrate Tay Lee Ly.

Of the six Nigerians (including a woman) who introduced themselves to Karpal in August 1990, three men — Oladotun Lukmanu Umaru, Tunde Apatira and Adekunle Johnson Oshodi —would end up on the gallows.

Umaru was charged with trafficking in 353.2 grams of heroin at 12.05 a.m. at the Butterworth District Hospital in 1990. Like Umaru, Apatira (498.2 grams) and Oshodi (407.5 grams) were also alleged to have been carrying the drugs in their stomach when they were arrested in the early hours of 13 August 1990 at the Butterworth District Hospital.

According to Karpal, there was only one thing more difficult than defending someone found with drugs attached to their body, and that was defending someone who was alleged to have swallowed them.

The one woman member of the Nigerian tour party Fatimu Lolade Lawal was the first to be freed. She was discharged by the Magistrate's Court in Butterworth in 1991 when deputy public prosecutor Zamri Ibrahim told Magistrate Ahmad Azhar Mohamed Kechik he did not wish to pursue the joint charge of trafficking in 130.1 grams of heroin against her.

Olalaken Olatunde Mosuro was found in possession of 9.6 grams of heroin in Butterworth in 1990. He was charged under section 39A of the DDA and freed in 1993 when the prosecution failed to prove the link between two pellets of heroin found in a toilet bowl and the accused.

Olusoga Saidi Oni was charged with trafficking in a massive 2,297 grams of heroin at Penang Jail on 9 November 1990. He was apprehended with the others at Butterworth Railway Station on 12 August 1990. On

12 August 1994 Oni wept and went down on his knees in gratitude before Karpal after Judicial Commissioner T Selventhiranathan freed him on the charge because of a break in the chain of evidence. Oni's major preoccupation in life at that time was to return to Lagos to see his daughter, who was born after he took up residence in Penang Jail.

A seventh Nigerian Michael Anayo Akabogu was also freed in the Penang High Court by Judicial Commissioner Dato' Jeffrey Tan Kok Wha on 10 February 1995, who agreed with the submission that the prosecution had failed to prove its case. Akabogu had been charged with trafficking in 1,074.4 grams of heroin at Penang International Airport in 1990.

In the 1995 Federal Court appeal case of Shukri bin Mohamad, Karpal highlighted an anomaly within the DDA on punishment for cannabis and Indian hemp. Under the Act 'cannabis' and 'cannabis (Indian hemp)' were penalised under different schedules by death and five years imprisonment respectively, even though similar weights were involved. He submitted that in the Shukri case the chemist had not specified whether he was referring to 'cannabis' within the meaning of section two of the DDA (punishable by death) or 'cannabis (Indian hemp)' listed in part three of the first schedule of the Act (punishable by up to five years jail).

The decision of Chief Justice Tan Sri Eusoff Chin in giving Shukri the benefit of the doubt in this case saw approximately 20 other convicted drug traffickers spared the gallows on appeal. Among those whose charges were reduced were Sua'ad Aziz, Mohd Ridzuan Abdullah, Mohd Nidhzam Ahmad, P Veerasamy and Abdul Manab Othman, who were all originally charged with trafficking in cannabis. Karpal prefers not to think of the people who were executed for trafficking in cannabis before he highlighted this particular anomaly in the Shukri case.

In the case of a 28-year-old Iranian Muhammad Khalafi from

Teheran, Karpal took the Shukri decision one step further. Khalafi was sentenced to death for trafficking in 439 grams of raw opium and 925 grams of cannabis resin. He was picked up at Kuala Lumpur International Airport in 1992. Karpal, commenting on chemist Chan Kee Bian's evidence, submitted on appeal a doubt as to the specific provision of the DDA the drugs in the Khalafi case should be classified under. Justice Dato' Faiza Tamby Chik agreed with him and Khalafi, allowing for his good behaviour, was on the next available plane back to Teheran.

Foreigners were not always on the wrong side of the DDA in Malaysia. There were a number of cases in the 1980s when agents employed by the United States Drug Enforcement Agency (USDEA) acted as agent provocateurs and subsequently gave evidence in open court.

The first woman executed in Malaysia on drug charges, coffee shop owner Lim Boey Nooi, was a client of Karpal. She went to the Pudu gallows in 1982 largely on the basis of evidence given in open court by two DEA agents who gave their names as William Feasor and Michael Powers. Also executed along with Lim for the same crime of trafficking in 974 grams of heroin were farmer Chang Liang Seng, noodle-seller Wong Ng Chin and carpenter Leong Teck Kee.

'Mr Feasor' introduced himself as an airline pilot during the negotiations at the Jaya Puri Hotel coffee house in Kuala Lumpur with Wong Ng Chin to purchase the 974 grams for RM80,000. 'Powers' gave evidence of Lim Boey Nooi's role in the crime. Her role was to deliver five packets of heroin to a room in the Jaya Puri Hotel. She was caught red-handed and arrested by Malaysian police waiting in an adjoining room.

In the Pardons Board appeal prepared on behalf of Lim Boey Nooi, Karpal submitted it was morally wrong for a law enforcement officer to provoke a crime and then for the judicial system to execute a person as a result of that provocation.

Police frame-ups have been a recurring theme throughout Karpal's career. He remembers well the case of Penang cake-seller Lim Beo Hean, who was framed for trafficking in 454 grams of heroin and 33 grams of heroin. In acquitting Lim Beo Hean after seven years in jail Sessions Court President Tengku Baharudin Shah Tengku Mahmud observed that the case was one where there seemed to be a 'rotten smell' right from the beginning. The court president accepted Karpal's submission that police had planted the evidence by sprinkling drugs all over Lim's car.

In another 1985 case, a 57-year-old coffee shop waiter Woon Kin Swee was stitched up by a police officer who planted a primed hand grenade on the carrier of his motorcycle. To their credit, prosecuting officers, satisfied that the police grenade was planted on Woon, released him soon after his arrest.

In Woon's and Lim's cases, evidence of a frame-up by police was clear. This could have had deadly consequences for both the accused persons for as far back as 1962, Malayan Chief Justice Tun Sir James Thomson said, "When a police witness says something that is not inherently improbable his evidence must in the first instance be accepted. If he says he saw a cow jumping over the moon his evidence is, of course, not to be accepted, but if he says he saw a cow wandering along one of the main streets of Kuala Lumpur (this sort of thing we all see every day of our lives) there is not the slightest justification for refusing to believe him."

It is one thing for informers and agents provocateurs to deviously fix people up, it is indeed another for police personnel to set people up when mandatory death sentences are applied. To be fair, police do uncover instances where informers endeavour to frame business rivals and enemies.

One of the more contemptible attempted frame-ups by a civilian that Karpal observed occurred when an Ipoh restaurant operator attempted to frame his successful business rivals in 1983. In this case a meticulous police investigation prevented four innocent people from going to prison. The instigator consigned a box containing 5.73 grams of heroin and 2.07 grams of cannabis by bus from Butterworth to the Rashid Restaurant. He anonymously tipped off Ipoh police, who arrested the bus driver, his assistant, a partner in the rival restaurant and a waiter, alleging his business rivals were engaged in trafficking.

When the police got to the bottom of this case the instigator was sentenced to two years jail. Dismissing the Ipoh restaurant operator's appeal Justice Datuk Ajaib Singh said in the High Court, "If not for the good investigations undertaken by the police four innocent people would have ended up in prison for anything from three to 14 years plus the mandatory six strokes of the *rotan*."

Law enforcement officers, informers and agents provocateurs are protected under section 49 of the DDA. Such protection, however, means nothing to the worldwide Chinese underground, and the practice of DEA agents regularly giving evidence in open court had all but died out by the end of the 1980s, reflecting the fact Chinese gangsters are perfectly capable of imposing their own death penalties.

One of Karpal's worst nightmares in a lifetime of legal battles occurred when he and fellow lawyers Rasiah Rajasingam and Jagjit Singh advised lorry driver Oo Leng Swee, mechanic Chon Ah Laik and tractor driver Teoh Weng Hock to plead guilty to a charge of trafficking in 3,441 grams of morphine and 2,880.3 grams of heroin. A plea bargaining deal struck in the Alor Setar High Court on 5 June 1980 resulted in the three men being sentenced to life imprisonment rather than the death penalty.

However, the sentence was appealed by the prosecution, who successfully sought the death penalty for the men on the basis that they also manufactured drugs. In allowing the appeal Lord President Tun Mohamed Suffian Mohd Hashim observed that *dadah* trafficking was an evil and lucrative business and people in the business depended on those who manufactured dangerous drugs. In condemning the trio the Lord President said the trial judge had taken everything into consideration, 'but he did not take into consideration the manufacturing aspect in which the accused were involved'.

Having to explain the repercussions of the successful prosecution appeal decision to the families of Oo Leng Swee, Chon Ah Laik and Teoh Weng Hock was one of the more difficult tasks Karpal faced in his career.

In Karpal's view the worldwide trend towards decriminalising drugs was not the answer for a country like Malaysia, a country still inundated with heroin, cannabis, and raw and refined opium. Malaysia would be committing suicide as a nation if it decriminalised drugs because the drug culture was so deeply rooted into the system, the lawyer said. Until alternative cropping arrangements are put in place in the Golden Triangle, Malaysia will always have a drug problem.

Reflecting the flow of drugs south to Malaysia via Thailand, Thais generally head up the annual drug statistics for the most number of foreigners arrested in Malaysia under the DDA. Over the past three decades Thai drug runners have earned this rather dubious distinction ahead of citizens from such countries as Myanmar, Indonesia and the Philippines.

Karpal's freehold four-storey building in central Kuala Lumpur stands testimony to the fact he was Malaysia's most successful criminal lawyer, and much of his hard-earned money stemmed indirectly from his country's hard-line attitude on drugs. He had no difficulty justifying a living from the back of other people's misery, saying he was quite happy to spend his working life trying to get people out of the mire.

For most people, going through a criminal trial is often the most traumatic experience of their lives. The expressions of gratitude from men and women freed from the jaws of death make it all worthwhile for the lawyers representing them. The archives of Malaysian newspapers contain many pictures of freed prisoners smiling, crying and hugging their lawyer after escaping the gallows on appeal. In these situations, when clients are totally beholden to their lawyer, there could be a temptation to take advantage of a situation.

Karpal did not mince his words when he said lawyers calling themselves professionals who took advantage of their clients in those situations, who used their position of privilege and power to obtain sexual favours from the accused's family, belonged in the gutter. Such people exist. When a person's life is at stake money can and does talk. Senior police officers can be bought but Karpal, who refused to act as a bagman for anybody, knew of a number of cases where families had paid out big money only to find themselves in the position of still having had to collect a body at the end of the court process.

Fortunately for Karpal life as a legal counsel in drug cases was not all doom and gloom, and rewards came in the most unexpected fashion. He especially remembered the time he received a call from Madam He Ken Kiok on the morning of 11 May 1994 to say that her husband Tan Kim Guan was scheduled to be hanged at Kajang Jail the following morning. The distraught Madam He did not need to remind Karpal that her husband was the man who, three years earlier, had elected to take the rope for his wife by pleading guilty to a joint drug trafficking charge.

Karpal felt the woman's grief over the phone and advised the widow-to-be to take her three children to visit their father and not to worry; he would do what he could. While Tan Kim Guan's family were sharing his last meal at Kajang Jail, Karpal was on the fax machine to the Agong and Attorney-General Tan Sri Mohtar Abdullah seeking a stay of execution pending reconsideration of the condemned man's appeal for clemency.

Karpal informed the Agong that Tan had told the High Court his reasons for pleading guilty — that since he was already sentenced to death on another trafficking charge, he had hoped his guilty plea would save his wife from the gallows and he wished to pay the penalty for what he had done. His bravery in the face of death obviously impressed the Agong.

Much to his amazement Karpal received a response from the monarch at about 8:00 p.m. that night advising a stay of execution had been granted. Madam He and her family did not know who to believe when Karpal phoned the Chinese temple where they were praying to advise they could remove their black clothing and temporarily store the coffin already purchased for their husband and father. The following morning Madam He and her family dashed to Kajang Jail to make sure Tan Kim Guan was still alive.

Life continued for Tan Kim Guan on Kajang Jail's death row until January 1995 when official confirmation was received by jail authorities from the Agong's palace that he had indeed been reprieved from the gallows. Tan provided the lawyer with his first official royal pardon on a hanging charge in 25 years of practising law in Malaysia.

Recalling the incident, Karpal shook his head and laughed disbelievingly. "He's my miracle man. It's fantastic actually. I still don't know how he's alive today," the lawyer had said.

The good news for those condemned to death since 2000 is that such royal pardons are now becoming more common in Malaysia.

12 EXECUTION

For those not as fortunate as 'miracle man' Tan Kim Guan, losing a capital punishment appeal for the condemned, in Malaysia in the 20th century, was a terrible moment. The condemned and their families knew there would be little chance of obtaining mercy from state pardons boards and they had to focus on the grim business of dealing with the hanging process.

It's a wonderful feeling, of course, for a lawyer and a client to walk away from the gallows via a successful appeal outcome. But if they all did, former hangmen like one-time Alor Setar prison Superintendent Yusof Bakar would have been out of work a long time ago in Malaysia. For judges, the imposition of the death penalty remains very much a matter-of-fact legal process.

Occasionally, very occasionally, judges do witness some of the gruesome scenes in their courtroom that people, like the retired Yusof

Bakar and his prison staff, were required to deal with on a regular basis. On 21 November 1984 in Penang Federal Court, judges Tun Abdul Hamid Omar, Tan Sri Wan Suleiman and Tan Sri Eusoffe Abdoolcader caught a glimpse of what prison officers have to routinely handle at the end of the final family visit on the eve of a hanging. The judges opted for a ten-minute adjournment after officially advising convicted drug trafficker Seah Teck Chuan that his appeal against the death sentence was unsuccessful. The piercing screams of grief from Seah's mother at the back of the courtroom proved too much for the judges. They retired to their air-conditioned chambers while relatives and friends dragged the distraught mother out of judicial hearing.

Karpal said the condemned themselves very often did not expect a positive outcome from their appeals and were in the main quite resigned to their fate when their appeals were turned down. He did not believe in holding out false hope for his appeal clients. Where there were grounds for optimism, as in the 1995 Federal Court appeal case of Shukri bin Mohamad over the mix-up of 'cannabis' (punishable by death) and 'cannabis hemp' (punishable by up to five years jail), he confidently advised them not to be too concerned.

As the ultimate approached, Karpal dreaded receiving notification from the condemned's family that they had been called for a final meeting with their relative on a specific date. In his dealings with his many condemned clients, Karpal had been surprised to see how they deliberately chose not to address the issue of their own death. All that would change however in the days leading up to the actual execution when the condemned were introduced to their hangman, and their weight and height were measured. At Pudu Jail at about 1:00 p.m. — 17 hours before they were scheduled to be executed — they were ushered into their cells in the *bilik akhir* (last room). From there they were then taken to the prison visiting area for the final visit with their families.

Alor Setar hangman Yusof Bakar told me his approach was to brief the condemned fully on what would happen to them the following dawn at the gallows. If they co-operated, he explained, their necks would snap cleanly between the second and third cervical vertebrae, their spinal cord would be separated from the brain, and death would be instantaneous.

Yusof Bakar says most of the men he executed asked him to go about his work as quickly and as efficiently as possible. They often asked him about the length of the drop, and he would explain to the lighter ones they would fall from seven to eight feet into the pit; to the heavier ones the fall would range from five to seven feet.

Yusof Bakar, who also had responsibility for hangings in Sabah and Sarawak, would go out of his way to be as helpful and as kind as possible to the condemned. He knew the prisoners' co-operation was essential if his work was to proceed smoothly and quickly. Psychologically he wanted them as calm and as co-operative as possible when he arrived at their cell doors early in the morning and cuffed their arms behind their backs.

In Malaysia a doctor, magistrate and senior prison official are required to be in attendance at a hanging, along with the hangman and his assistant. Where possible it is Malaysian prison policy to hang two prisoners together on the same gallows, the theory being that two people going simultaneously to their deaths can offer each other solace and strength.

Generally the families asked Karpal to attend the final visit, as Kevin Barlow's family did, in the hope the lawyer might be able to pull off a miraculous eleventh-hour reprieve. Over the years he had obtained a number of stays of execution, but rarely before the year 2000 did he actually prevent the hangman from going about his work at the Pardons Board clemency stage. Since 2000, there have been more royal pardons given to those previously condemned to death.

For Karpal there was nothing glamorous about the final family meetings where, very often, the condemned person took over the role of comforting his children, spouse, siblings and parents, all through a glass or metal grille barrier. He did not offer his clients any advice on the intensely personal subject of how they should face their inevitable deaths. He left the business of offering advice in this final hopeless situation to family members.

He had seen men and women trying to give their condemned brothers and sisters comfort, strength and support by urging them to be brave on the walk to the gallows trapdoor the following morning. He recalled a number of Chinese men giving their brothers similar advice along such lines: 'When the hangman is going to put you down, don't worry. You be brave. Just think you are going to go to the other side and God will meet you there. Don't cry.'

The lawyer had lost count of the number of times he had had to pick up totally distraught men offering such well-intentioned advice from the floor. The condemned prisoners themselves often try to help out in the final meetings by putting on a show of bravado. Karpal recalled one condemned man lighting a cigarette seeking to offer solace to his father. As he held out the cigarette, the father saw his son's hand shaking uncontrollably.

The worst part of these final visits came when the prison guards announced to the visitors they had to leave. The lawyer had nightmares of screaming Chinese mothers as the final goodbyes took place.

Australians Geoffrey Chambers and Kevin Barlow were allowed physical contact during their final visits with their families in small glassed partitions in Pudu's administration section before their executions. The norm, however, is for an Asian condemned prisoner's family to be seated on a bench in an alcove in front of a thickly barred metal grille in the prison's front compound. The condemned prisoners make their farewells from the other side of the grille while firmly entrenched in the administration building itself. Depending on security risk considerations, the authorities decide whether the condemned prisoner can have direct hand contact with his or her family.

When the family has departed, all that remains for the condemned prisoners when they return to the *bilik akhir* is a final meal and the comfort and solace offered by those who know one day they, too, will have to take the final walk out onto the gallows. In later years KFC washed down with Pepsi was a favourite final meal for many of Karpal's clients.

Karpal never ceased to be amazed at the calm demeanour some of his clients showed in their handling of the ultimate punishment. He remembered, in particular, one outwardly unperturbed Chinese man insisting on making a final financial transaction on the eve of his death.

Prison authorities owed him RM20 in back pay for 66 days work at 30 sen per day and he was adamant on being paid the money personally. Karpal was puzzled as to why the RM20 should have featured so highly on this man's list of priorities considering he had just 14 hours of life left. Nevertheless, he obliged the man by obtaining the money from the prison paymaster and duly handed him two crisp red RM10 bills.

The man then said to his lawyer, "Mr Karpal Singh, look here. I've got RM20 from my prison earnings. Do you think that can be added on to the money the prison is spending for my final meal so I can have a really good meal?"

"He thanked me for it. He told me he didn't want that RM20 to go to waste. That fellow was normal. He was fine. As a Chinese this was just normal commercial stuff which had to be sorted out before he died. His attitude was he was not going to leave his money lying around unaccounted for. Death for him was something he expected from his lifestyle. He took a chance, gambled with his life and lost," Karpal said.

That man went to the gallows well fortified and knowing he had squared the ledger with the prison authorities.

In hangman Yusof Bakar's experience, men and women to be hanged at dawn did not sleep during their final night of life. There were no lights inside the *bilik akhir* cells on Pudu's death row, where the prisoners slept on the concrete floor. Rather, naked light bulbs were mounted outside the seven-bar grilles above the cell doors and shone vertically down on the condemned, enabling prison wardens to maintain a final watch vigil over their charges.

While their peers further down the corridor sang to them in an effort to keep their spirits up, Yusof Bakar recalls the condemned repeatedly asked their warders, 'What's the time? How long have I got?'

At Pudu the *bilik akhir* was separated from the remainder of death row by a solid metal door (covered in roofing iron). This door was generally closed during a hanging so that others awaiting their turn on the gallows could not view the final journey of their fellow condemned brother or sister.

The hangman and his assistant arrive outside the condemned man's cell about five minutes before the scheduled time for execution. The prisoner is handcuffed behind his back and a loose-fitting hood is placed over his head.

In an ideal world, the prisoner co-operated by walking to the large single trapdoor capable of accommodating three people at one time. Once positioned on the trapdoor it was the hangman's job to pull the noose tight under the prisoner's left jawbone. For those whose legs did not have the strength to hold them in their final moments, a small two-legged support would be offered to enable them to rest their bodyweight. The executioner's assistant pinioned the legs and then, following the command from the senior officer, the lever was pulled, plunging the prisoner (or prisoners) to an instant death into the pit below.

The echoes from the sound of the trapdoor opening would reverberate around Pudu, sending shockwaves of terror into the minds of the men and women awaiting their own 6:00 a.m. appointments at the gallows.

The bodies were left hanging for an hour to ensure they were 'hanged from the neck until dead' in keeping with their sentence.

This of course is the ideal-world hanging scenario.

Karpal had heard all the stories about those final moments. When the time came for the final walk some prisoners — just as deposed Iraqi dictator Saddam Hussein did in Baghdad — walked quietly and with dignity to their deaths. Some of his clients, however, had to be carried to the trapdoor and physically held over it until it opened. Others walked to the trapdoor and once there did everything they possibly could to prevent the hangman from placing the noose around their necks. Whichever way they faced death, the result was always the same.

Relatives and lawyers standing outside the Pudu Jail gates waiting for news knew it was all over when a truck, with a body or bodies on the back, droned along the narrow concrete road running around the inside of the prison walls and out through the main gates en route to the Kuala Lumpur Hospital morgue.

Karpal agreed with former Australian Prime Minister Bob Hawke that hanging was barbaric. He knew because he had to help more than 50 mainly condemned men and their families get through the process. It was not easy for anyone involved, including people like Yusof Bakar. The prison service personnel he used to routinely deal with got absolutely no satisfaction out of having to execute a prisoner by hanging, no matter what crime they had committed.

If governments must continue to execute people, Karpal believed there were far more humane ways of going about it than by hanging. While firmly opposing the death penalty, Karpal said the Malaysian

244 KARPAL SINGH: TIGER OF JELUTONG

government, an institution rightly proud of itself for its economic advances, should consider bringing its method of execution in line with its progressive thinking in other areas. Sedation followed by lethal injection was Karpal's answer to doing away with the pain suffered by condemned prisoners and the sometimes grisly strong-man scenes acted out atop the gallows. Karpal argued Malaysian executioners would find their job less distressing if the condemned were first sedated before being fed a lethal cocktail of drugs. While in no way condoning the death penalty this would be a far more humane way of administering the capital punishment penalty.

His strongest argument against the death penalty was the prospect of just one innocent person going to their death. It had not escaped his notice that those on his client list who made it all the way out onto the gallows were very often uneducated people from poor backgrounds. At the end of 2012, Amnesty International estimated there were about 900 prisoners on death row in Malaysia, with most of them having been sentenced to death for drug offences.

At a time when the worldwide trend away from the death penalty was well under way Australian Kevin Barlow proclaimed his innocence to the very end, as did a Penang man, who was one of three condemned in a High Court drug trafficking case.

When he was sentenced to death this Penang man shouted from the dock, "Look here Judge, I didn't do it. I didn't do it."

"Take him away," the judge instructed police and prison guards at the conclusion of the case. This man, too, proclaimed his innocence to the very end. Karpal believed him.

Mandatory death sentences for the possession or control of firearms, murder and drug trafficking certainly solves the individual offender's recidivism problem but, in Karpal's view, have not been a noticeable deterrent.

(*above left*) Toilets inside Pudu Jail's death row; (*above right*) This metallic screen separated prisoners from their loved ones the day before they went to the gallows. Family members sat on the bench while the condemned sat on the other side in Pudu Jail's administration area.

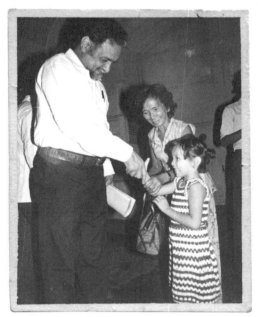

Australian Kevin Barlow's death row cell in Pudu Jail. Barlow and his travelling companion Geoffrey Chambers both went to the gallows on the morning of 7 July 1986.

Karpal on early morning deathwatch vigil outside the main gates of Pudu Jail with a condemned man's sister. *Photo courtesy of* The Star, *Malaysia.*

There is also the toll the death penalty takes on the family of the prisoner to be killed by the state. In Malaysia the lives of the condemned person's family are placed in limbo for ten years — the average length of time the court processes take — and very often parents and siblings can think of little else but the welfare of their loved one as he or she slowly works their way through the legal system.

In a number of his appeals for mercy to various pardons boards Karpal had focused on the length of time his clients spent on death row and the sheer terror they underwent while waiting for years for the 24-hour notice they would receive of the end being nigh.

Concern for the condemned person's family led Karpal to believe Singapore had got it right (at least in the area of the death penalty process) with the High Court, Court of Appeal and execution stages often all completed within a year. In Singapore the dead person's family can then at least get on with their lives.

In all his years of dealing with the condemned Karpal came across just one instance of a condemned person's family abandoning him while awaiting execution.

A tradesman was sentenced to death for shooting in the direction of a policeman while resisting arrest in 1986. He wrote to Karpal in 1998 asking for his assistance to reunify him with his family. 'All I want to do,' he informed the lawyer, 'is to ask my family for forgiveness before I die.' The condemned man's plea fell on deaf ears. When the man's son was contacted by a representative of the Malaysian Chinese Association after his father had been on death row for nine years, the 21-year-old said the family had long ago given the father up for dead. In a surprising statement from a culture where filial piety plays an important part, particularly during Chinese New Year celebrations, the son said there would be no visit to the father at the Sungai Buloh prison by the family, nor would there be any question of forgiveness for him.

The case of the spurned tradesman highlighted for Karpal the torment suffered by men and women who knew for certain they will die on the gallows.

A death row prisoner in Malaysia who lost his or her final appeal before 2000 knew for sure death was just round the corner from the *bilik akhir*. In Karpal's view the condemned were also worse off than the terminally ill for at least, in cases where middle or old age had been reached, a terminally ill person had the satisfaction of knowing they have had the opportunity of living life to the full.

Every so often, however, things happen to restore his faith in human nature. One such instance is the case of two Chinese men on drug trafficking charges. The older man adamantly said to his very much involved younger accomplice, "I'll take the rap. I want you to live. I've had my chance in life. There's no point in both of us dying." The lawyer went out of his way to give the older man months to reflect on his decision and recalled the younger man's disbelieving, grateful and bewildered reaction when the Attorney-General agreed to drop the charges carrying the death penalty against him. Karpal had seen no braver trafficker go to the Pudu gallows.

Over the years Karpal had seen a number of occasions when lives, including Kevin Barlow's, could possibly have been saved by this ultimate gesture of laying down one life for another. But when it came to the basic human instinct for survival Karpal recognised and understood the right of everyone to cling on to the hope of continuing with life.

In five decades of looking for loopholes in capital punishment legislation Karpal had seen enough to know the Malaysian government cannot categorically say it had not executed at least one innocent person. On the other side of the coin he had also represented clients with a death wish whom he has had to talk out of pleading guilty.

Karpal said if the death penalty must continue to have sway in

(*left*) The entrance to the *bilik akhir* in Pudu Jail; (*middle*) the gallows at Pudu Jail; (*right*) after being executed, the bodies of prisoners were taken out of this doorway, loaded on a truck and taken to the morgue.

Malaysia, courts should be given the discretion to choose between the death penalty and life imprisonment in capital cases. In other words, the mandatory death penalty should be substituted with death or life imprisonment and the 'rarest of the rare' principle for the imposition of the death penalty applied.

"It is in the public interest this be so. With the mandatory death penalty, criminals will not hesitate to kill their victims, having regard to the natural instinct of self-preservation, particularly in kidnapping and firearms cases which carry the mandatory death penalty," Karpal said.

He said there were sentences for the duration of natural life under the Arms Act 1960 and the Firearms (Increased Penalties) Act 1971. A sentence of natural life is, in fact, a sentence of living death and criminals coming under this category will not hesitate to kill to avoid arrest and prosecution. Further, said Karpal, those convicted and sentenced to imprisonment for natural life would not hesitate to escape from prison and, in the process, kill prison guards or for that matter anyone else in their way for the simple reason they had nothing to lose except their lives.

Such lives are often regarded as not worth living within the walls of a prison by those sentenced to natural life. Karpal had seen a number of clients become 'irrational' under the pressure of death row. Once they had lost their appeals most of his terrified clients, holding out little hope in their sentence being reduced by a pardons board, want to hang as soon as possible.

Not all executions in Southeast Asia take place on state sanctioned prison gallows. Chinese triad gang members, too, are perfectly capable of conducting their own unofficial executions. The triads have become generally more sophisticated in their approach since the days when they released snakes in restaurants and shops of those who refused to pay them protection money. There was, however, nothing sophisticated regarding the way in which three members of the Sio Sam Ong Secret Society eliminated a bridegroom's brother and five of his friends in the early hours of a wedding day.

Bridegroom Tan Kim Teoh was on top of the world as he and his friends relaxed over a pre-wedding dinner steamboat meal in the compound of his Sungai Petani family home on the night of 15 September 1992. The bridal car had been decorated and festivities were well under way when shortly before midnight, Tan left the group and went to a nearby Chinese temple to offer thanks to his ancestors. He returned one hour later just in time to see two gunmen walk into the compound of his mother's home and shoot dead six of his wedding guests, including younger brother Tan Kim Guan.

The other five people systematically executed via close-range bullet wounds were Chan Chok Veng, Chong Mooi Phang,

A victim lies dead in the case of 'six funerals and a wedding', 1992.

Chew Chine Yee, Ooi Chean Chee and Thong Chee Meng. Bridegroom Tan managed to dodge the bullets and flee to a neighbour's house, where he called the police.

Despite the mass slaughter of friends and family, Tan's sad wedding service continued on 16 September 1992, an event referred to in Sungai Petani as the case of the 'six funerals and a wedding'.

The police inquiry quickly focused on members of the Penang-based Sio Sam Ong Secret Society, Mok On Fook and Chong Peng San, in particular. These two were shot dead by police soon after the Sungai Petani killings, in Butterworth and Penang respectively. Soon after, gang member Cheah Boon Tat and a number of other gang associates fled to Bangkok.

Interpol tracked Cheah Boon Tat down and extradited him to Malaysia in August 1993 where he was detained under the Emergency (Public Order and Prevention of Crime) Ordinance 1969 for alleged involvement in secret society activities.

In December 1995 Cheah, represented by Karpal and his son Jagdeep, escaped the gallows when he was acquitted in the Alor Setar High Court on a charge of murdering the six wedding guests. Judicial Commissioner Datuk KN Segara ruled the defence should not be called. He said the prosecution had produced no positive evidence linking Cheah Boon Tat to the scene of the crimes or the weapons used in the slaughter.

The young man was, however, rearrested for secret society activities and returned to the Simpang Renggam Detention Camp in Johor Bahru. On the question of motive the court heard how Cheah allegedly participated in the shootings because he believed one of the wedding guests had given information to police leading to his arrest, along with six others, on a drug charge in 1989.

Karpal, too, had been involved in cases where police took the law into their own hands and imposed their own death sentences. One such case involved an air-conditioner mechanic. On 12 May 1995 Kuala Lumpur police beat Lim Guat Leong to death while he was under detention at the Police Remand Centre near Batu Caves. Karpal knew about police tactics used at the centre as he had been detained there twice himself in the 1980s under the Internal Security Act. Unpleasant memories of the venue flooded back when Lim's brother, Lim Guat Seong, phoned the lawyer with news of the police killing. The dead man's widow and brother commissioned Karpal to ensure the authorities did not sweep the circumstances of the death under the carpet.

The police killing had its origins during the March 1995 Hari Raya holidays. While most Malaysians were enjoying their holidays, a group of industrious thieves burrowed their way purposefully into the Maybank Finance Company's strongroom in Kuala Lumpur. In a highly successful heist the group known as the 'tunnel rats' made off with RM30 million worth of cash, jewellery and other valuables taken from safe deposit boxes. The pressure came on police from finance and insurance companies to crack this case.

Forty-two-year-old Lim Guat Leong was described as a suspect when police picked him up from his Kuala Lumpur office on 27 April 1995. Police later changed their description of him from 'suspect' to 'witness'.

From the outset of this case Karpal was met with a wall of secrecy and cover-up. Lim Guat Leong's widow Yeoh No Na was informed of her husband's death approximately 24 hours after he died. Kuala Lumpur Police Chief Datuk Ismail Che Rus' initial comment on Lim's death was that no action would be taken against investigating officers, as there was a lack of evidence surrounding the death.

Police urged the family to cremate the body as soon as possible after the autopsy was performed at the Kuala Lumpur University Hospital on the afternoon of 13 May 1995. On Karpal's advice Lim's body remained in the morgue at the centre of a three-week long game of push and shove involving police and family. Yeoh No Na and Lim Guat Seong agreed with Karpal that they would not accept their late husband and brother's body for cremation until they had received a copy of the post-mortem report.

However the hospital declined to make a copy of the report available to the family on the grounds it would infringe the Official Secrets Act. Karpal wanted to know why what was normally a formality, namely the supply of a post-mortem report to the family of a deceased person, should suddenly become shrouded in mystery and intrigue. He advised hospital authorities that if they did not provide the family with a copy of the report he would commence legal proceedings to obtain it. He further advised hospital authorities that if the hospital did not make a copy of its post-mortem report available the family was quite prepared to commission a Singapore pathologist to conduct a second post-mortem. Karpal accused senior policemen of shielding officers 'who had employed third degree methods' on Lim Guat Leong while he was on remand.

On Friday 2 June 1995 the family was finally provided with a copy of the autopsy report. They claimed Lim's body on Sunday 4 June 1995 before cremating him at the Sungai Besi Chinese cemetery. The autopsy revealed the 42-year-old died from internal bleeding caused by violent blows to many parts of his body, including his back, buttocks, hands, ribs and testicles. Numerous kicks, punches and blunt objects had struck him.

The Attorney-General Tan Sri Mohtar Abdullah requested a report from police on the death and on 11 October 1995 he released a statement expressing complete dissatisfaction with the police inquiry into the killing. He ordered a judicial inquiry, as police had declined to identify who had been responsible for Lim Guat Leong's death. The inquiry revealed that the mechanic had been interrogated for 96 hours on one occasion.

At the end of the hearing Judge Jalaludin Saleh found 11 policemen, including Kuala Lumpur's Deputy Head of Criminal Investigations at the time, were criminally involved in Lim's death. The two most junior officers named were prosecuted and sentenced to 18 months jail in 1996 for voluntarily causing hurt. In Karpal's view Lance Corporal P Shanmugam and Lance Corporal Muhari Mohamad Jani were the fall guys. The real culprits were not charged at all, he said.

Lim Guat Leong's brother filed a motion urging the High Court to review the sentence against the two policemen responsible for the death. Following this appeal they were sentenced to three years jail. Justice KC Vohrah described the sentences of the Sessions Court judge as being 'manifestly inadequate'.

Justice Vohrah said the two policemen should have been sentenced to five years jail. They were subsequently sentenced to three years because their service records were good.

In January 1996 the Inspector-General of Police Tan Sri Abdul Rahim Noor made a statement saying police investigations into Lim Guat Leong's death were carried out without fear or favour.

Karpal taking a rest in the Dewan Rakyat, 1986.

13 LEGAL VICTORY

The whitewashed walls of Pudu Jail's Block D, surrounded by barbed-wire and attached to a death row annex, evoked fear in the minds of most Malaysians. This prison is now just another Kuala Lumpur demolished building site hole in the ground waiting for the construction of yet another skyscraper.

But from 1970 to 1993 approximately 180 people died on the gallows there before the more modern Kajang Jail outside Kuala Lumpur took over the gruesome task of looking after the special needs of people sentenced to death. During the same period official statistics reveal 349 people went to their deaths on the gallows of all Malaysian prisons.

Across the road overlooking the jail was the Ibu Pejabat Kontinjen Polis Wilayah Persekutuan — the Kuala Lumpur police contingent headquarters — which still stands. The prison's main gates have been preserved by the bulldozers, presumably to be incorporated in future construction plans for the site.

One man who suffered regular nightmares of having his life snuffed out in the pit of the jail's former century-old British-built hanging chamber was Penang race course worker S Arulpragasan. He was arrested in Butterworth in 1986 and sentenced to death by the Penang High Court in 1992 for trafficking 1,396 grams of cannabis.

When a security guard reported Arulpragasan to the police in 1986, anti-narcotics branch officers swarmed over the truck he and driver Mohamed Kabir were operating. Two bags were found behind the driver's seat. One contained clothing and a bank book in Mohamed Kabir's name, the other contained a bank book in 18-year-old Arulpragasan's name. This second bag also contained a pair of underpants and some green leaves. Upon further analysis the contents of this bag turned out to be the incriminating cannabis. Both Mohamed Kabir and Arulpragasan were detained; Kabir was released soon afterwards.

At his trial Arulpragasan argued he had been set up and the bag with the cannabis in it was not his. When he was condemned to death, after five years on remand in jail waiting for his day in court, Arulpragasan began to take a serious interest in who would handle his death sentence appeal in the Kuala Lumpur Federal Court. He became yet another desperado with no one else to turn to other than the man they call 'boss' on Malaysian death rows.

Karpal, the criminal appeal specialist, was the man many on death row viewed as their last chance throw of the dice of life. If he won he was a saviour; if he failed the condemned could at least take some satisfaction in the knowledge their lawyer would have challenged the law in a way that could potentially benefit their death row colleagues later on.

Arulpragasan and his generally cash-strapped peers agreed that most inmates facing capital punishment were not too fussy about who represented them at the High Court level. Many would be quite content to do things on the cheap at a lower court level. But when it came to Supreme or Federal Court crunch-time appeals, Karpal was the man many of them decided to trust with their lives.

This trust manifested itself in the large pile of appeal files strategically placed on the red carpeted floor of his Kuala Lumpur law library. The court records of the files of murderers and drug traffickers, their hopes, aspirations, judicial and human trials, all ended up on the floor of his library. It remained a system only the lawyer and his filing clerk of 15 years standing, Shafi-In, truly understood. Shafi-In had the ability to put his finger on any file in the four-storey office building when his boss put the pressure on him to find something, no matter how obscure the request might have sounded to others.

When a man or woman's life was on the line Karpal would take their case if they approached him, regardless of their ability to pay. He did not, however, have the time to look after the interests of the poor small-time criminal who would undoubtedly also have benefitted from his services. Those people just had to do their time, as his legal practice

Karpal's long-serving filing clerk in Kuala Lumpur Shafi-In keeps tabs on all the files involving Karpal's many trials and tribulations.

philanthropy was by and large limited to life-and-death situations and people like Anwar Ibrahim who, members of the international community believe, are sometimes prosecuted for political reasons.

Five nights a week the lights regularly did not go out in his Kuala Lumpur and Penang law libraries until 11:00 p.m. The round-the-clock late-night sessions were required to prepare for the following day's court cases. The families of clients whose loved ones found themselves in 'impossible' life-and-death appeal situations regularly flocked to the Jalan Pudu Lama office in Kuala Lumpur for a 5:00 p.m. appointment.

On Sunday nights at 6:00 p.m. in Penang, there was also a similar procession of concerned clients outside his Green Hall office. People sometimes came because they wanted an assessment of the prospects of loved ones on death row.

Arulpragasan's desperate family joined the patient queue of appeal case people wanting to see Karpal for a few minutes at his Penang office in late 1992. He told the family he would take the case if Arulpragasan agreed to help him challenge the law in a particular area he intended to work on. Arulpragasan agreed. It was to be the best decision of his life.

Four years after his release in August 1996 Arulpragasan outlined the thoughts of death row inmates in Penang Jail on lawyers and a life lived on borrowed time.

On death row we all try to keep each other as happy as possible. There is no such thing as seniority among the inmates… there is as far as the authorities are concerned. We all prayed together and we have a common goal.

One thing death row teaches you is there is only one God. We wanted to survive… We discussed lawyers all the time and kept a list in there. Karpal is the best appeal lawyer in Malaysia.

They know he will go all out to save the life of the prisoner. He will do his best for them. Win or lose they are satisfied. Another thing about Karpal, he does not care if you are rich or poor. Even if you have no money, money is not the prime consideration.

To people on death row that is very important. One of the reasons Karpal ends up with a lot of appeals is there are certain lawyers who will not take the appeal unless they have the money up front.

When people lose their appeals they know they are going to die. Some of them come back from the court and curse God.

If you lose your appeal it takes about two years before you are executed. People lose hope in that time. They lose faith.

Whenever anybody left us after losing their appeal to go to Taiping, Pudu or Kajang to be executed we made sure there was very good rapport before they left.

Everybody understood because one day the same thing could happen to them. We all thought about the end but nobody spoke about it.

I used to think I would hang.

Arulpragasan also discovered a god in the Kuala Lumpur Federal Court on 27 July 1996 when his appeal was finalised before the first seven-man bench ever to sit in Malaysia.

The judicial issue the Arulpragasan appeal would clarify once and for all in the minds of the legal fraternity was whether the standard of proof in criminal cases should be '*prima facie*' (on the face of things) or 'beyond reasonable doubt' (requiring a higher standard of proof). For some years in Malaysia there had been confusion with different judges interpreting the law under both standards before making a decision on whether a defendant should be called upon to enter his defence.

In Arulpragasan's case the Federal Court, by a majority of four to three — with Chief Justice Tan Sri Eusoff Chin, Court of Appeal President Tan Sri Lamin Yunos, Federal Court judges Datuk Wan Adnan Ismail and Datuk Edgar Joseph Jr in the majority, and Chief Justice of Malaya Tan Sri Anuar Zainal Abidin, Federal Court judges Justice Tun Mohamed Dzaiddin Abdullah and Justice Mohamed Azmi in the minority — opted for the 'beyond reasonable doubt' scenario.

Accordingly the court quashed Arulpragasan's conviction on the basis that the defence should never have been called at his High Court trial as the prosecution had not proved a 'beyond reasonable doubt' case against him.

After 11 of his best years in jail, four of them on death row, Arulpragasan's handcuffs were removed. He leapt out of court not entirely sure he would continue to live but, at least for the moment, he was free.

Apart from the obvious joy a lawyer feels in saving a client's life, the Arulpragasan decision was special. Karpal was once again at the cutting edge of the law, just as he had been when he argued Teh Cheng Poh's case before the Law Lords of the Privy Council — Lord Diplock, Lord Simon of Glaisdale, Lord Salmon, Lord Edmund-Davies and Lord Keith of Kinkel — back in London in 1978. Eighteen years earlier he had been by himself in London when he won the epic Teh Cheng Poh case. There was deep personal satisfaction in 1996 in having seven judges consider his case. Assisting him with the appeal were sons Jagdeep, Gobind, brother Manjit and long-serving staff member Manoharan Malayalam (a man who would later be called upon to prove his credentials under ISA detention at Kamunting). The decision on Arulpragasan provided a glimmer of hope for many others on death row, just as the Teh Cheng Poh decision had done for the communists 18 years earlier.

History was about to repeat itself as the Criminal Procedure Code Amendment Act, firmly reintroducing the *prima facie* standard of proof, was promptly legislated by the Malaysian parliament. But unlike Teh Cheng Poh, Arulpragasan would live. Teh Cheng Poh's life, of course, ended on the scaffold.

The legislation, introduced to parliament in 1996, was not backdated as it had been when Prime Minister Tun Hussein Onn's government dashed the hopes of death row inmates by backdating the Emergency (Essential Powers) Act in 1979. The case of Arulpragasan, who lived by

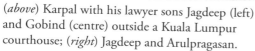

(*above*) Karpal with his lawyer sons Jagdeep (left) and Gobind (centre) outside a Kuala Lumpur courthouse; (*right*) Jagdeep and Arulpragasan.

The decision was 'beyond a reasonable doubt' and as a result, Arulpragasan escaped the noose. He is pictured here thanking Karpal outside the Federal Court on 27 July 1996 (from left to right) lawyer Manoharan Malayalam, Arulpragasan's ecstatic father, the reprieved man himself, Gobind (behind Arulpragasan), onlooker Badrul Zaman, Karpal, Ramkarpal and Jagdeep.

a vote of four to three, would therefore continue to provide some cause for hope among the death row inmates waiting for their own appeals to be heard.

In presenting his argument to the seven-man Federal Court bench, Karpal referred to the 1993 Khoo Hi Chiang appeal case. This appeal case stemmed from two men, Khoo Hi Chiang and Lee Shui Hooi, driving down to Malaysia from Haadyai, Thailand in a car with a modified fuel tank containing 42.23 kilogrammes of raw opium.

The appeal court, comprising Lord President Tun Abdul Hamid Omar, the Chief Justice of Borneo Tan Sri Mohamad Jemuri Serjan, Justice Datuk Edgar Joseph Jr, Justice Tun Eusoff Chin and Justice Tun Mohamed Dzaiddin Abdullah, upheld the death penalty against the two men.

But the court also agreed with Karpal's submission that the High Court judge had erred in applying the wrong standard of proof test by calling for the defence at the end of the prosecution case. The judge had applied Lord Diplock's Privy Council minimum evaluation *prima facie* test introduced to Malaysia in 1981 via the Singapore Haw Tua Tau case. On 24 December 1993 the five-man Malaysian Supreme Court bench ruled the judge should have applied the more stringent 'beyond reasonable doubt' test.

The bad news ('operation successful, patient still dies') for appellants Khoo Hi Chiang and Lee Shui Hooi was that the Kuala Lumpur Supreme Court also decided that no matter which test the judge applied at the end of their prosecution case, the result would have been the same — the two men would have been called upon to make their defence.

They left the court with handcuffs on and very much gallows-bound. Having obtained the required standard of proof change in Malaysia, Karpal turned his attention towards challenging Lord Diplock's Haw Tua Tau *prima facie* guideline decision in the Singapore Court of Appeal.

Before doing so, however, he needed an appellant prepared to act as a human guinea pig who would allow him to mount the challenge in Singapore's Court of Appeal.

There was no shortage of subject matter to work with and the lawyer's Singapore challenge had its origins in a shootout between two Chinese gangsters, Lee Kok Chin and Ng Theng Shuang from Penang, and a Sikh security guard. On 19 November 1992 the two Chinese men, brandishing pistols, ran into the Tin Sing Goldsmiths Shop on South Bridge Road in Singapore. One of them warned the security guard Karamjit Singh, "Don't shoot or I will shoot you."

Ignoring the warning, Karamjit began removing his Smith & Wesson pistol from its holster and was shot in the right thigh by one of the gangsters. Despite the wound the security guard returned fire before diving behind a counter to take cover. When one of the gangsters approached him, Karamjit fired again, prompting another volley of gunfire from the armed robbers, whereupon the two men dashed out of the shop and jumped on their motorcycle.

The wounded security guard followed them out of the shop and there was a third exchange of gunfire as the crash-helmeted robbers rode off. During this exchange Karamjit shot rider Lee Kok Chin dead with a bullet through the heart. Pillion rider Ng Theng Shuang, who would eventually become Karpal's appellant, in turn shot Karamjit in his right ankle. With bullet wounds in his thigh and ankle Karamjit was in no position to continue the chase.

Ng Theng Shuang then commandeered a car and made good his escape, leaving behind his dead partner

An inauspicious beginning to an appeal case in Singapore. Lee Kok Chin lies dead on a Singapore street after being shot by Sikh security guard Karamjit Singh.

in crime and the motorcycle on the footpath not far from the scene of the attempted armed robbery.

Besides Karamjit, jewellery shop salesman Ou Kai San was wounded in the hold-up. He was shot in the chest, the bullet lodging in his neck. Like security guard Karamjit, described by some onlookers as very brave for his relentless undertaking of the counter-attack against the two Chinese, Ou Kai San made a full recovery following an operation at the Singapore General Hospital.

A year after the hold-up Ng Theng Shuang was arrested by Malaysian police on 23 November 1993 on minor offences and handed over to the Singapore police in Penang on 29 December 1993. Ng then faced three charges, under Singapore's Arms Act, of shooting Karamjit, shooting Ou Kai San and armed robbery of a station wagon.

Shooting charges in Singapore carry a mandatory death penalty and Ng Theng Shuang's case highlights a significant difference in the handling of capital punishment offences between Malaysia and Singapore. Ng was convicted on the three charges by the Singapore High Court on 15 September 1994, lost the appeal on 4 March 1995 and went to the gallows at Changi Prison in August 1995.

In Malaysia an average defendant can expect to live for at least five years from the time of their High Court condemnation and most would have already been in jail for five years before their case gets to the High Court. In Singapore, if a defendant facing the death penalty is found guilty in the High Court and loses in the Court of Appeal the execution generally takes place about nine months after the High Court conviction.

To Karpal the Singapore system of quick-marching condemned prisoners to the gallows is far more humane than the Malaysian system, which puts the lives of the accused and their loved ones on hold for a decade while going through the drawn-out legal processes.

The fingerprint and videotape evidence against Ng Theng Shuang linking him to the shootout and the getaway station wagon was damning. Karpal had little difficulty in persuading Ng to mount a points-of-law challenge to the High Court decision. Put simply, he was already a dead man on the facts of the case.

Singapore's Chief Justice Yong Pung How was unimpressed by the challenge to the prosecution's standard of proof. In his view the five-member bench of the Malaysian Supreme Court laid emphasis on the words 'would warrant a conviction' as outlined in section 189 of Malaysia's Criminal Procedure Code.

Justice Yong Pung How said his Malaysian counterparts had ignored the crucial words 'if unrebutted' in dealing with the procedure to be followed at the close of the prosecution case. Referring to Ng Theng Shuang's specific appeal on the standard of proof he sent the appellant to the gallows with the following words: 'From an evaluation of the evidence adduced by the prosecution, there was a *prima facie* case made out against the appellant on each of the charges. The trial judge had correctly called on the appellant to enter on his defence.'

Karpal's legal sortie in Singapore and his endeavours to evoke change in the legal arena there ended with this standard of proof appeal.

In the range of emotions Karpal experienced on a regular basis, the joy of a client who escaped the gallows on appeal was professionally most encouraging and rewarding. It is quite common for people reprieved from the gallows on appeal to shed a tear and just sit in the dock, absolutely dumbfounded. Initially many of them are unable to come to grips with their newfound freedom, particularly if they have been in jail for ten years or more. One man who had initial difficulty believing he was free was Sierra Leone national Akpojotor Usman Oscar, who was the last defendant facing the death penalty to have his case heard under the Arulpragasan 'beyond reasonable doubt' standard of proof in Malaysia.

Before Oscar's Alor Setar High Court trial began in 1996 Karpal had unsuccessfully approached the Attorney-General's office seeking a reduction in the charge against his client from trafficking in 487.67 grams of heroin to possession. He also suggested, in the incriminating knowledge that the heroin was found in Oscar's shoes, ten strokes of the *rotan* be thrown in for good measure on top of a 15-year jail term. After explaining his pre-trial position to Oscar, Karpal later had the unfortunate task of advising him the Attorney-General wanted his client's neck. There would be no deal.

Before the trial the lawyer and his client could not have known the prosecution would make it easy for them, for the police told the court they sent 'slabs of heroin to the chemist' who, in turn, later described the substance he received and analysed as 'powder'.

At the end of the prosecution case Justice Datuk KN Segara acquitted and discharged Oscar on the 'beyond reasonable doubt' Federal Court Arulpragasan grounds of there being no prosecution case to answer. The lawyer was almost as surprised as his client by the development.

Oscar understandably expected to hang going into the trial, after the best-case deal scenario explained to him by his lawyer — 15 years plus a ten-stroke whipping — was rejected by the Attorney-General's office. The last place Oscar expected to be on the evening of Sunday 15 December 1996 was sitting in an Alor Setar restaurant as a free man having a celebratory drink with his lawyer.

Foreigners gaining freedom in the unexpected fashion of the Sierra Leonean Oscar have the additional problem of getting their passport returned from the authorities. Many in this situation do not want to run the risk of being re-arrested under the Dangerous Drugs (Special Preventive Measures) Act 1985 by going back to the prison to collect their passports and personal possessions. Instead, in a culture where money can generally buy anything, they purchase a false passport and catch a bus out of the country as soon as they possibly can. Karpal did not advocate nor condone this type of behaviour but he understood why many of his clients, with their necks still very much on the block, resorted to it.

The Arulpragasan decision also indirectly saw two Turkish men with links to the anti-Israeli Hezbollah Islamic movement escape the gallows in an intriguing 1996 case. When Kocaslan Hidayet, a then 24-year-old Hezbollah member, appeared in the Tapah Magistrate's Court in August 1994 he didn't do himself any favours when he repeatedly told the court, 'Allah Hu Akbar, Allah Hu Akbar (God is great, God is great), I chop head, he not guilty.'

Hidayet had been charged with murdering 'retired Canadian Air Force Colonel John Gately' on 12 February 1994 at the Perak township of Tapah, a township well known to tourists travelling on the road to Cameron Highlands. Charged alongside him was fellow Turk Olmez Orhan, who was represented by Karpal. Surjan Singh Sidhu represented Hidayet in the preliminary stages of the case.

The early defence strategy involved getting Orhan freed on the basis that there was no point in two men going to the gallows for a crime when one was quite prepared to hang for it. Hidayet created a lower courtroom sensation by telling Magistrate Yaacub bin Haji Chik he had been 'commanded by God' to decapitate Gately.

According to Hidayet, Gately was not a retired Canadian Air Force colonel at all. In between exclamations of 'Allah Hu Akbar' he told the court Gately had been an Israeli general in a former life. Gately's dental records tabled in court, beginning in Vancouver in 1981 as a 56-year-old, lent some credibility to what the Hezbollah man was saying.

Given he represented the other defendant Orhan at the preliminary court hearing stage, it suited Karpal for Hidayet to be making self-incriminating comments. It prompted the lawyer to write to the Attorney-General's office suggesting the charge against Orhan be dropped on the basis of Hidayet's very public confession. But when the Attorney-General responded saying both men were to face trial, and Hidayet subsequently approached Karpal to take on a joint defence, the lawyer found himself with a problem.

Orhan had been well known to Karpal in a previous existence when he passed himself off as a Mr Hacoglu. The lawyer had defended 'Mr Hacoglu' in 1987 and prevented him from being extradited to Turkey, where he was wanted by Turkish authorities following a jail escape there. When the Kuala Lumpur High Court set 'Mr Hacoglu' free on Wednesday 1 July 1987, saying he was not the criminal Turkish authorities thought he was, the Turk promptly disappeared from Karpal's life via Thailand's black-market passport sanitation department. Before leaving the country for Australia, 'Mr Hacoglu' informed his lawyer he was mightily impressed by the Malaysian justice system. The good news was he would be back with his family 'maybe in five years' time or so'. True to his word, although two years behind schedule, 'Mr Hacoglu' called in unannounced at Karpal's Kuala Lumpur office one day in early 1994 for no particular reason, inquiring after his health and extending best wishes.

So it came as no real surprise when a man now officially identified as Olmez Orhan contacted Karpal from Pudu Jail in mid-1994 asking whether it might be convenient for the lawyer to pay him the courtesy of a prison visit. In prison, following the preliminary Magistrate's Court hearing of the murder of 'retired Canadian Colonel John Gately', Orhan obviously had an opportunity to brief his very committed Hezbollah friend Kocaslan Hidayet on what his lawyer had been able to achieve on 'Mr Hacoglu's' behalf in 1987.

It was no surprise Orhan called his lawyer 'Sir Karpal Singh'. He viewed him as a miracle worker. Well he might for when the one-time 'Mr Hacoglu' appeared in court in Malaysia in 1994, Interpol was still on the lookout for one Olmez Orhan, a man who had escaped from Ankara Prison on 30 April 1979 while serving a life sentence for murder. In Pudu Jail the two Turks agreed it would be in their best interests to be jointly represented by the man they referred to as 'father'.

When the case went to trial at the Ipoh High Court in October 1996 'father', however, had a problem on his hands — namely how was he to expunge the memory of Kocaslan Hidayet's much publicised words 'Allah Hu Akbar, Allah Hu Akbar. I chop head, he not guilty' from the minds of Justice Datuk Pajan Singh Gill and one of the last juries to sit at a Malaysian criminal trial.

Going into this trial, with his two sons Gobind and Jagdeep assisting him, Karpal knew all was not lost by any means. This was evident early on in the trial when Hidayet's 'I chop head' statement was ruled inadmissable in preliminary trial proceedings. The court heard how Gately's headless body had been found with both hands stretched out in a pool of blood approximately 30 metres from a Tapah cowshed. Following a police interrogation, Orhan had no trouble leading police to the victim's head after his arrest.

A number of prosecution witnesses also provided evidence that they had seen the Turks travelling in a Proton car with the victim — bloodstains had been found in the car hired by Orhan, the victim had been strangled before being decapitated, and the three men had earlier checked into a hotel together before the Turks checked out hurriedly one morning in 'the manner of criminals running away from the scene of a crime'.

At the end of the ten-day prosecution case Justice Gill dropped a bombshell when he agreed with Karpal's submission that the Turks did not have a case to answer. He decided the prosecution had not provided evidence to link the victim's death to the Turks.

Justice Gill said, "At most, the accused and the deceased were together in Penang, Kuala Lumpur and the Cameron Highlands prior to Gately's death. This evidence is insufficient to prove the accused caused the death." The judge said the prosecution had not presented a 'beyond reasonable doubt' case in line with a standard of proof precedent in the Arulpragasan 27 July 1996 drug trafficking Federal Court appeal decision.

When the trial's sudden and unexpected end was fully explained to the Turks, Hidayet asked incredulously, "Does this mean we not guilty?"

Karpal explained he was a free man after the jury followed the judge's direction to free them. Outside the court there were more cries of 'Allah Hu Akbar' from Hidayet. Orhan kissed the hand of the man who had been instrumental in 'miraculously' obtaining his freedom for a second time.

While in no way condoning his actions, Karpal nevertheless respected Hidayet's honesty. Hidayet admitted he had killed a man, earlier told the Magistrate's Court exactly why he did it, fully expected to hang for a deed he was proud to have committed, and was completely puzzled as to how he could so suddenly find himself acquitted. As the lawyer and his freed clients went their separate ways Hidayet was still saying to anyone prepared to listen, 'I kill Israeli general… because he kill our people. I chop off head.'

Olmez Orhan did not seem to be quite as puzzled by it all as Hidayet. He'd seen Karpal in action before and once again expressed public gratitude to the Malaysian legal system. Before his departure from Malaysia, Orhan presented Karpal with a poignant wooden plaque. On it were inscribed the words: 'Truth is like surgery, it may hurt, but it cures. Sincerity is the best policy.' When he received this gift Karpal wondered about John Gately's family. He felt deeply for them and understood perfectly why none of them attended the trial or publicly came to Malaysia to check on the circumstances surrounding the death.

Karpal realised 'John Gately' must have been quite a man to have earned a place on the Hezbollah hit list. Was 'John Gately' really an Israeli officer, he wondered, or could this have been a case of mistaken identity? He did not expect the Mossad to clarify this for him during his lifetime.

While he was happy for his Turkish clients, Karpal did not take any special personal credit for the not-guilty decision. He realised there may have been political overtones to this case and knew it would be politically very difficult for Malaysia to hang two self-professed Hezbollah members for killing a man they claimed to be a former Israeli general.

Another bizarre case, this time bordering on insanity, came along in 1977 and involved a 15-year-old Chinese youngster. The teenager summarily executed four Indian men — Ganapatukairi, Sommunaidu, Jaganathan and Apparao — at the Chong Wing Chan Estate in Rompin. The youth was driving through the estate on his motorcycle when he accidentally ran over and killed a chicken crossing the road. The four Indian men came out of a nearby house and remonstrated with the teen for killing the chicken.

The youngster was unable to provide Karpal with a logical reason why he shot the four men. "I told them if the chicken is dead you may as well join him. So I shot them dead," the youth told his lawyer.

The youth's age — he was a juvenile at the time of the murders — prevented him from being sent to the gallows. He was found guilty of the four murders by the Seremban High Court and detained at the pleasure of the State Ruler in Council.

The case which played a significant part in placing Karpal on the road to a career in national politics was that of a 13-year-old boy, the most unlikely person Karpal had ever defended on a capital punishment charge. Lim Hang Seoh was the client who also had the most impact on Karpal's own professional life. Lim was a schoolboy aged 13 years and 11 months when he was arrested in Penang on 14 February 1977 for possession of a Browning pistol and 20 rounds of .25 ammunition.

During his visits to Penang Jail before Lim's August 1977 High Court trial, Karpal found difficulty understanding the rationale of a system capable of imprisoning a schoolboy among hardened criminals. It also irked him that the same system should seek the death penalty against one so young for possession of a small pistol and ammunition.

It did not help Karpal, too, that the kid made him laugh every time he visited the boy in jail.

"Hey, Tuan [Sir], did you bring me some food? Have you got me some chocolates? Why is there no play area in here?" the boy would invariably ask his lawyer.

He would look at Lim and smile, thinking, 'What sort of a creature is this? Give me a big creature any day. He's a naughty boy! Nobody hangs naughty boys, do they?'

The lawyer recalled the boy did not want to know about the issues of the case. All he was concerned about was chocolates, so Karpal made sure he was well protected, fed and cared for within the jail.

The jailers also took special care of the youngster. The word went out among the Chinese gangsters in the jail that anyone who laid so much as a finger on this boy would be better off dead. Some among the gangsters too had teenage sons themselves and they looked out for Lim with fatherly concern. In sum Lim was having a charmed life in jail.

Lim's imprisonment among an adult male population was a consequence of the Juvenile Courts Act 1947 being subservient to the Essential (Security Cases) Regulations 1975 (ESCAR).

Karpal urged the authorities to place the boy in the Henry Gurney Boys Home near Malacca, but they would not hear of it. He was kept in jail on the official line that a 13-year-old boy who could run around Penang with a pistol and ammunition in his pocket could also take his chances along with the other gallows-bound alleged ESCAR offenders.

The boy's Penang High Court trial — the first in Malaysian history where a juvenile was charged under the ISA — was presided over by Justice Fred Arulanandom. In his defence Karpal submitted on Lim Hang Seoh's behalf that the boy was given a sum of money by a gangster to keep a plastic bag. The gangster threatened to beat him if he opened the bag. The boy maintained he was totally unaware of the contents of the bag.

Justice Arulanandom said he was satisfied beyond any doubt that the boy knew he was carrying a pistol and ammunition. Anyone harbouring doubts about the determination of the authorities to wipe out communism in Malaysia had them removed by the court's decision to sentence Lim Hang Seoh to death.

In his decision the judge said, "In the eyes of the law, if a person is charged under the ISA and tried under the ESCAR there is no difference between a juvenile and an adult. This is one thing which this trial should prove to society, especially to those under the age of 18 who may feel that they are still privileged and will receive a different type of treatment from adults."

In passing sentence on 25 August 1977 Justice Arulanandom put on a black cap and said to Lim, "You are hereby sentenced to death. You will now be taken to a place of hanging where you will be detained and then hanged by the neck until you are dead."

The boy grabbed hold of Karpal's gown and pulled it saying, "That man, he said, he said they are going to hang me!"

Karpal responded as reassuringly as he could, "Nobody is going to hang you, boy. You don't worry. You take it easy." In reality he was not so sure.

Meanwhile, the youngster was taken back to Penang Jail where he was given his own cell among the big boys on death row. The other condemned Chinese gangsters, in particular, were not happy to have him in their midst. "What's he doing here with us? It's like having our son in here with us. Are they mad enough to hang a mere boy?" the big-time criminals domiciled alongside the boy asked.

Lim Hang Seoh's case received front-page nationwide publicity, particularly during his Federal Court appeal on 4 October 1977 heard by Lord President Tun Mohamed Suffian, Chief Justice Tan Sri Sarwan Singh Gill and Justice Tan Sri Datuk Michael Chang Min Tat.

In his submissions to the Federal Court Karpal said Justice Arulanandom should have placed himself in the boy's position when considering the circumstances of the case and not apply the test of a reasonable man on a 13-year-old boy. Furthermore no fingerprint evidence showing Lim had actually touched the gun or the ammunition was placed before the court.

The learned judges dismissed the appeal. Karpal could not believe he was responsible for the life of a by then 14-year-old boy who was well and truly on the road to the gallows.

While Malaysia's Chinese population was prepared to give the judiciary the benefit of the doubt that a genuine mistake had been made at the High Court level, they expected common sense to prevail in the Federal Court, and when it did not, there was talk of race riots far worse than that of 1969 if the government executed the young fellow.

Karpal proceeded with plans to appeal the case to the Privy Council, where he appeared six times in his career, while helping to coordinate a nationwide campaign securing support for Lim's right to life. This campaign, initiated by the DAP, had universal support from the Malaysian population, reflecting a mood of total opposition to the Federal Court's decision. Approximately 100,000 signatures were collected.

The campaign sparked national outrage against the government. Parents by the hundreds stopped Karpal on the streets of Penang expressing their horror at the thought of a 14-year-old being executed by the state. Everywhere he went there was sympathy for the boy, even from the nation's number one executioner of the day. The lawyer knew the support for Lim Hang Seoh was there, but he could not afford to take any chances.

Lim Hang Seoh, pictured here after losing his Federal Court appeal under the ESCAR. At the eleventh hour the Agong commuted Lim's sentence of death to one of detention.

"Everybody has a 14-year-old boy in the house. They looked at their own sons and they thought, how can they do this? They all thought, my God, they're going to hang my son. I'm not going to let them do it.

"I knew this but on the other hand I could not take a chance. I had to organise the appeal to the Privy Council. The boy was going to be my Teh Cheng Poh and if the boy's case had made it to the Privy Council, Malaysia would have been the laughing stock of the world," Karpal said.

His national signature campaign even received backing from the influential Malaysian Chinese Association (MCA) and the national groundswell of support for the boy from the leaders of all communities eventually made the Malaysian government see sense.

On 6 October 1977 Attorney-General Tan Sri Abdul Kadir Yusof issued a statement saying he would ask the Pardons Board to exonerate Lim. The youngster's death sentence was eventually commuted and he was transferred to the Henry Gurney Boys Home outside Malacca where he was detained till age 21.

This political/legal campaign, fusing all of the lawyer's skills, would be just one of many in Karpal's career resulting in the saving of a life.

Heaven would have to wait for Lim Hang Seoh and hundreds of others like him whose lives Karpal has extended.

During the 1978 federal election campaign for the Jelutong seat Karpal's political opponents would often pass disparaging remarks about a Sikh daring to put himself forward in a Chinese-dominated electorate. But the Jelutong voters recognised it took special fighting skills to save Chinese youngsters, particularly Lim Hang Seoh, from the gallows. The people of Jelutong sent him to parliament for the next 21 years, where he pushed their causes to the limit as an opposition party legislator.

Since 2004 he had been the MP for Bukit Gelugor, Penang. After decades in parliament representing the people of Jelutong and Bukit Gelugor, he still viewed himself more as a lawyer than a politician.

14 ANWAR

Datuk Seri Anwar Ibrahim is a man very much at home in the palatial Islamic-domed Jalan Duta courthouse building in Kuala Lumpur. The former finance minister and deputy prime minister has spent a lot of time in docks and prisons over the past 15 years after having been charged on a number of energy-sapping cases since 1998. The three most significant cases against him involved a corruption case which began in September 1998 and two sensational sodomy cases, the first in 1998 and the second in 2008.

In 1998 Anwar was viewed widely as the heir apparent to Prime Minister Dr Mahathir Mohamad's leadership in the top job with the 1999 election looming. Instead he found himself dismissed from his job by Dr Mahathir on 5 September 1998. He was arrested and incarcerated two weeks later, on the night of 20 September, when approximately 200 security police forced their way into his plush home. At the time of the arrest Anwar held differing views on how Malaysia should react to the Asian financial crisis from others operating at the top of the UMNO totem pole. He was initially detained under the ISA, but on 29 September 1998 he was charged with four counts of corruption and with committing sodomy against his former driver Azizan Abu Bakar.

The corruption charges against Anwar focused on an allegation that he had misused his position as deputy prime minister. The charges alleged he had sought assistance from police officers to get a written admission from Azizan in August 1997 that he (Azizan) had not been sexually abused and sodomised. The star prosecution witness in the first sodomy case was none other than Azizan himself.

Karpal first became aware of the problems Anwar was facing within the ruling Barisan Nasional in unusual circumstances in August 1997. An obviously agitated man and woman, Azizan Abu Bakar and Ummi Hafilda Ali, accompanied by a small group of supporters, entered the swinging glass front door of his Kuala Lumpur office building. The lawyer's long-serving chief clerk George Fernandez greeted them in his usual genial fashion and proceeded to ask all of them to take a seat in the ground floor front office waiting area. But Azizan and Ummi Hafilda insisted on meeting Karpal promptly so Fernandez ushered them up two flights of stairs into the red-carpeted security of the lawyer-politician's office.

Karpal's first reaction was to ask the question he often asked people on their first meeting. "Well, what's the problem?" This was one of those rare occasions when their replies stunned him.

Azizan identified himself as Anwar's former driver while Ummi Hafilda explained she was a relative of Anwar's former private secretary. Karpal heard the same remarkably frank alleged 'sexual misconduct and sodomy' story, which would be put before the High Court during Anwar's corruption trial from November 1998 to April 1999. Azizan alleged Anwar had sodomised him, while Ummi Hafilda alleged a close female relative was having an affair with the high-flying politician. They told Karpal that in mid-1997 they had written to Dr Mahathir, outlining their allegations against Anwar.

They apparently visited Karpal's office because they feared for their personal safety although Azizan later told the High Court on 3 December 1998 that he and Ummi Hafilda went to Karpal for advice because they felt they could trust him.

Armed with this political dynamite, Karpal was in one of those classic 'what to do?' situations which confronted him from time to time.

On 22 October 1997, while speaking in Parliament as an opposition MP, he urged the Government to investigate allegations of sodomy against Anwar as a matter of public interest. His comments at the time were ridiculed by UMNO politicians, who leapt to Anwar's defence.

In the first sodomy trial Karpal initially represented Sukma Darmawan Sasmitaat Madja, who was jointly charged with Anwar, for an offence of sodomy against Azizan.

"It was in the course of the trial that I was invited by Anwar to join his defence team, which I did. Sukma was, thereafter, represented by my sons Jagdeep and Gobind. The fact Anwar wanted me to be his defence counsel, despite my position against him when he was in government, clearly shows he had confidence in me to effectively represent him," Karpal said.

By the time Azizan gave his evidence, Karpal was working with defence lawyers Raja Aziz Addruse, Christopher Fernando and Sankara Nair. Karpal was subsequently accused of being a 'snake' by his political opponents for agreeing to represent Anwar in the two sodomy trials following the meeting with Ummi Hafilda and Azizan in his office in 1997. He responded to the criticism by saying he met with them in his capacity as a politician, not as a lawyer.

At the end of the trial, Anwar was found guilty of corruption and sentenced to six years in jail on 14 April 1999.

In a second High Court trial in August 2000, again largely on the basis of Azizan's evidence, Anwar was convicted of sodomy in connection with a 1993 incident. He was sentenced to a further nine years jail on 8 August 2000. Anwar, with Karpal advocating on his behalf, was subsequently released from the massive Sungai Buloh prison outside Kuala Lumpur on 2 September 2004 after successfully appealing against his sodomy conviction. The release came when the Federal Court overturned the sodomy conviction 11 months after Abdullah Badawi succeeded Dr Mahathir as Malaysia's prime minister.

When Anwar was released in 2004 after six years in jail (the corruption conviction ran concurrently with the sodomy conviction), Karpal was asked about the quality of evidence that led to Anwar's incarceration on the sodomy charges. He declined to comment other than to refer to the judgement, which said prosecution evidence had not been believed as the Federal Court found there had been contradictory dates for the alleged sodomy activities in different statements placed before the court.

During the sodomy trial Karpal clashed with Justice Datuk Arifin Jaka over an attempt to subpoena Dr Mahathir as a witness. When the judge asked why the prime minister should be called, the lawyer replied that the issue was a matter between the defence and Dr Mahathir. He told the judge that Dr Mahathir was at liberty to apply to set aside the subpoena served on him. Karpal then asked the judge whether he was afraid of the prime minister. The judge requested Karpal repeat what he had said and added that he would record it as it amounted to contempt of court.

"I repeated every word I had uttered, which he recorded. Judge Arifin Jaka then asked me to withdraw what I had said and he would let matters rest, otherwise he would hold me for contempt of court.

I retorted that I stood by what I had said... I do not utter words for the sake of withdrawing them later," Karpal said.

As part of his role in the Anwar defence team during the corruption and first sodomy trial, Karpal also represented Anwar on the Royal Commission of Inquiry into his beating at the hands of Malaysia's Inspector General of Police Tan Sri Abdul Rahim Noor while in the national police headquarters lockup. Anwar had appeared in court with a black eye about a week after his arrest, prompting outrage among his supporters and the public. In his submissions to the Royal Commission, Karpal said Abdul Rahim should have been charged with Anwar's attempted murder. Mike Tyson (the former world heavyweight boxing champ) himself would have been proud of the job done on Anwar, the lawyer said.

In the build-up to the inquiry, Karpal had occasion to reflect that not a lot had changed in interrogation methods designed to exact confessions from suspects in Malaysia since 1972. In that year he had successfully conducted his first murder case defence, on behalf of three of seven defendants, who were all charged with the Kedah murder and armed robbery of Haji Ismail bin Haji Mahidin. The evidence in that case revealed that the defendants were forced to sit on large blocks of ice, beneath air-conditioners, while being routinely beaten and having cold water poured over them by investigating police officers. Until recent times Malaysians had reluctantly accepted such behaviour as being a normal part of police methods, but a younger more sophisticated generation of Malaysians is no longer prepared to put up with police methods akin to medieval brutality. There is an increasing number of cases coming before the courts where Malaysians are showing they will not tolerate suspects being battered and bludgeoned by police while in custody. Karpal said the bashing and sometimes killing of people — like Kuala Lumpur truck driver N Dharmendran who was found dead in his cell in May 2013 — while under police interrogation happened far too frequently in Malaysia.

Former IGP Abdul Rahim — described as a 'gangster' by Karpal during a supplementary budget debate in parliament in April 1996 — resigned his position in 1999 after acknowledging that he had indeed assaulted Anwar during a visit to the latter's prison cell. At the time of the attack, Anwar was both handcuffed and blindfolded. Abdul Rahim told the official inquiry that he was provoked into lashing out at Anwar, who allegedly described him as '*ni bapak anjing*' (the father of dogs). Anwar denied ever having made such a statement and the Royal Commission found, based on the evidence put before it, that there was no provocation at all from Anwar. The Royal Commission also heard in detail how another policeman in the lockup cell area at the time, CID Director Datuk Yaacob Mohd Amin, physically restrained his boss' sustained attack upon the defenceless Anwar by pulling the former IGP out of the cell by the belt of his trousers.

The Royal Commission found that the IGP had moved 'single-mindedly from his office on the 30th floor to cell number six (on the ground floor)... where he paused while subordinates carried out his sign instructions to both handcuff and blindfold Datuk Seri Anwar... he then moved straight from the grille door to the cell and assaulted Anwar immediately after he entered the cell. ... It must follow that this was a premeditated assault and that the intention was there ... from the time... Abdul Rahim commenced his journey from the 30th floor to cell number six,' the commission in part stated.

It found Abdul Rahim solely responsible for the police attack upon Anwar and for the additional pain caused to him during the period of 20 to 24 September 1998 when medical treatment was denied to him. Abdul Rahim was subsequently charged with attempting to cause grievous hurt to Anwar.

There were two other legal sequels to the infamous Anwar black-eye incident. The former police chief Abdul Rahim was jailed for two months after pleading guilty to an assault charge on Anwar at the Kuala Lumpur Sessions Court on 15 March 2000. In August 2005 he apologised to Anwar and paid an undisclosed sum in damages for the beating he gave him.

Anwar was able to return as leader of the parliamentary opposition in 2008, winning back his Permatang Pauh parliamentary seat in a by-election. His wife Wan Azizah, a medical doctor and MP in the Parti Keadilan Nasional, the party founded by Anwar, had held the seat for him. She was a constant figure in the front row of the public gallery dressed in traditional Malay attire, seated alongside other family members at all her husband's court appearances. Anwar's opposition coalition Pakatan Rakyat grouping, of which the DAP is a member, shocked many in the ruling Barisan Nasional by taking 82 parliamentary seats in the 2008 election. Although the Barisan Nasional took 140 seats, the result nevertheless gave Pakatan Rakyat control of Penang, where Karpal's comparatively young cellmate from his detention days at Kamunting Lim Guan Eng took over as head of the State Assembly.

Anwar's second sodomy case dominated political headlines in the country between the 2008 and 2013 elections. It resulted from allegations made by a young man Saiful Bukhari Azlan, who worked with Anwar as a volunteer before the 2008 election. After the March 2008 election he was taken on full time as Anwar's personal assistant. In late June 2008, Saiful signed a police report stating he had been sodomised by Anwar earlier that month in a Kuala Lumpur condominium. He also alleged there had been eight or nine earlier sexual assaults upon him by Anwar in the preceding two months.

Karpal's third lawyer son Ramkarpal played a prominent role in Anwar's acquittal at the High Court level through his handling of

Karpal with public prosecutor Datuk Mohd Yusof at the second sodomy trial, 2010. Assisting Karpal is his personal assistant Michael Cornelius, seated in the foreground is Ramkarpal. *Photo courtesy of Mark Trowell.*

the DNA evidence defence case. In his 9 January 2012 High Court acquittal decision Justice Datuk Mohamad Zabidin Diah said in part when delivering his verdict, "After going through the evidence the court cannot be 100 per cent certain that integrity of DNA samples was not compromised, and finds that it is not safe to rely on DNA evidence. … As such the court is left only with Saiful's testimony. As this is a sexual crime, the court is reluctant to convict based entirely on Saiful's testimony, which is uncorroborated. The accused is thus acquitted and discharged."

The High Court's decision was inevitably appealed on 10 July 2012, meaning Anwar went into the May 2013 general election with the appeal hanging over his head. Over and above the appeal, earlier in May 2012 Anwar was charged with civil disobedience for his role in helping to organise a rally in Kuala Lumpur on 28 April 2012.

Karpal, with his legal guerrilla hat on and supported by a close-knit coterie of brave lawyers, was once again back in business on Anwar's behalf. A significant motivating factor for Karpal in representing Anwar was to ensure he remained a free man and was legally electable for the next elections to be held in 2018. It was no mean feat keeping Anwar out of jail for the 2013 election.

Karpal and Anwar Ibrahim at the trial. *Photo courtesy of Mark Trowell.*

During Anwar's first sodomy trial Karpal found himself charged with sedition — an offence punishable by a five-year prison term or a RM5,000 fine — for remarks made in court on 10 September 1999 when he suggested that Anwar may have been the victim of arsenic poisoning. This information came to light when Karpal referred to a pathology report from a Melbourne laboratory indicating that high levels of arsenic had been found in Anwar's body. During the trial Anwar's wife Wan Azizah had noticed her husband was not looking well and arranged for a urine sample to be taken from him. In the interests of anonymity the sample was sent in the name of Subramaniam to a Kuala Lumpur laboratory on 18 August 1999, requesting a test for arsenic. The laboratory could not handle such a test and passed the sample on to Gribbles Pathology Malaysia, which in turn sent it to their Melbourne office for further analysis.

Karpal created international news when he told the court on 10 September 1999 that the Melbourne laboratory results indicated high levels of arsenic had been found in Anwar's body. Elaborating on the position in open court in front of the international media, Karpal said:

> If he is slowly being poisoned, something must be done
> about it … It could well be that someone out there wants to
> get rid of him … even to the extent of murder … I suspect
> people in high places are responsible for this situation.

He added that whoever was responsible should be charged with attempted murder.

Justice Datuk Arifin Jaka immediately adjourned the trial and sent Anwar to hospital for a thorough medical check-up. Further tests on various urine and hair samples undertaken in pathology laboratories in Malaysia, Australia and the United Kingdom revealed the presence of arsenic but the levels were not considered dangerous.

Karpal was to pay a high price for the international embarrassment caused to the Malaysian government by his comments on the arsenic issue. He found himself charged (and bailed) under section 4 of the Sedition Act, 1948.

Justice Datuk Seri Augustine Paul, the man who presided over the earlier Anwar corruption case, was appointed to handle Karpal's sedition case. The appointment did not engender a great deal of confidence in the defendant who, on 14 April 1999, had clashed with the judge shortly before the latter was about to deliver his judgement in the Anwar corruption case.

On that day the eyes of the world were on the Kuala Lumpur High Court following Anwar's 77-day corruption trial. Before Anwar went down on the charges, Karpal told Justice Paul he had filed a motion to cite the judge for contempt on behalf of fellow lawyer Christopher Fernando. Karpal said in open court:

In the foyer of the Jalan Duta courthouse (from left) Lim Kit Siang, Ramkarpal, Gobind, Karpal, Anwar and Wan Azizah.

That application should be heard first, to determine whether your Lordship is in contempt. If so your Lordship cannot proceed with the trial to deliver judgement. The remarks made by your Lordship [on 1 April 1999 in the High Court at Kuala Lumpur] against Mr Christopher Fernando are serious. You were from the University of Singapore, so was I, as was my learned friend the Attorney-General. I always thought we learned some law there. To have passed those [alleged] remarks calling Mr Fernando an animal, who ought to be shot... goes against the principles of natural justice... Such remarks should not be used against counsel.

In referring to Mr Fernando, the judge had earlier been reported as saying, 'If the way of speaking is like an animal, we can't tolerate it. We should shoot him. He has to change.'

Justice Paul apologised to Fernando in court before delivering his historic 14 April 1999 judgement. "If Mr Fernando feels upset about the remarks, I would like to tender my profound and sincere apology to him," Justice Paul said. At this stage the judge told Karpal to 'sit down'.

Karpal responded, "I will not be cowed by the court or anyone."

By taking the stand he did, Karpal was sending a none-too-subtle message to other forms of authority in Kuala Lumpur. Against this background he viewed the sedition charge against him as yet another establishment attempt to intimidate the lawyers on Anwar's defence team. He also viewed it as an attempt to finish him as a lawyer. He had lost his seat in parliament as the MP for Jelutong in the 1999 elections, and a conviction of a sedition charge could have meant a five-year prison term and/or a RM5,000 fine. He and Anwar had learned a hard lesson over the years that when there was trouble within UMNO, the ruling party's political opponents were vulnerable to full-on attacks. Put bluntly, there was just one set of political and legal rules in this particular game — smash or be smashed.

On the evening the sedition charge was laid against him, 4 February 2000, all members of Karpal's immediate family descended on the first floor of his Jalan Pudu Lama, Kuala Lumpur law office. "It was like their whole world had collapsed round them once again. Instead of them consoling me, I ended up consoling them," Karpal said.

There were times in his legal career when it might have been more convenient to have been a bachelor, like Sankara Nair, his fellow forthright lawyer on various Anwar defence teams. This was yet another such occasion. Karpal hated seeing his family having to suffer again, as they had during his 16-month imprisonment under Operation Lalang from 1987 to 1989.

His family feared further for his safety when Dr Mahathir spoke about Malaysian lawyers during a lighthearted interview in London just three months after the sedition charge. He said he was not against all lawyers, only some of them, people like Karpal for instance.

Karpal himself had learned to handle whatever was thrown at him by the political establishment over the years. He had learned through bitter experience that attack in such situations was often the best form of defence. He knew this would be the strategy he would have to implement to avert a possible conviction on the sedition charge. He made his mind up early on that he would go all out for Justice Paul from the dock.

What Karpal did not expect in the build-up to his 14 January 2002 sedition case hearing, however, was the level of support he would receive from the international legal community and members of the Malaysian Bar Council. These people were very concerned that a lawyer could be accused of sedition while making a submission in defence of a client. As a result the new Attorney-General Datuk Abdul Gani Patail found himself bombarded with submissions from members of the international legal community.

Comprehensive written submissions of support came from Michael Birnbaum QC and fellow British lawyer James Laddie; the Law Society of British Columbia, Canada; the Australian Bar Association and the Criminal Lawyers Association of Australia. In his submission Birnbaum said in part that great concern had been expressed in Malaysia and internationally as to the fairness of the Anwar case, the nature of the prosecution evidence and the restrictions placed on the conduct of the defence by the trial judge.

Present on the first day of the sedition case hearing on 14 January 2002 were a number of international legal observers including the United Nation's well-respected Special Rapporteur for the Independence of Judges and Lawyers Dato' Param Cumaraswamy, and representatives from the Canadian, Australian and British High Commissions in Kuala Lumpur.

Karpal, representing himself from the dock, applied for the international observers in the court to be granted official observer status. Justice Paul declined the request on the grounds that any member of the public was perfectly entitled to observe a particular trial in Malaysia. Karpal told Justice Paul that 'judges are obliged to uphold the rule of law and the constitution'. He reminded the judge how he had sentenced one of Anwar's defence lawyers Zainur Zakaria to three months in jail for contempt of court:

> In the appeal the Federal Court found that Your Lordship acted more as a prosecutor than as a judge… and with that finding it is more important that you are observed…. That will ensure that nothing goes amiss. Above and beyond this, our criminal justice system itself will be on trial. I have filed an application to have Your Lordship disqualified [from the case].

This remark drew a stern rebuke from the judge, who said the Federal Court's 27 June 2001 decision which overturned Zainur Zakaria's imprisonment also made it clear he had not protected or assisted the prosecutors. The spat between defendant and judge very quickly became largely academic, however, for in a surprise move Attorney-General Abdul Gani rose to his feet and told Justice Paul he was withdrawing the sedition charge.

Justice Paul was not about to let the defendant walk away entirely free from his sedition case courtroom. He said there was an explosive and detonative intention behind Karpal's critical comments from the dock. They were designed to rock 'the very chair on which I sit', Justice Paul said. He then referred the lawyer to the Malaysian Bar Council's disciplinary board for his 'open and blatant attack on the judiciary', calling Karpal's challenges an affront to his impartiality and saying they constituted 'the biggest threat and insult not only to me but also to the entire judiciary... They strike at the very core and foundation of the institution of justice and the democratic process as enshrined in the Federal Constitution'.

The Bar Council's disciplinary committee hearing did not proceed when, among other reasons, Justice Paul declined to appear before it. When Justice Paul died in 2010 Karpal diplomatically buried the hatchet. He described him as a good friend and 'one of the best judges we had'.

Karpal's second sedition case related to alleged seditious words spoken about the late Sultan of Perak at his Jalan Pudu Lama office in February 2009. The circumstances behind this case resulted in a major demonstration outside his Kuala Lumpur office. Approximately 100 riot police dressed in red crash helmets were sent to control this demonstration. The High Court Judicial Commissioner Datuk Azman Abdullah acquitted Karpal on the charge in June 2010. That decision was appealed to the Court of Appeal and the case went back to the High Court for further hearing. At the end of that second hearing, the same High Court Judge Azman Abdullah found Karpal guilty.

While Karpal's second sedition case was going through its various stages the Government indicated in 2012 it would repeal the Sedition Act, 1948. Karpal welcomed the move saying the legislation seriously affects freedom of speech and expression which should be 'a sacred fundamental right' in any society. In July 2012 he called on the Attorney-General to withdraw all charges of sedition in ongoing trials as an expression of *bona fides* over its reported intentions to repeal the legislation. Despite the Government's indication of repealing the Act, individuals, notably Opposition party members, are still being charged for sedition and Karpal's own case was ongoing at the time of his death.

Many in the international community believe Anwar's real crime

(*above*) Riot police outside Karpal's Kuala Lumpur office on Jalan Pudu Lama, February 2009; (*right*) Demonstrators from UMNO Youth had gathered outside the office in response to the lawyer's remarks concerning the Sultan of Perak. *Photos courtesy of Ng Shin Cheong.*

A senior policeman meets with Karpal in his office regarding the 2009 demonstrations outside his office. Looking on is fellow DAP MP Tan Kok Wai.

is that, even after spending six years in prison from 1998 to 2004, he remains a popular figure capable of leading a credible opposition coalition into the 2018 election. Regular attendees in the back of the High Court Sodomy II case hearings were diplomats from the United States Embassy, the Australian High Commission and many other members of the diplomatic corps based in Kuala Lumpur. After 14 years of graphic detailed newspaper headlines, even the Chinese taxi-drivers in Kuala Lumpur, who thrive on salacious gossip, were telling their passengers they had been 'sodomised out' by all the publicity. They wanted to know why dual sodomy prosecution lightning bolts should 'coincidentally' strike Anwar twice.

They were not alone in asking this hard question. More support for Anwar came from 50 Australian politicians on 12 February 2010. In his book *Sodomy II: The Trial of Anwar Ibrahim* (2012), Perth-based Mark Trowell QC noted MPs and senators from both major political parties in Australia had lodged a formal protest with the Malaysian High Commission in Canberra urging Malaysia to drop the charge against Anwar. Their protest letter in part read:

> Many friendly observers of Malaysia find it is difficult to believe that a leading opposition voice could be charged with sodomy a second time, and so soon after his party made major gains in national elections. It should be made known to the Malaysian government, that in our opinion, global esteem for Malaysia will be affected by these charges against Mr Anwar. We hope that Malaysia's authorities will not pursue these charges.

In response, Malaysia's Deputy Foreign Minister A Kohilan Pillay, who unsuccessfully stood against Karpal's son Gobind in the 2013 election contest for the seat of Puchong, said the Australian MPs should respect Malaysian law as the case was still pending in court.

Put simply, many in the international community viewed Anwar's trials and tribulations as being politically motivated. Anwar, after all, was a man who could put thousands of demonstrators on the streets of Kuala Lumpur, as he did before his arrest in the build-up to the 1999 election; one massive demonstration of support was held in and around the national mosque on 20 September 1998.

Observing Karpal presenting Anwar's case in the Jalan Duta courthouse was like watching a legal guerrilla at work. The lawyer frankly acknowledged there clearly were political overtones to his legal work when defending Anwar.

"It is high-octane guerrilla work. Every time I open my mouth in an Anwar case there's the possibility of contempt or sedition charges being laid against me. I have to be very careful what I say."

He viewed the repeat sodomy court cases against Anwar as strengthening the parliamentary opposition's political cause. It is possible Anwar could lead an opposition coalition to power during his lifetime. If he does, Karpal, were he alive, would have held no desire to become Malaysia's Attorney-General, but he would have seen a role for himself as a Minister of Law. Such a job would have given him an opportunity to rid Malaysia of the death penalty legislation.

Karpal's representation of Anwar over the past 15 years was a sign of the changing political climate in Malaysia. His political fan base included a growing chunk of the Malay population, even in his Bukit Gelugor, Penang electorate. During court adjournments at courthouses up and down the country it became the norm for Malays, particularly supporters of the hardline PAS Islamic political party, to approach him wanting their photographs taken with him. A decade ago these Islamic fundamentalists shunned him but they, too, have come to realise an

Karpal with Australian Mark Trowell QC who observed both of
Karpal's sedition trials in 2002 and 2012. *Photo taken in 2002.*

opposition coalition administration is the only way to wrest absolute
political power away from the sons of a fertile peninsula's soil. They also
realised that without Karpal and his team of lawyers Anwar's political
career would have ended a long time ago. At the time of writing, in the
immediate aftermath of Karpal's death in April 2014, Anwar continued
to be a source of pro bono work for Karpal's family of lawyers.

The Barisan Nasional-controlled newspapers made sure voters
knew the prosecution appeal in Anwar's second sodomy case would be
heard in July 2013 in the Jalan Duta courthouse. On 3 May 2013, two
days before Malaysia's 13th general election, a video of Saiful Bukhari
Azlan, the man who took the Sodomy II proceedings against Anwar, was
made available for public consumption. The recording, of Saiful taking
a retributive oath under sharia law while on a pilgrimage to Mecca,
was the second religious oath sworn by Saiful asserting that Anwar had
sodomised him in June 2008. Anwar's wife Wan Azizah dismissed it as

yet another attempt to discredit her husband saying the High Court had acquitted the would-be prime minister on the charge.

Karpal's worst fears for Anwar were realised on 7 March 2014 when the Court of Appeal overturned the High Court's earlier acquittal in the Sodomy II case. The man who led the opposition to its strongest ever performance in the 2013 elections was also hastilty sentenced on the same day to five years in jail on sodomy charges by the Court of Appeal.

On the face of it, if the sentence is upheld by way of a Federal Court appeal, Anwar's prospects of becoming Malaysia's first ever opposition prime minister would appear to be virtually zero.

When Karpal died in his Toyota Alphard on the highway between Kuala Lumpur and Penang in the early hours of Thursday, 17 April he was working on Anwar's Federal Court appeal.

Perhaps symbolically, too, he had with him at the time of his death, Anwar's Sodomy II case files.

15 LET GOD BE THE JUDGE

Taking an overview of his own tempestuous life, Karpal believed he had been able to achieve more via the law than he had as the perennial hardball opposition DAP politician. On 5 May 2013 he participated in his eighth national election when, as the national chairman of the DAP, he contested the Bukit Gelugor seat in the national parliament.

While he saw his contribution to Malaysian society as more legal than political, nevertheless his dual-pronged achievements in both fields had been significant and very much intertwined. Undoubtedly his biggest contribution to Malaysian society was in steering hundreds of clients away from the gallows via numerous legal challenges to capital punishment legislation.

He was also renowned for being a highly irritating opponent in the corridors of power in his use of the law and parliament's standing orders to keep fellow politicians honest. Articulating an unshakable, often solo,

Karpal with Lim Kit Siang
outside Parliament, 1996.

human rights message against the formidable machinery of state had not
been easy. Even so, his powerful legal and political messages concerning
alleged corruption and abuses of power had consistently been espoused
over the years.

Along with his lifelong friend in the DAP Lim Kit Siang, Karpal was
a human rights watchdog in a society where the fundamental political
rule is one of 'might is right'. Karpal's response had been to bend the
rules he very often himself challenged in the first place.

Armed with a keen sense of humour and his Sikh legal sword, he
spent a lifetime working to modify the laws of a legal system which
evolved from Muslim rulers and British colonialists.

For a man who lived his life righting wrongs on behalf of others, his
first-floor Kuala Lumpur law library was an alpha and an omega for the
lives and hopes of many. One area of his professional life which had no
publicity concerned the many women who regularly consulted him over
sexual harassment issues. The male transgressors, many of whom were

captains of society, quietly paid out millions of ringgit in compensation to his clients. For the old (and sometimes not so old) bulls knew, once Karpal took on a watching brief in a case he would not let go.

To pull off the deals surrounding such cases, Karpal knew he had to be above suspicion himself. He was all too aware that for every satisfied and financially well-rewarded client there was someone equally dissatisfied and out of pocket on the other side.

Yes, he did have numerous enemies in politics and the law as a result of his work and yes, execution-style killings were not uncommon events on the streets and roads of Malaysia. He was somewhat surprised his political and legal careers were still intact after a lifetime of challenging so many of Malaysia's sacred cows. Throughout his political career there had always been a sword of Damocles of some sort hanging over his head. Going into the 5 May 2013 election it was yet another sedition case against him.

He did not expect to see his long-term goal of racial equality for Chinese and Indians recognised under the country's Constitution being achieved during his lifetime. But it was an objective he believed his lawyer-offspring might one day realistically help to achieve.

Clearly his family had benefitted and will continue to benefit financially from the father's frequent political and legal battles. But they also paid a heavy price via the loss of innocent childhoods, particularly when their father was incarcerated in Kamunting under the ISA.

From the large table in his Kuala Lumpur law library Karpal had quietly guided and directed the submissions, strategies and arguments of the young lawyers in his employment.

His own family of lawyers knew the father would dominate one of Malaysia's largest privately-owned criminal law firms until the day he died. For Karpal, even at 73 years of age and with life in a wheelchair, retirement from his political and legal roles was not on the agenda.

This created new challenges for second lawyer son Gobind, who decided to go it alone outside the family law firm's protective umbrella. Gobind left the family firm with Karpal's blessings, as the latter understood better than most that a lawyer has to do what a lawyer has to do.

While it must have affected him somewhat to see the son most like him leave the family shingle the father was not about to deprive a lawyer son of the same opportunities he himself had enjoyed. There was, for instance, real satisfaction and fun to be had from owning his own law firm and representing a client like Arthur Cheah, who in 1981 wanted a lawyer who would not choose to be a common man or a follower.

Cheah, a pilot in the Singapore Air Force, approached Karpal after refusing to salute the Singapore flag while parading with his military colleagues in 1981. He justified this lack of patriotism by informing his superiors he was a Malaysian citizen. He was soon afterwards charged with failing to take care of an official document and allowing a businessman to obtain photocopies of the minutes of secret Singapore Air Force meetings between 23 October 1972 and 2 May 1974. Clearly those in authority in Singapore wanted to teach the spirited Cheah a lesson.

Many in Singapore's legal fraternity did not wish to shatter their own well-supplied government rice bowls by defending a mercenary Malaysian flyer who, in reality, saluted just one flag at the time — one which possibly had a Singapore dollar inscribed on it. Desperate to find a lawyer willing to take on his case, Cheah contacted Karpal, who readily agreed to handle his first-ever case in Singapore.

On judgement day in July 1981, Cheah packed a toothbrush and shaving gear and flew down to Singapore, where he expected to be detained at Changi Prison for some time. When he was acquitted on both charges for lack of evidence Cheah joined Karpal for a drink before they boarded the shuttle flight back to Kuala Lumpur. Karpal rarely took a drink but, like everything else in his life, when he did it was usually a good one in the company of friends and for a good reason.

Karpal told his new-found friend how important this case was to him, even in comparison to the many murder, ISA, ESCAR and constitutional cases he had handled — because it was personal. For in winning the case he had squared the ledger with Singapore's first Prime Minister Lee Kuan Yew, the man who indirectly had him banned from his university hostel during his student days on the island republic.

Here again, as a 41-year-old at the time, there were no half measures for Karpal. The lawyer respected and understood Cheah's rebellious stance and his general passion for life. The two men celebrated long into the following morning upon their victorious return from Singapore.

Like thousands of other clients Cheah knew Karpal would never cower before any judge. The lawyer and his wife Gurmit, a smart hardheaded businesswoman in her own right, were self-made multi-millionaires — their orchard in Penang, office buildings and homes in Kuala Lumpur and Penang all illustrate this fact. Gurmit was the driving force in converting Karpal's legal charisma into real estate dollars and cents.

But money and power did not change Karpal's surprisingly simple, largely legal-loner, quiet and patient, ascetic lifestyle. He was a man who, some say, had become overly immersed in politics and the welfare of his clients over the years, but it was his choice to adopt such a lifestyle. Despite his outwardly tough exterior he had a keen sense of humour and appreciation of human foibles. This was evidenced by the fact that throughout his political career, there had always been a touch of the 'upon my beard' irreverent rascal about him.

His biggest political opponent over the years was undoubtedly Dr Mahathir, the one-time Alor Setar medical doctor turned prime minister, who had him imprisoned under the ISA from 1987 to 1989.

Yet after Dr Mahathir stepped away from the full-time political scene Karpal professed to actually missing the man. The reason for this was simple from his perspective. He had spent a lifetime endeavouring to score much publicised, king-hit political points off Dr Mahathir. With Dr Mahathir now retired, there was no longer anyone to play an enjoyable game of political hardball with. Headlines, therefore, were harder to get from a media where the concept of press freedom was still dependent upon newspaper owners being granted publication rights.

On the debit side, apart from two ISA imprisonments, there were just three court findings of any real substance against Karpal personally. One was the fine of RM250 after a Magistrate's Court conviction for participating in an unlawful DAP assembly in Alor Setar in 1984. The second was the RM100,000 (plus interest and costs) payout the Federal Court ordered him to pay in damages to parliament's former Malaysian Indian Congress Deputy Speaker DP Vijandran at the end of a libel case. Karpal had little difficulty justifying both these payouts. "When you go to war there are always casualties. Even generals go down from time to time." The third, of course, was the February 2014 High Court conviction for sedition.

On the positive side there can be no doubting how the lives of thousands of clients in a tough legal environment had been enhanced via his fearless, take-it-to-the-limit criminal advocacy. He derived satisfaction just knowing there were hundreds of people alive, whether in jails or walking the streets of Malaysia, simply because they entrusted him with their death penalty appeals — people like S Arulpragasan, Khoo Hi Chiang and Goh Kim Looi. For such people Karpal had proved himself time and time again as the lead counsel in Malaysia's court of last resort. Wherever lives and political careers had been on the line in Malaysia over the past five decades the bearded Sikh was never far away — Anwar Ibrahim was proof of this.

Throughout it all, though, the most important thing in Karpal's life was his own family. Those who rode roughshod over family values, particularly Sikh family values, could expect no favours from this lawyer if they came up against him. This aspect of his personality was obvious when he discussed a family values brief while on a 1996 trip back to his Sikh roots in northern India.

Sitting relaxed in the spacious lounge of a Jalandhar-based retired military man's home, his eyes were drawn to a photograph on the wall in front of him. It was a 1989 picture of a smiling, beautiful young woman

Two of Karpal's latter life legal success stories, Goh Kim Looi and Khoo Hi Chiang, pose in front of the Green Hall site in Penang where the family home of the young Karpal once stood.

elaborately dressed for her wedding. The beauty in the photograph was a picture of joy with her red *bindi* on the forehead (a decorative mark signifying a married woman), a large gold ring through her nose and a gold *tikka* (a piece of jewellery that hangs down the forehead) on her head. For Karpal, the picture evoked thoughts of his own only daughter Sangeet and he knew nothing would be spared to ensure her wedding was special. It captured for him the joyful anticipation a young Sikh woman feels for a new husband on her wedding day. It accentuated the importance of family life and told a story in bright colour of lavish affection showered upon an only daughter by loving and devoted parents.

But a lot had happened in the seven years since the young woman in the photograph had taken the young man from Jalandhar as her husband. Soon after the wedding the young couple left for Southeast Asia, where she was treated as a domestic servant and an object of ridicule because her retired military man father had produced just ten lakhs of rupees (RM1 million) by way of a dowry, instead of the eagerly anticipated 50 lakhs. The daughter-in-law's position in her new home became completely untenable when the first child she delivered turned out to be a girl. It is a sad fact of Indian life that daughters are often viewed as economic burdens, with the prospect of the dowry that has to be paid always lurking round the corner in their young lives.

Defeated and humiliated, the young Punjabi mother fled to the sanctuary of her parents' home in Jalandhar with the baby. Her shame was shared by her parents, for it is expected of a Sikh wife to remain in her husband's home until her oldest son lights her funeral pyre.

The lawyer met the young woman and when she had retired for the evening, Karpal put his lawyer's hat on and gave her father one of his typically forthright categoric assurances he always gave people with their backs to the wall.

"Don't you worry, sir. We'll feed this fellow to the dogs bit by bit if he doesn't come to his senses," Karpal said.

This was the sort of fighting talk, fuelled by a dram or two of whisky, the veteran of three wars against Pakistan and one against China understood clearly. A son-in-law who would destroy an only daughter's happiness must himself be destroyed, unless the young man and his family could first be brought to their senses.

Entered Karpal Singh!

The former military man recounted to the author in 1999 of his total astonishment, when soon after his meeting with Karpal the son-in-law unexpectedly turned up in Jalandhar 'on his knees begging for forgiveness and offering lakhs of rupees'. The monetary offers were spurned by the old soldier on the grounds that a daughter's and grand-daughter's happiness could not be purchased by buying off her parents. Nevertheless, the final settlement in the fairytale ending to this case saw a very financially secure young woman and her baby daughter reunited with her husband and his family in Southeast Asia. Honour and pride had been restored to an old soldier and his Sikh family.

This was a case Karpal enjoyed working on as he, too, had big plans for daughter Sangeet's own wedding day. Little did he know it at the time of his 1996 trip to Jalandhar, that from a very subjective personal perspective, such Sikh dreams of playing his full part in his daughter's Sikh wedding ceremony would be shattered by a car crash.

The nose to tail prang occurred when he was returning to his Penang home from the airport in a taxi driven by Soib Abdul Rahman in the early hours of Saturday 29 January 2005. A car behind them, driven by Penang banker Lau Yee Fuat, ploughed headlong into the boot of the airport taxi. Seated in the back seat of the taxi Karpal came within a whisker of having his upper spinal cord permanently separated from his brain.

The family leadership in this latest life-long crisis would immediately be handed to his wife Gurmit. She was the first person to come to his assistance as he lay spreadeagled and paralysed in the back of the car. Gurmit had been in the happy process of putting up decorations for Sangeet's wedding when the driver pounded on the front door with news of the accident. Her life, too, changed forever at that moment.

Since late January 2005 the real pain for Karpal had been far from physical. It was more the deep anguish of knowing his family once again had to suffer. The wedding was postponed twice in the hope that the father would be well enough to give his daughter away. But given the seriousness of his injuries there would be no question of him participating fully in Sangeet's marriage to medical doctor and bone specialist Simmrat Singh on 1 January 2006. The lawyers' lawyer preferred not to talk about the wedding of his only daughter.

The 700 people who attended the reception in the Grand Ballroom of the Eastern & Oriental Hotel on the Penang waterfront had no idea of the psychological and physical pain Karpal suffered when he was lifted from his hospital bed and prepared to go to the hotel. At the back of Karpal's mind, his daughter's wedding was always going to be the traditional Sikh one he and Gurmit missed out on 36 years earlier, courtesy of his own mother's traditional hardline views that Sikhs should marry strictly within their own castes. Finally she — the same woman who gave Karpal his steel-trap mind and created the fighter he was — agreed to disagree over her son's marriage arrangements all those years ago.

Suffice it to say that on 1 January 2006 the spirit within the battered body of the bride's father, coupled with Gurmit's stoicism and unfailing love for her family, ensured the only daughter had the very best on her wedding day. Karpal was distressed that he was physically incapable of giving Sangeet away; this role he delegated to his oldest son Jagdeep.

Throughout his lifelong battle with the political and legal establishments, Karpal's family was always at his side when the going got rough. The roughest it ever got for them was in the days after the accident when Karpal was medically classified as a category 2–3 tetraplegic.

Some of Karpal's friends, no doubt with his best interests very much in mind, said it might have been more merciful for the son to have suffered the same fate as the father back in 1974 in Punjab. But Karpal did not subscribe to that theory. He was grateful the Sikh divine hand he believed in gave him an opportunity to survive and watch his 11 grandchildren grow up.

It was testament to his tenacity that on 14 February 2007, two years after his accident, Karpal presented his evidence from his wheelchair in the witness box in a matter-of-fact manner. At the conclusion of his evidence the defendant's counsel Bala Mahesan said simply, "Mr Karpal Singh, I have known you 42 years. You have given your evidence very

(*above*) Sangeet at her wedding ceremony held at the Police Gurdwara on 1 January 2006. She is pictured surrounded by her brothers (from left) Gobind, Ramkarpal and Jagdeep, and in photo on the right, with her husband Dr Simmrat Singh; (*right*) With her father at a press conference in their Penang law office, 2011.

clearly. I have no questions, Your Honour." Such was the measure of his recovery and professionalism.

Karpal was awarded RM2.018 million by Penang Sessions Court Judge Chan Jit Li as compensation for the injuries which had left him wheelchair-bound. Even at the conclusion of this case there was controversy when the Bar Council took exception to the judge's actions — she came down from the bench at the end of the case and gave the disabled lawyer a hug.

"It was not a bear hug. Her action was a spontaneous one coming from one human being to another who is disabled. What she did was an act of compassion in open court for which she should not be defaulted in any way. Chan Jit Li should not be punished in any way for having acted as a human being," Karpal said in support of the judge.

Those who knew Karpal realised the accident presented him with the fight of his life. He underwent special treatments and therapies, including trips to India and Singapore for spinal surgery. There were ongoing signs his daily physiotherapy treatment was working. He was able to sign letters and cheques and feed himself with his left hand; for a while he had to use his thumbprint to sign correspondence.

While undergoing rehabilitation he heard all the conspiracy theories doing the rounds about who and what might have been behind the accident. On that subject he came to his own conclusion long ago — he lost the game of chance everyone plays when they venture out in a car onto a road, particularly a Malaysian road.

On 14 February 2007 before leaving his Penang home to give his evidence Karpal went out of his way to point out to the author a simple rain tree across the road from his home.

"This tree knows everything. It witnessed the accident," he said.

This particular rain tree had, at one stage, been chopped right back but now vibrant branches are growing from it. The tree was a source of inspiration for him. Such thoughts were the lawyer's way of letting those around him know that the accident had cut him back to the basic fundamentals of life. It was his way of saying he knew he had to start again, to adapt to a new form of existence in a wheelchair. He looked out to the rain tree often. Ironically his home near the accident spot was one special place on earth where he found peace.

Karpal pondered on the irony of it all. With the exception of two notable detentions under the Internal Security Act, all his political and legal foes had failed in their endeavours to imprison him. It took an out-of-control driver to truly imprison the man, this time in his own body. Imprisoned alongside him with a loyal spouse's lifetime sentence was his wife.

"At least during Operation Lalang we had people to fight. The pain then was mental. This time it was both physical and mental. It was difficult to fight but we did it," Gurmit observed.

Karpal likened himself to a client who had been handed down a natural life sentence. But he came to terms with his predicament and no longer looked for clemency. The wounded lawyer was resigned to not walking again but viewed every second of the life left to him as a bonus.

He spent a year of medical seclusion in bewilderment and feeling sorry for himself. But the fighter in him took over; he slowly regained his spirit and returned again to his legal and parliamentary duties. The turnaround was nothing short of miraculous. Trips to parliament were soon followed by trips to his Penang and Kuala Lumpur office buildings, where wheelchair lifts were installed. He immersed himself in his legal and political work to take his mind off the pain.

The lawyer rarely travelled by plane within Malaysia as he found it more comfortable and convenient taking to the road in his modified Toyota Alphard. This meant extra work for his personal assistant Michael Cornelius and driver Fahmi, whose jobs saw them traversing great distances each year on Malaysian highways. The two support staff worked round the clock as a tag team, taking their boss on his rounds of parliament, law offices, court houses, prisons and homes and seeing to his every need. They were indispensable to his lifestyle.

Despite him being in a wheelchair Karpal's opponents still took every opportunity to go at him. On 30 April 2008 the independent MP for Pasir Mas Ibrahim Ali called upon the MP for Bukit Gelugor to stand while addressing parliament. This comment subsequently saw Ibrahim the target of 30 wheelchair-bound members of MADD (Malaysians Against the Discrimination of the Disabled) who demonstrated in the foyer of parliament and demanded an apology. Ibrahim refused to apologise, saying he was merely retaliating against Karpal who had earlier on in the debate called him a 'frog'.

Clearly, Karpal's physical disabilities had not made an iota of difference to his approach to life.

Even in death the verbal and written assaults upon Karpal continued.

Soon after Karpal died in the early hours of 17 April 2014, Langkawi MP Datuk Nawawi Ahmad's minders posted a picture of Karpal's battered face on the Internet. Alongside the death-mask were posted comments reflecting the fact the deceased Bukit Gelugor MP was totally opposed to the implementation of *hudud* law in Malaysia. The photograph was accompanied by a comment which read: "*Siapa nak sambut cabaran Karpal Singh? Sila bagi nama he he.*"

It was a reference relating to the fact that Karpal, many years earlier, had said the creation of an Islamic state in Malaysia would take place "over [his] dead body". The implication behind Nawawi's Internet posting was that with Karpal gone, the time was now right for *hudud* law to be introduced widely throughout Malaysia.

Nawawi subsequently apologised for the insensitivity surrounding this posting, which understandably had caused a furore and an outpouring of outrage among Karpal's friends and supporters.

In the wake of Karpal's funeral service during the three days of prayers at the Sikh temple in Penang, the lawyer's oldest brother Baksis Singh, the man who had paid for Karpal's university education half a century earlier, was asked if he had anything to say about Nawawi's remarks.

"I am just a simple man," the senior member of Karpal's family said. "Let God be the judge of him."

(*above*) DAP supporters outside Karpal's Penang home on 5 May 2013. To the left of this group on the road was the scene of his 2005 accident and the large rain tree from which Karpal drew inspiration; (*bottom left*) Baksis Singh in front of one of the first houses in Penang that Karpal lived in; (*bottom right*) Karpal with Michael Cornelius, his personal assistant who attended to his every need, in a picture taken in May 2013.

16 THE WHEEL TURNS

The Buddha and the Singh were back in business again on the night of the 5 May 2013 general election in Penang. This time, though, the Buddha in the frame was not Karpal's old nemesis-turned-friend from the controversial Penang State Assembly days, Lim Chong Eu. The only Buddha-like personage within range on election night was one Cheong Fatt Tze, a Chinese educational philanthropist from the early 1900s whose statue stood proudly within the confines of the Chung Hwa Confucian School. It was to this school in the Chinese heartland of Penang that Karpal made his way to learn the news he had retained his Bukit Gelugor parliamentary seat with a massive 41,778 vote majority. His loyal supporters were ecstatic to learn he had polled the best he had ever done in his eighth successful general election contest.

Opposition leader Anwar Ibrahim's Pakatan Rakyat coalition, comprising the DAP, PAS and his own Parti Keadilan Rakyat (PKR), had also obtained over 50 per cent of the popular vote, and by contrast the ruling Barisan Nasional recorded its worst ever performance in 13 general elections held in Malaysia's 56-year political history.

But the dream of the embattled Anwar Ibrahim leading his three-party opposition coalition to a historic victory did not materialise that night. His PKR party had won 30 seats, PAS 21 and the DAP 38, which gave the opposition a total of 89 seats in the new parliament, in comparison to 82 seats it held in the 2008 election. The ruling Barisan Nasional won 133 (60 per cent) of the seats after securing just approximately 47 per cent of the overall popular vote.

Karpal knew from his own bitter experience that whenever there were problems within Barisan Nasional ranks, there would be trouble for the opposition forces in the wake of the election. There had been huge rallies in support of Anwar's coalition, including one in Penang with an estimated 100,000 people present at the Esplanade on the night of Friday 3 May 2013, in the build-up to the election. These massive flag-waving opposition rallies across the country, which rocked the political establishment, had been largely ignored by the Barisan Nasional-controlled mainstream media outlets.

Such was the traffic build-up surrounding the Penang rally that Karpal had to be unceremoniously pushed, shoved and carried for a kilometre in his wheelchair just to get to the venue itself before addressing the huge crowd alongside Anwar. With his Melbourne-based older brother Santokh, 74, following behind him the trek to the Esplanade was indeed a trip down memory lane for the lawyer-politician.

Santokh in Penang, 5 May 2013.

Karpal was wheeled past the spot near where the two brothers were forced to bow the deepest of deferential bows to guards during the Japanese Occupation of 1942–45. They also passed the spot where their Green Hall family home once stood before being bombed to the ground by American airmen serving in forces controlled by another man in a wheelchair, President Franklin Delano Roosevelt.

There would, of course, be no nationwide fairytale ending on election night for Anwar Ibrahim's embattled Pakatan Rakyat opposition coalition. This fact was obvious to see when Karpal arrived at the Chung Hwa Confucian School with a sizeable entourage of supporters in his wake on the night of his largest ever personal political victory; he was accompanied to the official counting house from his Jalan Utama campaign headquarters by about 200 supporters.

Karpal was adamant he wanted all of them to be able to enter the school's large assembly hall area for the official vote announcement. But the lockdown contingent of police and electoral commission staff on duty at the school gates, who were under strict orders to allow only pre-approved pass holders to get through the firmly shut gates on that night, had other ideas. Karpal was unimpressed that even his youngest Kuala Lumpur-based banker son Mankarpal was among the throng left trapped outside the gates as he argued with the authorities to allow his supporters entry. In the finish police and electoral commission staff, tired of the lawyer's non-compromising submissions, pulled the gates open. To cries of 'Ubah, ubah, (change, change) Karpal Singh. Ubah, ubah, Karpal Singh', the supporters marched in behind the man in the wheelchair to hear the official vote count proclamation read out.

Karpal's family, as they had always done since the 2005 accident, had overseen the logistics of moving their special elderly and demanding 'baby' at every stage of his latest campaign. While sons Gobind (a sizeable chip off the old block who is also not shy about being banned

(*above left*) Karpal and second son Gobind, who would become the MP for Puchong in 2008. In the 2013 election Gobind retained his seat by a majority of 32,802 votes; (*right*) Karpal on election day, 5 May 2013.

from parliament) and Jagdeep were busy defending their respective DAP seats in the federal parliament (Puchong) and Penang State Assembly, Ramkarpal, working alongside his mother Gurmit and sister Sangeet, had masterminded the Bukit Gelugor campaign; youngest son Mankarpal looked after the media during the campaign. Gobind and Jageep retained their seats with healthy majorities in the 2013 election.

In thanking his family and supporters he was gracious in victory and more than happy with the extent of his winning margin and those of his colleagues. But at the back of his steel-trap mind there were other concerns, highlighted in an Al-Jazeera television documentary in the build-up to the election, which concerned him. This programme had focused on vote-rigging, election bribes being paid to poor voters in marginal electorates, corruption and cronyism at the top levels of Malaysian business, politics and society generally.

Earlier that day, when he cast his vote at the Penang Free School, Chinese grandmothers leaned over him to hug him while their husbands commented in Chinese, "Ahhh, Karpal Singh. The old tiger is out today." For even when it came to casting his own vote he did so while pushing his rights within the boundaries of existing political and electoral regulations.

At the Penang Free School election booth, he set out to make a political point by using his own vote to highlight what was to him an unfair aspect of the electoral system. Sangeet had pointed out to her father the night before that there was a specific provision 'to avoid identification' in the voting process. Explaining this to a puzzled-looking polling booth staffer that, in his opinion, voting papers could possibly be traced to the voter, thus establishing how individual people had voted, Karpal cited provisions of the Elections (Conduct of Elections) Regulations, 1981 Act. Under these regulations voters had a legal right to select their ballot paper and not simply accept whatever ballot paper was given to them by polling booth staff.

Karpal insisted on receiving a 'random' ballot paper from the polling booth attendant. He instructed the attendant to produce ten random ballot papers so he could select one upon which to exercise his vote. This, of course, was all too much for the attendant who immediately brought in her supervisor to deal with the problem voter. The supervisor instructed the polling booth attendant to make ten random ballot papers available and Karpal cast his vote accordingly.

"Everyone should do this at the next election. That way they will be guaranteed anonymity at the ballot box," Karpal said.

His massive majority in Bukit Gelugor reflected the fact that the Chinese population had deserted the Barisan Nasional — 'who eat money' according to one Chinese taxi driver spoken to on election day — in droves since the 2008 elections.

The tiger roars again with his 41,778 Bukit Gelugor seat majority at the May 2013 election.

Immediately after the election opposition leader Anwar Ibrahim refused to concede defeat saying, "[The ruling coalition] has robbed us of our elections and I want to present the case on behalf of Malaysians." For that reason he had a duty to expose irregularities the opposition had uncovered in up to 31 seats. Anwar, at 65, still remains the opposition's main leadership hope of achieving power in the 2018 elections. In the weeks after the election he organised a number of large rallies protesting against these irregularities and Karpal knew it would not be long before an establishment crackdown occurred.

The vitriol came to a head in late May 2013 when a number of opposition figures, including MPs, were arrested and charged with sedition for their respective roles in organising the nationwide demonstrations. It was a move which evoked memories of the 1987 Operation Lalang crackdown which led to his two-year detention.

Karpal knew as he headed back down the highway from Penang to Kuala Lumpur the day after the election his own personal fight had to go on. It had to, for on his immediate legal work agenda were two prosecution appeals — 'politically motivated' in the minds of many in the international community — against Anwar in the press-dubbed Sodomy II case and himself in his second sedition case which had to be defended. The second sedition charge was brought against him following the 2008 election when he simply suggested a ruler was not above the law.

At the time of writing Anwar, too, was just a 'losing Sodomy II appeal case' away from yet another lengthy term of imprisonment which would effectively destroy his prospects of becoming Malaysia's first opposition prime minister at the next election in 2018.

"They've still got us both within shooting distance," Karpal joked.

There was also a third case on the lawyer's mind, involving one of the most bizarre murder mysteries in the nation's history, which Karpal was determined to see through all its potential lengthy legal stages.

The case on Karpal's mind involved a 28-year-old Mongolian woman Altantuya Shaariibuu, who was blown to bits in a remote Selangor forest with high-powered C4 military explosives by two Malaysian policemen one night in October 2006. Following the High Court verdict, Karpal was appalled and disgusted at the manner in which the policemen went about their work in first of all covering Altantuya with the malleable, ductile plastic explosive before detonating it and blowing her to smithereens — all that was left of her body were approximately 400 small bone fragments.

The policemen, Chief Inspector Azilah Hadri, 31, and Corporal Sirul Azhar Umar, 36, were both sentenced to death for Altantuya's murder at the end of their Shah Alam High Court trial in 2008. However, in August 2013 the Court of Appeal found the circumstantial evidence against them was not enough to sustain the High Court's earlier guilty verdict for Altantuya's murder. The Court of Appeal found a heinous crime had been committed but the guilt of Azilah and Sirul Azhar had not been satisfactorily proved. The Court of Appeal gave the benefit of the doubt to the appellants. The prosecution intends appealing the Court of Appeal decision to the Federal Court. Azilah and Sirul Azhar were freed following the Court of Appeal's decision. They were both members of the country's Special Actions Unit, whose responsibilities included looking after Malaysia's top politicians.

Karpal had a watching brief in this case on behalf of the Mongolian government and Altantuya's family. He went to his death puzzled as to why the policemen would carry out such an execution-style killing on an attractive young woman when neither man appeared to have a personal motive for disposing of her in such a brutal fashion.

The third defendant in this case was the well-connected Kuala Lumpur-based political analyst Abdul Razak Baginda, 46. He walked from the high-sided wooden court dock a free man at the end of the prosecution case. He had been charged with abetting the two policemen in Altantuya's murder but Judge Datuk Mohd Zaki ruled in mid-trial that Baginda had no case to answer.

Prior to her death the High Court heard how the Mongolian beauty had been a fluent linguist. The court heard how, for two years, as well as being his lover, Altantuya worked as a professional interpreter for Baginda, the executive director of the Malaysian Strategic Research Centre. Evidence was presented in court how the couple had met when Baginda was abroad on a business trip as a very well-paid government middleman to broker a deal involving the purchase of submarines from a French company.

The court also heard in evidence how Altantuya sought to blackmail Baginda when their affair turned sour. The political analyst, who had earlier hired a private investigator to keep watch over his house, had also contacted an acquaintance in the police force. This acquaintance introduced Baginda to Chief Inspector Azilah Hadri. Following this introduction Baginda met with Azilah Hadri to discuss how the Altantuya problem might be resolved. Baginda told the court he had met up with Azilah Hadri but had specifically advised him not to do anything which might harm Altantuya.

Problems between the former lovers came to a head on 19 October 2006 when Altantuya made a nuisance of herself outside Baginda's home. Previously she would be accompanied by two friends on money extortion missions designed to create maximum embarrassment to Baginda outside his family home, but that night she was on her own. Azilah Hadri and Corporal Sirul Azhar Umar then turned up; they spoke with her before taking her away. The High Court heard in evidence how they drove her to a forested area where she was blown to bits.

CCTV screen grab of Azilah and Sirul in the foyer of Hotel Malaya, 18 October 2006.

However, unbeknown to the policemen, Altantuya had left a note in her hotel room — the Hotel Malaya in the heart of Kuala Lumpur's vibrant Chinatown tourist area — with instructions on who should be contacted should something happen to her.

Following the murder conviction of the police officers, Atlantuya's father Setev Shaariibuu, through his lawyer Karpal, filed a civil suit for damages. The suit, if it is heard, could become Malaysia's version of the OJ Simpson case. (The former American football star was acquitted of murdering his ex-wife Nicole Brown and her friend Ron Goldman in October 1996. Later both the Brown and Goldman families successfully sued Simpson for substantial damages in a civil

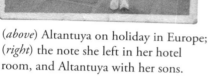

(*above*) Altantuya on holiday in Europe;
(*right*) the note she left in her hotel
room, and Altantuya with her sons.

case.) Altantuya's father believes his daughter's spirit will not rest until
justice is done in Malaysia and instructed Karpal to sue Azilah Hadri,
Sirul Azhar Umar, Abdul Razak Baginda and the Malaysian Government
for RM100 million in a civil suit once all the death penalty appeals had
been disposed of. At the time of writing, the prosecution's Federal Court
appeal against Azilah Hadri and Sirul Azhar Umar had not been heard.
It had been scheduled to begin on 23 June 2014.

Setev Shaariibuu was ordered to pay RM30,000 security for costs
to Abdul Razak Baginda and the Malaysian Government, which he has
done. Baginda had earlier applied for RM250,000 as security for costs
and the Malaysian Government had applied for RM1 million. However,
on 30 March 2010, the High Court at Shah Alam slashed the security
for costs for Baginda and the Government to just RM30,000.

Karpal said the main reason he took this case on was to secure some sort of future for Altantuya's two sons.

"We owe it to those young boys," he said matter-of-factly.

He acknowledged Abdul Razak Baginda was found not guilty of being an accomplice in Altantuya's murder at the High Court level and also recognised that all appeals from the criminal case to the Court of Appeal and the Federal Court must be finalised before the civil case could begin. Karpal was also very much aware that the two policemen Azilah and Sirul had been found not guilty in the Court of Appeal. Over the years the lawyer learned the appeal process could be very lengthy but he was ready for the wait. In taking on this case Karpal stood very much alone in Malaysian legal circles.

Meanwhile, the 2013 election was also a personal triumph for Karpal's lifetime friend from Kamunting days, Lim Kit Siang. The 72-year-old Lim Kit Siang shocked the political establishment by winning the Malay heartland Gelang Patah seat in Johor.

His son Lim Guan Eng is the Chief Minister of Penang State, a DAP stronghold, while also performing the job of DAP Secretary-General. Lim Guan Eng was in a jubilant mood on election night and had no doubts about the national DAP chairman's future role within the party, including the possibility of him standing again in the Bukit Gelugor seat in 2018.

"That's a decision for Karpal... he'll make up his own mind," said Lim Guan Eng, himself a former Kamunting inmate before being subsequently imprisoned under sedition legislation later.

The crippled DAP national chairman was showing no signs of slowing down the day after the election. As proof of this he spoke of the family's almost completed plans to build a new family home for him in Kuala Lumpur overlooking parliament buildings, one that could accommodate his disability.

Penang Chief Minister Lim Guan Eng and his wife Betty Chew greeting Karpal at the Wadda Gurdwara in Penang on the occasion of the Sikh New Year, 13 April 2008.

On the previous evening he euphemistically told about 50 journalists and photographers covering his landslide victory at the Chung Hwa Confucian School, "I'm still fit enough and there is fire in my belly. A good lawyer dies in the saddle. The same applies equally to a politician. They should work to the last."

The Tiger of Jelutong signed off from this victorious election night press conference by simply saying, "If you slow down you die. In this life you have to fight."

While Karpal's personal fight was far from over on election night of 5 May 2013, surrounded as he was at the time by an atmosphere of personal election victory euphoria, no one considered the unthinkable prospect of the voters of Bukit Gelugor having to return to their Penang polling booths a year later, on 25 May 2014, for a by-election.

EPILOGUE

Throughout his life Penang was always Karpal's spiritual home and whenever he had a big matter to work on he would return there. It was a place where he found the peace and quiet needed to focus his mind on important issues at hand in a relaxed atmosphere.

On the night of Wednesday 16 April 2014, Karpal was making preparations for yet another overnight road trip up the highway from Kuala Lumpur to Penang.

There were three matters on his mind as he sat in his wheelchair in his first-floor office in Kuala Lumpur.

One was the High Court hearing of a murder case set down for consideration in the Penang High Court the following day. The 2013 Valentine's Day killing in Penang, where 31-year-old engineer Cheong Teik Keon was charged with the stabbing murder of his 24-year-old girlfriend Tan Ching Chin, evoked comparisons to South Africa's

Oscar Pistorius trial. It was, however, just another bread-and-butter capital punishment murder trial for Karpal.

The second matter on Karpal's mind was the preparation of the petition of appeal for the Federal Court hearing in Anwar Ibrahim's sodomy case. The third was his son Gobind who had been warded at Pantai Hospital on a minor medical matter.

As usual Karpal methodically worked his way through all the issues on his plate, as well as attended to the normal caseload of clients sitting in his downstairs waiting room.

Before leaving his office at about 8 p.m. to visit Gobind in hospital, Karpal and Anwar had a lengthy telephone conversation. Michael, as usual, would have been required to hold the phone to Karpal's ear as the conversation progressed between them.

Whilst they initially came from opposite ends of the Malaysian political spectrum, Anwar and Karpal had come to understand each other completely.

Karpal harboured doubts that his High Court sentencing on a sedition charge and Anwar's sentencing in the Sodomy II case Court of Appeal ruling — both of which occurred within a week of each other in March 2014 — may have been politically motivated. It crossed his mind that the ruling political establishment may have wanted to sideline two key opposition coalition figures in the build-up to the 2018 election.

Anwar's sentencing carried with it a five-year term of imprisonment. He was freed on bail following this decision pending the outcome of the winner-take-all Federal Court appeal. The timing of his sentencing prevented him from standing in the Kajang by-election for a state seat in the state of Selangor.

Winning this by-election seat would have provided the opposition leader with a possible means to become the chief minister of Selangor, the wealthiest state in Malaysia, and thus the opportunity to prove to voters that he was capable of governing the country. Anwar assuming the chief minister's position would also have provided the opposition coalition with the perfect base to take power nationally in the 2018 election. The prospect of Anwar stepping up from a chief minister's job to the prime ministership in 2018 was one which might not have been all that attractive to the ruling Barisan Nasional.

Many in the international community, including the Inter-Parliamentary Union, Lawyers for Liberty, Human Rights Watch and LAWASIA questioned the impartiality and independence of the Malaysian judiciary following the two 2014 appeal decisions affecting both Karpal and Anwar.

Little wonder then that Karpal told Anwar he was worried about the latter's pending Federal Court appeal when the two men spoke by phone on that Wednesday night. Anwar recalled Karpal saying he was particularly troubled by the speed with which the appeal records had been sent to his Kuala Lumpur office.

The two men understood that they were both looking down the barrel of terms of imprisonment should they lose out on their respective appeal processes. Anwar's conviction, if upheld in the Federal Court, means he will have to serve at least two-thirds of the five-year prison sentence, namely three years and four months. He will also be unable to stand for a parliamentary seat for up to six years after completing his sentence. He could be out of action for the next two parliamentary elections.

The last discussion between Anwar and Karpal ended with the lawyer's usual positive trademark parting shots: "Not to worry, Anwar. You carry on. Don't worry. I'll do my best!"

A week before this conversation took place I had arranged for a colleague of mine from Wellington, Aimee Gulliver, to interview Karpal in his Kuala Lumpur office. She was working on secondment for the *Malaysiakini* wire service. The interview was to be the last substantive one Karpal ever gave.

Prophetically it was sub-headed: "Despite facing jail on a sedition charge, he (Karpal) will fight to the last for a better Malaysia."

Little wonder then that the interview, published 11 April 2014 on the *Malaysiakini* website, focused on the Appeal Court problems he and Anwar were facing. Gulliver's story read:

FOR KARPAL, NO BACK DOORS, NO DEALS, NO SURRENDER

Nearly 30 years on from one of the first of many threats on his life, Karpal Singh still refuses to slip quietly out the back door.

Then, he was urged by police officers to secretly leave a courtroom to avoid the danger posed by a man, claiming to have spiritual powers, who threatened to attack Karpal for suing the sultan.

Karpal refused, saying, "If I go through that back door now, I will go through back doors all my life."

The 73-year-old lawyer-politician maintains the same stoicism today, in the face of yet another attempt by the government to not only kill his political career, but also to put him in jail.

The sentence for his recent sedition conviction, a RM4,000 fine, precludes Karpal from holding political office and imposes a five-year disqualification period on running for Parliament again. Malaysia has no upper-age limit to enter Parliament, and Karpal calculated he would be 82 when he would be eligible to return to politics.

"They are not doing it fairly; it is not the right way to do it," Karpal said of the attempt to remove him from politics. But he plans to give the government "a run for their money" on appeal.

"I will fight them to the Federal Court, and if at the end of it I have to go, then that's too bad. I've got nothing left to lose."

He laments the loss of the Privy Council as Malaysia's final court of appeal, as "you could expect justice" from the English judges, who were objective to the political implications of the verdict.

Antiquated British law

Yet for the enviable justice administered by British courts, it is an antiquated British law that Karpal has been convicted under.

"Sedition was a law brought by the British, way back in 1948. I don't think any other country has sedition anymore, because what it amounts to is criticism of the government, which is allowed in a democracy. But here, you have no right."

Malaysia kept the offence of sedition because "they want it as a political weapon against critics of the government, an easy way out," Karpal said.

It is the second time he has been charged under the same legislation; the first, for a statement he made in court in the defence of Anwar Ibrahim, then facing charges of sodomy. It was the only known charge of sedition brought against a lawyer for remarks made in court in defence of a client in any country in the Commonwealth. In the face of intense pressure from the international community in Karpal's defence, the government backed off.

"I think they were waiting for some other chance, which I think they thought they have got now."

The government has filed a cross-appeal on Karpal's sentence, seeking to imprison him. The maximum penalty available under the law is a three-year jail term.

"Yes, they want to put me inside. They want a custodial sentence. Can you imagine it?" he asked, laughing.

The threat of incarceration does not worry the veteran politician — "not at all."

"If they put me inside they are dead."

"Internationally, there will be a hue and cry, especially with me in my state," he said, referencing the wheelchair he has been forced to use since 2005, when a car accident left him with spinal injuries and severely limited mobility.

Political martyrs

The jail term sought by the government carries an additional penalty — the five-year suspension on holding political office would, in that case, apply from the date Karpal was released from jail.

Yet Karpal knows both he and Anwar — sentenced to five years imprisonment on the latest sodomy charges — would become political martyrs if imprisoned.

"Once you do that injustice, then the ballot box will bring about the justice which you have denied others. But these are challenging things. It makes it more interesting, but also very dangerous at times."

In the face of seemingly never-ending challenges, few would begrudge Karpal a peaceful retirement away from the persecution he has suffered for decades at the hand of the government, as an ever-present thorn in their side.

But he already has plans for his first act should the opposition win its hard-fought battle to come to power in Malaysia.

"The first thing I will ensure is that all convictions made against us will be set aside, declared invalid. We won't go for a witch-hunt, but we will make sure to nail the buggers who did wrong to us. That will be nice," he said, with a small smile at the idea of finally being vindicated after so many years.

Asked why he stays in Malaysia in the face of so much adversity, Karpal's answer is simple.

"They want to make it as difficult as they can for us here so we'll go away. But we will not go — that would be giving them what they want, and that would be wrong.

"We have to stay and fight."

That interview was classic Karpal Singh.

A week later Karpal was still fighting when he left his Kuala Lumpur office with his wife of 44 years Gurmit, Michael Cornelius and their recently arrived driver from India, V Selvam. The four drove to Karpal's new home near Parliament House at about 10 p.m. and had dinner there after visiting Gobind.

Before leaving for Penang, Karpal asked Michael to take him for a walk in his garden. It was a place he had come to love in the last six months of his life. He loved the independence his large, new, wheelchair-friendly house gave him. It boasted a spacious garden. Even when Michael was looking over him from a discreet distance, he was able to breathe through his nose as he navigated his mechanised wheelchair through the garden.

At about midnight Karpal and his third lawyer son Ramkarpal left for Penang together with Michael, V Selvam and the family's Indonesian maid Selfiana Rengga.

Karpal was in the front passenger seat while Michael sat behind him in the second row of seats. Ramkarpal sat behind the driver on the right-hand side. The maid sat alone, at the back of the vehicle, among the Anwar and Valentine's Day murder trial case files.

The seating configuration would determine who would live or die.

Ramkarpal and his father spoke about their impending caseloads and the political issues of the day before Karpal dozed off.

At one point early in the journey Karpal woke and asked Michael to adjust his seating position and to readjust his pillow.

That was the last thing Michael ever did for his boss.

Ramkarpal, however, was having difficulty sleeping and regularly checked his emails on his iPhone. As their Toyota Alphard approached the old tin mining town of Kampar, Perak, Ramkarpal casually looked up from his phone and saw the vehicle on a direct course to plough into the back of a truck travelling up the highway in the left lane. He yelled out to the driver to take evasive action.

It was too late.

The right rear of the truck's tray sliced open the left-hand side of the Toyota Alphard, resulting in the instant deaths of Michael and the man he had served so loyally and faithfully in recent years, the Tiger of Jelutong.

Alive, slightly hurt, and temporarily shattered in the back seat was the man who would become the next MP for Bukit Gelugor — Ramkarpal Singh.

On Sunday 20 April, Karpal was given a state funeral by the DAP-controlled state of Penang. An estimated 100,000 people turned up to pay tribute to him as the hearse carrying his body made its way through the streets of Penang on the way to the crematorium.

On the night of Friday 25 April, I drove down from Penang to Ipoh with the MP for Puchong, Gobind Singh, who addressed a rally held to honour the memory of his father.

In front of about 3,000 people Gobind said his father had given people strength and hope to push on. "There will only ever be one Tiger of Jelutong. He was my father, Mr Karpal Singh," said the man now known as the "little lion of Puchong".

On 25 May 2014, Ramkarpal Singh joined his older brother in Parliament as the MP for Bukit Gelugor after winning the seat left vacant by his deceased father.

Ringing loudly in the ears of both his lawyer-MP sons were the words of the father in the last substantive interview he ever gave. They too had no choice; they had to stay and fight.

That is why they together with their sister Sangeet plan to appeal their father's High Court sedition case all the way through to the Federal Court if necessary. Their own heritage demands it of them. The precedent for their appeal commitment had been set almost 40 years to the day, back in May 1974, when Karpal and his older brother Santokh dropped everything and flew to India looking to protect the interests of their own father, Ram Singh.

Filing clerk Shafi-In was already dusting off the justice-for-father files when the appeal plans of the adult offspring took on yet another dramatic new twist with the death of Sultan Azlan Shah on 29 May 2014. The 86-year-old Sultan was the 'distinguished' catalyst behind Karpal's conviction and sentencing in the High Court's respective February–March 2014 consideration of the sedition case.

Karpal surrounded by his legal entourage headed for yet another Jalan Duta courtroom drama in Kuala Lumpur in early 2013. On his right is his prominent DAP lawyer-son Gobind. Pushing his wheelchair was a man who a year later would lay down his life for his friend and boss, Michael Cornelius. *Photo courtesy of Mark Trowell.*

If nothing else the deaths of Karpal and Sultan Azlan Shah, within six weeks of each other, ironically proved one thing: that there was indeed one law for all at the end of the day. The men — one who was once disparagingly referred to as a 'bullock carter's son' and the other, a privileged royal son of Malaysia's soil — could not escape their own mortality.

Suffice to say when Karpal's life story ended abruptly, he was up against Malaysia's (former) ninth king and a former Lord President of the Federal Court.

For both men it was a winner-take-all fight to the death. Such an approach suited Karpal. Indeed he'd spent a lifetime perfecting it.

ACKNOWLEDGEMENTS

Since 1988, completing Karpal's life story became not only a hobby but a seemingly unending race. Just when I thought I had an appropriate ending, another major milestone case or unusual political situation would see 'the tiger' prowling in unknown territory just over the horizon.

But finally the end to this 'Believe it or not' Ripley story came like a thunderbolt out of the night sky when death caught up with Karpal in the early morning of Thursday, 17 April 2014 on the North-South highway between Kuala Lumpur and Penang.

I received the news of Karpal's death from early morning text and Twitter messages from Singapore and Malaysia. The first one I read came from the very capable and thoughtful managing editor of this book, Mei Lin Lee in Singapore.

"The death of Karpal's passing saddens me. It's so much deeper for you. Take care please. Mei Lin," she wrote.

I read that text while sitting in a car at a service station in Hunterville, a small rural town in the heart of the Rangitikei District of New Zealand's lower North Island. Also in the car was a long-time journalist friend and colleague of mine, Paul Moran, whom I had worked with on the *Dominion Newspaper* in Wellington in the early 1980s. We were both travelling to my house in the central North Island town of Raetihi to spend Good Friday and Easter Saturday together to discuss the old times and colleagues in the newspaper business.

Paul could see that I was stunned when Mei Lin's text landed. Nothing was said. He walked away, thoughtfully leaving me alone for five minutes and found an excuse to do some shopping at a nearby supermarket. For the remainder of Thursday, Paul watched and listened as I became a 'go to' guy for the Malaysian media while reflecting on a man whom I had known and written about for over a quarter of a century.

It was a source of pride that Karpal had chosen me to be his biographer when he was inside the Kamunting Detention Camp near Taiping in 1988. We both realised when we first discussed the writing of this book that this was a job for someone living outside Malaysia. I remember vividly Karpal telling me with a smile on his face, "Tim, if you want trouble, you have come to the right place!"

As well as mourning the deaths of Karpal and his personal assistant Michael Cornelius, there was one thing in particular on my mind amidst the radio and newspaper interviews. It was something I knew Karpal would have wanted me to say as he was not a man to die wondering. It was important that I should publicly make clear who it was that Karpal had wanted to succeed him in his Bukit Gelugor electorate seat.

At the time of the launch of the first edition of this book in Kuala Lumpur in September 2013, Karpal went out of his way to tell me, if and when he was finally convicted of sedition, how he wanted his third son Ramkarpal to succeed him. I relayed this story, which prompted outbursts of nepotism from many quarters, to another Kiwi journalist colleague Aimee Gulliver, who was working in Kuala Lumpur at the time of Karpal's death.

She handled the story with style and suffice to say the DAP's Secretary-General Lim Guan Eng named Ramkarpal as the candidate for the Bukit Gelugor seat on 10 May 2014. When Guan Eng made that announcement the undertaking I gave to Karpal to write his book, inside the barbed wire of the Kamunting Detention Camp 26 years earlier, had been honoured.

Against that background, I now have many people to thank who helped me arrive at the Sikh Temple in Penang for the three days of prayer, in late April 2014, to honour the life of Karpal Singh. I thank, in particular, the temple committee for their hospitality.

My boss at the now no more New Zealand Press Association Graeme Jenkins began my involvement with the Karpal Singh life story by sending the Donoghues to Hong Kong in the mid-1980s. My current boss Bernadette Courtney, editor of the *Dominion Post* in Wellington, gave me time off to finish the job.

In writing this book, I was hosted by hundreds of Malaysian and Punjabi people on numerous trips to Malaysia and on a single trip to the Punjab. The people, particularly of Jalandhar and at the village of Samna Pind just outside Amritsar, know who they are. So, too, do the people of peninsular Malaysia who opened their doors and briefed me with humour on the latest 'Karpatology' snippets and happenings. I thank them all.

In researching this book, I also relied heavily on discussions with many brave members of the Malaysian Bar who operate in a difficult legal environment. I also wish to thank Karpal's older brothers Baksis and Santokh for their assistance. My friends Santokh and Professor Teo Soon Beng, who were often called to the Soho Bar on Penang Road when

I was in town, and their friends at the Soho, who not only organised my travels and accommodation but provided valuable insights and humour.

I also relied heavily on the work of various newspaper journalists and photographers from the *New Straits Times*, *The Star* (who can forget Tunku Abdul Rahman's weekly columns in the 1980s?), *The Sun* and the *Malay Mail*, and Datuk Mohammad Nor Khalid, more commonly known as Lat, of the *New Straits Times*.

I am also very much indebted to the professionalism of the editors of the *Singapore Law Reports*, *Malayan Law Journal* and *Malaysian Current Law Journal*, on whom I relied heavily for the reporting of the numerous cases referred to in this book.

Veteran Kiwi photographer and friend to all Peter Bush, who was based in Taiping while serving among the Commonwealth troops involved in the forlorn hunt for the wily Malayan communist leader Chin Peng, helped keep me focused on historical issues during my visits to Malaysia.

I must also mention the support and professionalism exhibited by the managing editor of Marshall Cavendish, Mei Lin Lee, her editor SL Leow and Steele Roberts in Wellington for their collective professionalism and guidance in putting this book together.

I am also very much indebted to Perth-based Mark Trowell QC for his Foreword which so capably summarises Karpal, the lawyer and the man. I very much value too the support and hospitality shown for the project by another Perth-based lawyer Ron Cannon who, like Trowell, went out of his way to understand and appreciate the various nuances of the Malaysian legal system.

I would of course also like to thank an indomitable, now deceased tetraplegic Karpal, his wife Gurmit and their adult offspring Jagdeep, Gobind, Ramkarpal, Sangeet, Mankarpal and their own respective growing families for so generously sharing a husband's and father's extraordinary life story. It has been a long and enjoyable journey since we all first travelled together from Penang Island to the Kamunting Detention Camp with Karpal's young children then singing "we're going to bring the old man home" in the back of the car. The record now shows they did indeed bring the 'old man home' every step of the way throughout his life.

When I first visited Karpal inside the detention camp, his most high profile clients were Lorraine Cohen and her son Aaron. Both were from New Zealand and they were the reason why I flew to Penang from Hong Kong and met Karpal in the first place. I owe Aaron and Lorraine (a posthumous) debt of gratitude for the introduction.

Lorraine Cohen was on death row, having been sentenced to death for trafficking in heroin by the man known in Australia and New Zealand as the hanging judge, Tun Mohamed Dzaiddin Abdullah. At that time it seemed impossible to me that she would outlive Karpal. The public prosecutor was also seeking a cross appeal death penalty against Aaron Cohen, who had been sentenced to 20 years jail and a whipping for possession of 34 grams of heroin, at the High Court level.

But the Cohens, who bravely retained Karpal's services even while he was twice detained under the Internal Security Act in the late 1980s, turned out to be a Karpal Singh success story. On appeal they were both convicted of possession of heroin for their own use and sentenced to 20 years in Penang Jail. In June 1996, after spending 11 years in Penang Jail, they both flew out of Penang following a royal pardon.

Ironically Lorraine Cohen did outlive her lawyer. She died of cancer in Auckland on Tuesday, 27 May 2014, some six weeks after Karpal's death.

Now that Karpal and Lorraine are both dead, it is time for me to move on from this real life-and-death story to another assignment in the journalistic game of life-and-death assignments.

To wrap up, suffice to say, I have admired the in-house gallows humour of Karpal and his extraordinary family, been privileged to closely study their hard-headedness, patience and fortitude over the years in overcoming many trials and tribulations. I also marvelled in recent years at the round-the-clock unswerving support Karpal received from his personal assistant Michael Cornelius, a humble man who gave his life for his boss.

Following the prayers at the Sikh Temple, I bade farewell to Karpal's family at their Jalan Utama home in Penang, before once again returning to New Zealand and a small Maori township, a world away in Raetihi. Ramkarpal was there with his mother Gurmit, Karpal's lifelong campaign manager, wife and protectress. She was the woman who helped her husband plan each often seemingly impossible charted course. This record shows, together they stood tall and saw it all through, regardless of the consequences. Amidst their grief there was the certain knowledge that Ramkarpal's first election victory in the Bukit Gelugor electorate would be a landslide, and indeed it was — by a majority of 37,659 votes. His destiny, like his brother Gobind's, was to become a Federal MP in the Malaysian Parliament.

Finally, now that the 'totara has fallen', a word of thanks for the love and support of my wife Gabrielle, without whom this long overdue book would not have been written.

Arohanui

TIM DONOGHUE

RAETIHI, NEW ZEALAND

JUNE 2014

SELECTED REFERENCES

Bush, Peter and Thomas, Paul. *Peter Bush. A Life in Focus*. New Zealand: Hachette New Zealand Ltd., 2009.

Chen Man Hin, Dr and Lim Kit Siang. *25 Years of Struggle. Milestones in DAP History*. Kuala Lumpur: DAP, 1991.

Das, K. *Questionable Conduct Over that May Day Caper*. Kuala Lumpur: K. Das, 1990.

Galbally, Frank. *Galbally! The Autobiography of Australia's Leading Criminal Lawyer*. Australia: Penguin Books, 1990.

Majid, Mimi Kamariah. "Dangerous Drugs Laws" in *Malayan Law Journal*, Kuala Lumpur, 1995.

Pannick, David. *Judicial Review of the Death Penalty*. UK: Gerald Duckworth & Co. Ltd., 1982.

Salleh Abas, Tun and Das, K. *May Day for Justice*. Kuala Lumpur: Magnus Books, 1989.

Trowell, Mark. *Sodomy II – The Trial of Anwar Ibrahim*. Singapore: Marshall Cavendish Editions, 2012.

Williams, Peter, QC. *Judicial Misconduct. Kuala Lumpur*: Pelanduk Publications, 1990.

Yatim, Rais. *Freedom Under Executive Power in Malaysia*. Kuala Lumpur: Endowment, 1995.

INDEX